# NONVIOLENT STORY

# NONVIOLENT STORY

*Narrative Conflict Resolution
in the Gospel of Mark*

ROBERT R. BECK

ORBIS BOOKS

Maryknoll, New York 10545

The Catholic Foreign Mission Society of America (Maryknoll) recruits and trains people for overseas missionary service. Through Orbis Books, Maryknoll aims to foster the international dialogue that is essential to mission. The books published, however, reflect the opinions of their authors and are not meant to represent the official position of the society.

**Library of Congress Cataloging-in-Publication Data**
Beck, Robert R. (Robert Raymond)
    Nonviolent story : narrative conflict resolution in the Gospel of
Mark / Robert R. Beck.
        p.    cm.
    Includes bibliographical references and indexes.
    ISBN 1-57075-061-0 (alk. paper)
    1. Bible. N.T.  Mark – Criticism, interpretation, etc.
2. Nonviolence. 3. Violence in the Bible. 4. Narration in the
Bible.    I. Title.
BS2585.2.B435    1995
226.3′06–dc20                                    95-42415
                                                        CIP

# Contents

FOREWORD *by Ched Myers* . . . . . . . . . . . . . . . . . . . . . . . . . IX

PREFACE . . . . . . . . . . . . . . . . . . . . . . . . . . . . . . . . . XIII

ACKNOWLEDGMENTS . . . . . . . . . . . . . . . . . . . . . . . . . . XVII

1. LOUIS L'AMOUR AND THE MYTH
   OF CONSTRUCTIVE VIOLENCE . . . . . . . . . . . . . . . . . . . . . 1

   The Freedom Medalist                                          1
   The Narrative Form                                            2
      *History and the Yarn*   2
      *The Yarn and the Agon*   4
      *The Agon as Narrative*   6
   The Narrative Outlook                                         8
   Civilizing Violence                                           8
      *Men, Women, and Violence*   8
      *Menace of Nonviolence*   9
   Myth and the Narrative Quality of Violence                    11
   Gospel: An Alternative Story?                                 14
      *Two Versions of Reality*   14
      *A Thesis*   17

2. ON READING ANCIENT TEXTS . . . . . . . . . . . . . . . . . . . . . 19

   The Absent Writer                                             20
      *An Urgent Message from the Evangelist*   21
      *Opaque Texts*   23
   Genre                                                         24
      *The Historical versus the Literary Projects*   26
      *The Problem of Unshared Cultural Contexts*   28
      *Popular Narrative*   30
   Narrative Criticism and the Gospel                            32
      *Story and Discourse*   32
      *Plot and Conflict*   36

3. THE GOSPEL AS AGON .............................. 39

A Case for Mark's Plot                                            40
The Main Form: Blocking the Action                               43
  *Two Beginnings*    *45*
  *Cleansing Actions: Synagogue and Temple*    *47*
  *Anointing Actions*    *48*
The Dramatic Movement of the Plot                                50
  *Act 1: The First Week (1:14–3:6)*    *51*
  *Act 2: The New Family (3:7–6:6)*    *52*
  *Act 3: Feeding the Multitude and Other Stories*
    *(6:7–8:30)*    *54*
  *Act 4: The Road to the City (8:31–10:52)*    *55*
  *Recapitulation: The Time of Rising Action in*
    *Mark's Gospel*    *56*
  *Act 5: The Temple Action as the Narrative Climax*
    *(11:1–13:37)*    *57*
  *Prophetic Dismantling*    *59*
  *Act 6: Within the Times of Anointing (14:1–16:8)*    *60*

4. THE SYMBOLISM OF POWER ........................ 63

Mark's Symbolic Vocabulary                                       65
Act 1: Holy and Unclean Power in Mark                            70
  *Dangerous Language*    *70*
  *Dangerous Gates*    *72*
Act 2: Faith and Fear                                            75
Act 3: Opening a Door to the Gentiles                            79
  *Gentile Mission, or Last Chance for Purity Rules?*    *82*
  *The Climactic Event*    *83*
Bodily Healing as Social Metaphor                                85
  *Jesus' Symbolic Acts*    *87*
  *Nonviolent Action*    *89*

5. JESUS AND HIS DISCIPLES ........................ 92

The Teaching of Jesus                                            93
  *Precedents in Scripture*    *94*
  *Messiah: Christological Lessons*    *96*
  *Servant: A Nonviolent Christology*    *99*
The Teaching of Jesus as Subplot                                 103
  *Finding the Main Plot and the Subplot*    *103*
  *Imitation: The Heart of the Subplot's Conflict*    *106*
  *The Conflict Resolved?*    *108*
The Reader: Discipleship and the Structure of Irony              109

6. THE AGON AND NONVIOLENT PLOT RESOLUTION . . . . . . . . 114

   Richard Horsley's Spiral of Violence                     115
   Gene Sharp's Three Moments                    116
   Sharp on the Gospel                    119
   Three Narrative Moves                    120
   The Move on Jerusalem                    122
   Moving from Temple to Garden                    123
   Garden to Cross: Nonretaliation                    125
   An Empty Tomb: An Unclosed Story                    127

7. BREAKING THE MYTH OF VIOLENCE . . . . . . . . . . . . . . . . . 130

   Ways That Stories Tend                    130
     *Popular Stories*   *131*
     *A Story Formula*   *132*
     *Poetic Justice*   *135*
     *Innocence and Purgation*   *136*
   The Gospel Refusals                    137
     *The Quality of Innocence*   *139*
     *The World of Gift and Debt*   *143*
     *Violence and Moral Outrage*   *146*

EPILOGUE: TAKING STOCK . . . . . . . . . . . . . . . . . . . . . . . . 149

APPENDIX A: EXEGETICAL OUTLINES . . . . . . . . . . . . . . . . . . . 153

APPENDIX B: NARRATIVE TRANSFORMATIONS . . . . . . . . . . . . . 157

APPENDIX C: JESUS AS PROPHET —
            NOTES ON THE TEMPLE ACTION . . . . . . . . . . . . . 159

APPENDIX D: THE STORY FORMULA . . . . . . . . . . . . . . . . . . . 164

   The Terms                    165
   The Formula                    167

NOTES . . . . . . . . . . . . . . . . . . . . . . . . . . . . . . . . . . . . 169

BIBLIOGRAPHY . . . . . . . . . . . . . . . . . . . . . . . . . . . . . . . 193

SCRIPTURE INDEX . . . . . . . . . . . . . . . . . . . . . . . . . . . . . 199

GENERAL INDEX . . . . . . . . . . . . . . . . . . . . . . . . . . . . . . 202

# Foreword

The historical problem of violence continues to be the most pressing issue of our time. This is evident by any index: the spread of the international arms trade or of urban gang-banging; our fascination with vicarious brutality, from cinema verité to celebrity murder cases; or the epidemic levels of domestic battering and homelessness. As we near the end of the millennium, the most sophisticated technologies are still guided by the most ancient belief systems: blood-feuding, retributive "justice," and the politics of domination.

Christian theology, if it is not to become irrelevant, must struggle to understand and overturn the practices and justifying ideologies of violence. It must provide a "radical" critique that exposes the deep historical and cultural *roots* of our assumptions that enemies should be killed and that lethal force may be used toward righteous ends. Fortunately, a small body of recent literature has begun to engage this very task.

Walter Wink's *Engaging the Powers: Discernment and Resistance in a World of Domination* (Fortress Press, 1992) analyzes how the historical logic of "might makes right" and the efficacy of militarism have wrought a "domination system" that is much greater than the sum of its individual social, political, psychological, and spiritual components. Underpinning this system, however, is what Wink calls the "myth of redemptive violence," in which "good" triumphs over "evil" through the use of "righteous" and superior violence. He traces this myth from its origins in the cultic narratives of ancient Babylon to its expressions in contemporary popular culture, from Superman to the Power Rangers. Wink then contends that Jesus' practice of non-violence and love of enemies represented a fundamental defection from this myth, thus offering a way to break the historical spiral of violence.

Similarly, Gil Bailie's *Violence Unveiled: Humanity at the Cross-roads* (Crossroad, 1995) studies how societies make enemies into scapegoats, so that their destruction serves a ritual function of "cleansing" the victor's body politic and reinforcing its group boundaries. Ideologies of "sacrificial" violence lie at the heart of every attempt to justify morally the objectification and destruction of perceived enemies. Bailie also contends that the New Testament narrates a countermyth that specifically rejects scapegoat ideology. The world is redeemed by Jesus' death on the cross, God's self-sacrifice that undermines any legitimation of sacrificial violence.

Robert Beck's *Nonviolent Story* builds upon the important contributions of Wink and Bailie by examining more closely *how* narratives legitimate and perpetuate myths of redemptive violence in the hearts and minds of people. Before violence is ever committed its justification has already been secured in our individual and collective consciousness by the socializing power of stories about the destruction of "bad guys" by "good guys."

Beck reminds us that "like walking or talking, listening to stories is complicated work made deceptively simple." Using the example of the popular western novellas of Louis L'Amour, he shows how the traditional "agonist" plot structure functions to persuade the reader to identify *with* the protagonist and *against* the antagonist. Then comes a fatal narrative transformation. In order for the threat of evil to be defeated, "The hero drops the ways of virtue and adopts the practices previously monopolized by the villain." The antagonist is vanquished by his own methods of violence or deception, which the protagonist uses to "restore equilibrium." We justify this as "poetic justice" and revel in the "purgation" of the antagonist, who has become the personification of evil.

We know this seductive formula well, from Saturday morning cartoons to movies like *Rambo* and *Star Wars,* from the official history of World War II to the press coverage of the Gulf War. It lurks behind our criminal justice system and our foreign policy and determines our reading of both the past and the future. It is precisely this story line, reproduced ubiquitously in popular narratives great and small, that keeps us loyal to myths of redemptive violence. And that loyalty drives the spiral of violence while precluding alternative approaches to conflict resolution.

Like Wink and Bailie, Beck sees the gospel as a rejection of this classical plot formula. Jesus the protagonist explicitly rejects the option of righteous violence as the oxymoron it is, and chooses instead to suffer and die in order to redeem his antagonists. Using the Gospel of Mark as his primary text, Beck portrays Jesus as a nonviolent resister of evil and injustice, but one who turns away from "the last temptation: that compassion vitiate itself by moving to violence."

Beck is a keen "narratologist" who offers real contributions to our understanding of Mark's intricate structure and plot dynamics. For example, he identifies three "moments" in Mark's narrative in which the term "robber" appears, correlating them to the crucial turns generic to an agonist plot. At the peak of the "rising action" of the plot, Jesus "exorcises" the temple ("You have made this place a den of robbers!" [Mk 11:17]), representing the climax of his nonviolent challenge to his opponents. At the point of his arrest in the plot's "falling action," however, Jesus is overtaken by the countermoves of his opponents ("Have you come against me . . . as if I were a robber?" [14:48]). Now comes the most crucial and consequential plot-turn. Instead of asserting the antagonist's "prerogative" to retaliate with superior force in order to vindicate the "good," Jesus takes up his cross ("and they crucified him between two robbers" [15:27]). Such insightful analysis punctuates this work.

Beck is a good teacher and practitioner of narrative criticism. Equally significant, his study of Mark confirms how important "political hermeneutics" are for biblical research. But most important of all is the fact that Beck has addressed his craft to the central question of our times. In so doing, he has helped us in our struggle to understand the narrative taxonomy of the myth of redemptive violence. And his reading of Mark further encourages us in our struggle to embrace the alternative of militant nonviolence and suffering love that alone has the power to redeem our history.

CHED MYERS

# PREFACE

Was it Dorothee Soelle who first taught me the principle that, since the Holocaust, theology must begin with the knowledge of suffering? I believe it was, though I can no longer name the place. Certainly her example leads away from an uncommitted, "neutral" theology that can conceal beneath its polished, idealist surface an unrecognized complicity with genocide. The Gospels have been used to launch racial pogroms as well as relief programs, support structures of slavery as well as liberation movements. Usually we can recognize attempts to use the Gospels to support servitude as forms of blasphemy. But not always.

Mention of the Holocaust serves to remind us that Christian anti-Semitism enjoyed Gospel warrants for centuries. To guard against such misrepresentation here, I make my disclaimers now. There is no basis for anti-Semitism in the Gospel of Mark; all parties are Jewish, and the conflicts take place entirely within a Jewish horizon. To avoid such twists of implication, I refer to Jesus' opponents, as I must do repeatedly, as the Judean authorities. This is to be understood as a political and religious reference, naming those parties in the Gospel who adopt the role of antagonists to Jesus' role as protagonist.

The Gospel of Mark is a violent story. It is, if you will, a murder story. It is an account of justice miscarried, in which the protagonist is legally framed. But it can also be viewed as an account of nonviolent action, which is what this book presumes to assert. There is, however, a nonviolence that is tantamount to a license to victimhood. There is a nonviolence of the "martyr complex," and even another of passive resistance. Such nonviolence is not what this book is about. It is instead about nonviolent action, a nonviolence that is often confrontational. Just as I will try in these pages to avoid the complacencies of abstract theology, so I will try to remember that nonviolence is a program of resistance.

A major hurdle for any discussion of nonviolent resistance is our cultural prejudice against it. We generally understand nonviolence in terms of avoiding conflict or giving in to pressure, as in the popular image of the doormat. One does not wish to be indiscriminately walked over. Furthermore, our dislike of any kind of bullying, personal or international, frequently expresses itself as an acute sensitivity to the injustices in our world. Evil, we are sure, must be resisted. And nonviolence is simply inadequate to that task.

Yet refusing to use violence is not the same as avoiding all conflict. In fact, nonviolent resistance in the mode of a Gandhi or a Martin Luther King, Jr., may mean moving deliberately into conflict, even while refusing the satisfactions of violence in working through the differences. For us the notion that nonviolence can be a form of active resistance against unjust social structures tends to seem exotic and unreal. We believe that any effective opposition to oppressive or unwelcome power requires violence: either we are nonviolent and therefore ineffective, or we are effective and therefore violent. This conviction is at the heart of what I call the "myth of constructive violence." By this phrase I want to include the many forms of our confidence in violence as a beneficial tool. Sometimes I use alternative phrases such as "therapeutic violence," "redemptive violence," or, in the first chapter of this book, "civilizing violence." What these have in common is a belief in the constructive value of violent action. My contention will be that the Gospels — and here I am looking mainly at the Gospel of Mark — reject this myth.

This is not to deny that violence is effective. It clearly is so, within a narrow field of accomplishment. But what does it effect? What are its achievements? We are safe, I think, in assuming that it is in the work of *destruction,* not construction, that violence excels. In these terms, "constructive violence" is an oxymoron, contradicting itself. What will interest us in these pages is the myth, the story line, that makes it seem believable. Certainly destruction does have its practical virtues. It clears the slate by removing a construction or any unwelcome constructing persons or groups. The effect of destruction is to require new construction, preferably along the lines favored by the destroyers. In this way it can boast a certain kind of usefulness for solving problems.

Furthermore, destruction is quick and easy, yet comprehensive. Perhaps one of its most awe-inducing aspects is its ability to disrupt in moments what has taken years, even centuries, to put in place. In its noncreative impotence it can alter circumstances completely. This is one of the main reasons it is useful. It saves time by avoiding processes. In addition, it can control outcomes; it is expedient. The virtuoso of violence wins not only the war but the peace afterwards as well. The convenience of destruction is that it doesn't get bogged down in honoring claims of relationships. It can move ahead with the task at hand without apologies, without endless consultations, without the necessary bookkeeping of human obligations. While destruction carries out its effect in some ways independently of its intent, it would seem to be at heart an intended activity. Which is to say it is a human act. This is why it is an inverted form of construction. Something similar may occur in the natural realm, apart from human intention, but it is not destruction.

But if destruction is a human act, it is not such in the same way that violence is. *Violence* would seem to include something more. We might say that violence is *destruction directed toward persons*. It is this sense of things that is evoked in Mark's Gospel when the Pharisees and the Herodians meet "in order to destroy him" (3:6). All destruction is human, but violence is personal. As a human act, destruction is an anticreative act. Correspondingly, as destructive of persons, violence is a betrayal of the care we owe one another. While its use may be imagined by those who employ it as an exercise in care, as in the case of defense of family or country, the betrayal structured in the very act implies the contradiction mentioned above. It is this that directs our attention to the cultural myth of violence.

The temptation to enlist violence on behalf of our causes is woven deep into our cultural fabric. To show this I will invoke, in the first chapter, the example of one of our more popular authors of western stories, Louis L'Amour. While I enjoy his work, I cannot accept the vision he offers of constructive, civilizing violence. In his view, as with so many, violence is honored as an integral part of the difficult work of bringing civilization to the American continent. It is the myth of violence as civilizing instrument. L'Amour allows us to distinguish between the "agon," the central struggle in the action of the plot, and the "narrative outlook," the ideological point of view adopted by the narrator as regards the nature of power most effective for achieving the goals of the plot.

In chapter 2, "On Reading Ancient Texts," I try to situate the present effort in the context of the emerging discipline of Gospel narrative studies. Reading a message that comes to us across a great divide of time requires paying close attention to the text. Here I hope to provide a justification for my frequent strategies of textual analysis. I also distinguish between the reader-oriented literary analysis adopted here and the historical project of determining the "author's intent."

Finally, this chapter proposes popular forms of literature as the most suitable genre analogue for Mark's Gospel.

The next three chapters look at the literary patterns of conflict in Mark. Chapter 3, "The Gospel as Agon," explicates the struggle between Jesus and the Judean authorities as the main plot of the narrative. Chapter 4, "The Symbolism of Power," shifts the perspective from the agon to the narrative outlook in order to reexamine the plot. Here the focus of interest is the ideological message carried in the narrative's symbolism of the holy and the unclean. The fifth chapter, "Jesus and the Disciples," identifies the other prominent conflict among the Gospel characters as the subplot of the narrative. The imitation of Christ is the challenge to join the protagonist in the struggle of the main plot.

Chapters 6 and 7 explore the nonviolent resolution of conflict in the closing events of Mark's narrative. Chapter 6, "The Agon and Nonviolent Plot Resolution," proposes a close analogy between the political theory of nonviolent action and the climactic drama of the Gospel. Chapter 7, "Breaking the Myth of Violence," finds us returning to the framework of the narrative outlook to show how the Gospel refuses to take certain steps outlined in the patterns of constructive violence. Together these two final chapters illustrate that the Gospel narrative makes a deliberate move away from the patterns of destructive reprisal characteristic of the myth of violence.

# ACKNOWLEDGMENTS

Although this book follows the convention of its genre in adopting the narrative voice of the intrepid solo academic hero, the Lone Ranger of truth scouting unknown territories of theory, I know that many people helped to bring it to realization. The project began in different places. One such place was a musical about Mark's Gospel, which first explored for me in an explicit way its narrative and dramatic values. I am in debt to the many who contributed their theatrical, musical, and MIDI (Musical Instrument Digital Interface) abilities to that celebration.

A more sober starting point is a long-time reflection on the practice of certain faith-based communities of resistance, such as Jonah House and the Community for Creative Non-Violence, which see in the Gospel a blueprint for confrontational action. The remarks and presentations of Liz McAlister, especially during annual Holy Week actions in Washington, D.C., began a number of these thoughts. And I must acknowledge the example of Frank Cordaro, friend and former student, who continues to test the Gospel narrative in practice. Much of what I say here has been learned from his street-smart hermeneutic.

The ideas grew in the conversations among other communities committed to the values of nonviolence and resistance to the more destructive of our cultural tendencies. I want to thank the members of the Dubuque Catholic Worker community, the Anawim community, and the Monday night Bible study group for providing the space and occasion for exchange on some of these themes. In many instances I can no longer separate what is theirs from what is mine.

Many friends have helped; many have been willing to read what I've written and point to things I've neglected or forgotten. I particularly want to thank Andy Auge, Karla Braig, Patti Jung, Janet O'Meara, Paul Fuerst, and Mary Ann Zollmann, each of whom put their mark on the project in various ways. Loras College, with the encouragement of its academic dean, Kenneth Kraus, allowed me sabbatical time to organize my thoughts. Ruth Jackson and the Visitation Sisters willingly arranged my chaplain duties to open up some work-

ing time and never ceased praying for the success of the project —
especially Sister Paschal Kelly. Steve and Brenda Oreskovich provided
a peaceful haven in Montana for various stages of composition and
revision. I have to thank Louise Kames for convincing me finally that
if I were serious about the project I would take the necessary time off
to complete it. Her friendship and encouragement have been invalu-
able in keeping me believing in the book. And I want to remember my
parents — my father, Paul, who has read what I've written and deems
it good, and my mother, Mildred, who died while I was writing it, but
was pleased that I had finally got on with it.

*Chapter One* ⎯⎯⎯⎯⎯⎯⎯⎯⎯⎯⎯⎯⎯⎯

# LOUIS L'AMOUR AND THE MYTH OF CONSTRUCTIVE VIOLENCE

## The Freedom Medalist

At the beginning of his book *Bendigo Shafter,* Louis L'Amour proposes a rather complex act of imagination for his reader. The dedication reads:

> To the hard-shelled men who built with nerve and hand that which the soft-bellied latecomers call the "Western myth."

Most of us who read Louis L'Amour no doubt belong to the group that he calls the "soft-bellied." We can assume he knew that. As a writer who published over 240 adventures of short-story length and 90 novels, nearly all of which have enjoyed continual reprinting,[1] he must have known most of his readers were only surrogate gunslingers. It is interesting to think about his expectations of the reader. He knew that we, at least for the duration of the telling, counted ourselves among the adventurers, not the armchair jockeys. And yet most of us do our reading in armchairs, not in the saddle. It is powerful testimony to the imagination to suggest that we could be expected to repudiate the activity of reading even while we were engaged in it.

The pictures of L'Amour on his books invariably show him in a Stetson hat. The hat tells us that the truth he has to impart is the truth of experience. Even though it comes to us from a book, it is not book learning. It is authentic and direct; it is not derived. In the brief bio printed in the back pages of each of his Bantam issues we learn by his own testimony that he wanted to write from the time he could talk. But it is not his apprenticeship in writing that we are told about. The credentials it offers are from the school of action.

Louis L'Amour is no academic hothouse plant. He left home at the age of fifteen to begin a series of adventures that ranged from the inevitable (seaman, lumberjack, officer of a tank destroyer in World

War II) to the exotic ("elephant handler, skinner of dead cattle" —
which I presume means more than working in a meat-packing plant).
He was a professional boxer, winning all but eight of his fifty-nine
fights. This experience served him, for instance, in writing works such
as *Lando,* about a prizefighter. L'Amour published his first book-
length story in 1958, after a series of short stories, and he died in
1988, with numerous works still projected.

In his Bantam bio we read:

> The recipient of many great honors and awards, in 1983
> Mr. L'Amour became the first novelist ever to be awarded the
> National Gold medal by the United States Congress in honor
> of his life's work. In 1984 he was also awarded the Medal of
> Freedom by President Reagan.

These are not literary awards. At least they are not what we usually understand by such awards, that is, recognition for expanding the
possibilities of the literary art. L'Amour was not honored for pioneer-
ing new dimensions for the human spirit but rather for confirming old
convictions — cultural verities that have come to be collected under
the symbolisms associated with the pioneers of the Wild West. In conferring the Medal of Freedom on L'Amour, President Reagan was not
simply conferring public recognition upon a favorite writer; he was
rewarding an American for performing a useful social function.

## The Narrative Form

### History and the Yarn

A clue to what this social function might be is found in L'Amour's
"Sackett" stories. In an ambitious project, which publishers cannot
avoid calling a "saga," L'Amour presents us with ten generations of
the Sackett family doing their part to civilize the North American
continent. The saga is constituted of seventeen of L'Amour's cus-
tomary tales (the canon of this saga is somewhat indeterminate —
L'Amour had planned at least nine more works), this time given a setting in frontier history. A *Sackett Companion* has been published that
provides supplementary information, maps, and a family tree.[2]

When L'Amour speaks of "history" in connection with his saga,
he means it in a particular way. The Sackett name is historical, but

not L'Amour's treatment of it. Historical sites and events are employed, but only as a background for typical examples of L'Amour's stories. The historical event here is not the story, but simply the occasion for it. The story being told is the familiar Louis L'Amour formula story.

An example of L'Amour's attitude toward history is found in his defense of the climactic mastodon scene in *Jubal Sackett*. What warrants the appearance of a mastodon in a story about the American West in the 1630s? Here's what L'Amour has to say about the matter in an appendix:

> MAMMOTH, MASTODON, etc.: According to scholars mammoths died out around 6000 B.C. Nonetheless, American Indians record hunting and killing them. Many Indian tribes had accounts of seeing or hunting the mammoth. Near Moab, at Hys Bottom close to the Colorado River, there is a petroglyph of a mastodon. And in the Four Corners area near Flora Vista a small boy found two slabs on which were carved many glyphs, including pictures of two elephants. They have been called fakes, which is the most convenient way of getting rid of something that does not fit current beliefs.[3]

What is interesting here is that the apparatus of scholarship — footnotes, appendices — is used to dismiss the work of scholarship. L'Amour's "history" is the Reaganesque history of pleasant anecdotes: spinning a good yarn.

In extending his adventure stories to the arena of history, L'Amour makes implicit historical claims. And inasmuch as the history involved is the history of the settlement of the continental United States, these are claims of "civilizing" activity. But at the heart of the saga, there where the action is, L'Amour has effected a crucial substitution. He has substituted the yarn for the event. The familiar pleasures of the yarn are presented as containing the truth of the historical settlement of the country. Despite the author's disavowals about the western myth, it seems he has been busily extending the range of the genre into historical fiction and even staking a claim for its role as instrumental in founding the United States — a narrative function usually attributed to myth.

The yarn at the heart of the Sackett series is an action story. Following the genre of the western tale, the characters are fixed: heroes are good; villains are evil. There is no possibility of redeeming or converting the bad man. What generally distinguishes the good guys from the bad is an allegiance to something larger than self-interest, along with a self-deprecating sense of humor usually missing on the other side. The villain's lack of humor contributes considerably toward our experience of that character as disagreeable. Along with his rough amiability, the L'Amour hero can generally be said to have certain rangy, flat-stomached, chisel-cheeked beauty, self-perceived as ugliness. Sometimes a bad man is later revealed to be a good man. But this is explained as a change in our perception, not in the makeup of the character. That such a misperception is possible, given the distinct differences between the two sides, suggests powerful similarities linking them. Despite the absence of real character changes in these stories, heroes such as Matt Coburn, the gunslinging hero of *The Empty Land,* can worry about slipping over the thin line that separates the good from the bad.

### The Yarn and the Agon

In these stories the good guys share with the bad guys something fundamental, namely, a certain sense of the world. The action of the plot unfolds in a context of mutual respect that, though often grudging, is nonetheless deep. It has much in common with the athletic arena, the agon of Greek culture. It is a man's world of testing and combat, a special arena sometimes referred to as the "real world." It is a world that derives much of its sense of reality from the intensity of its experiences.

"Agon," a term that came to mean any contest between equals, is familiar to us from the language of conflict in drama. The protagonist, the hero of the piece, and the antagonist, the villain, are locked in an agon that provides them with their titles. Anthropologists as well as literary critics have borrowed the notion. Agonistic cultures, such as those of the first-century Mediterranean world, are marked by the pattern of "challenge and response" in social exchanges outside the family. Every encounter of males from different families, good or bad, is interpreted as a challenge to honor. The rules of this "game," as Bruce Malina typifies it, go a long way toward describing the shared world of the "agonists" of stories, the protagonist and the antagonist, with particular reference to L'Amour's story world.[4]

The game of challenge and response in agonistic societies is a dialogue of actions. Malina identifies three phases: a challenge, the interpretation of the challenge, and the response. The *challenge,* in

Malina's words, "is a claim to enter the social space of another." It can be positive or negative. A gift presents a predicament that needs a response as much as a threat does. Praise, like insult, creates an imbalance, and therefore a tension, between parties. Whether positive or negative, it is a challenge to the honor or self-esteem of the receiver and his family.

The *interpretation* of the challenge by the receiving party is an important moment for a number of reasons. The seriousness of the challenge needs to gauged. Misinterpreting an opponent's threat would signal a weakness in the faculty of judgment, not to mention a suspicious emotional instability. Nor would underreacting improve matters, for that would open one's name and family to abuse. Furthermore, the interpretive moment is crucially important because it is only social equals that can play this game, so the relative status of the antagonists must be determined. It is insulting for an inferior to pretend to an equal status by issuing a challenge. Add to this that the onlookers are part of the game, and their assessment must be factored in. While I might be inclined to dismiss an upstart challenger, the crowd's response may persuade me to take the matter more seriously. These instances suggest why Malina and others place emphasis on the moment of interpretation, even though it is not an action in itself.

The *response* follows upon the interpretation. Once I have evaluated the challenge to my honor, three options are available to me. I may actively reject the challenge, as with a scornful reply. In this case it would implicitly label the challenger my inferior, requiring him to redress the insult in some way. At the other extreme, I could simply fail to produce a response. Passive rejection, however, implies weakness and dishonor. To refuse the gambit is not to refuse the game, but rather to lose it. One cannot refuse the game and continue on as if nothing had happened; there are no rules for that. In the middle ground between active and passive refusals is the simple act of accepting the challenge. I do this by offering a counterchallenge. And so the exchange continues, as it enters a new round. For now the counterchallenge invites an evaluation and response.

If fact, although Malina scrupulously restricts his anthropology to the first-century Mediterranean world, the dynamics he describes are readily recognized by most Americans. While males are more likely than females to be contestants in the agon, women find a place in the pattern since it is carried by the culture as a whole. Versions of the pattern appear in almost every public arena, from bar fights to freeway driving, from neighborhood spats to spectator sports. This access based on our own experience argues strongly for the claim that the first-century Mediterranean world and our own world share important features of this cultural pattern.

In addition, the pattern of challenge and response tells us something about the use of violence in larger social interactions. Political violence is instrumental, and instrumental violence — employed for a purpose, not gratuitously — can be understood as one form of challenge and response. Such violence is almost always located within a social "narrative," in the position of response to a perceived, and evaluated, threat. In the assessments of recourse to violence under these circumstances, we are vigilant that violence be constrained by a set of rules, permitting some actions as if by concession, forbidding others as if by exchange for those conceded. We understand how, in certain circumstances, it is socially required. We see how it is dialogic, as steps in a dance, with its moves and countermoves.

All morally justified, violence has the character of a response to a challenge — an evil that usually takes some part in the justification. In this sense, we can say it unfolds in a manner similar to the agonistic exchange. "Proportionality" in the just-war theory, for instance, implies a prior action to which a response is deemed necessary. This response must be proportionate. In John Yoder's words, the evaluation of the just-war theory "calls for the evil likely to be caused by warfare to be measured against the evil it hopes to prevent,"[5] an evil facing it as a challenge. The theory itself emerges as a sort of grammar in the dialogue of international violence. L'Amour's story world is surprisingly instructive in these matters as well.

*The Agon as Narrative*

In this anthropological pattern of the agon, human behavior converges with narrative by way of its crisply structured system of behavioral constraints. Without speculating on the underlying reasons, we can perceive a kinship between the agonistic pattern of anthropology and the protagonist-antagonist relation of conflict in the world of drama and narrative. Some of the narrativelike qualities of the game of challenge and response are worth noting. At a most basic level, the game unfolds in time. It is essentially *durational*. According to Stephen Crites,[6] duration is the primary quality of human experience, relating it deeply and intimately to the temporal arts, especially that of narrative. In the agon, this can be seen in the dialogic structure of the exchange. It alternates statement and answer, but in a behavioral mode. It is a conversation in symbolic action, a dance of gestures.

Connected to this is the way in which the exchanges are strictly *rule-bound.* While the confrontational dialogue develops in terms of alternate responses, the options for any possible response are narrowed drastically. For instance, the game cannot simply be refused. According to the rules, that response would be counted as losing.[7] To cite a possible contemporary setting for the kind of activity described here, any adolescent male unfortunate enough to have been caught in the orbit of a parking lot fight, whether peripherally or as a featured player, knows the whirlpool effect of the dynamic. Should one be inclined to back out, one quickly discovers that there is no social vocabulary for doing so. The dynamic is heavily weighted toward producing a fight.

A third narrativelike aspect of the dynamic is its thirst for *satisfaction.* Stories move toward the equilibrium that brings rest at the end of the tale. In the agon, honor must be satisfied. But, of course, in achieving this goal, a new demand is raised on the opposing side. An ascending spiral is created, an escalation of the honors at stake. Like a pump valve, this dynamic drives the tensions toward increased pressure. In the world of stories we encounter a similar impetus toward satisfaction. Here too we stand on one side of the conflict, sharing what is commonly called the narrator's point of view. Accordingly, we side with the protagonist — the party favored by the narrator. Mercifully, the plot of a story will stop once reader satisfaction is reached. But there is something notably artificial about the rounding-off of narrative plots. In contrast, life goes on. And as for narrative plots, it is seldom hard to imagine another story beginning at the end of a narrative plot, emerging from the losing side. In this it imitates the agonistic encounter that solves the present confrontation only to lay the basis for the next one.[8]

In the stylized world of L'Amour's western novels, the agon governs the whole of the plot but finds its special moment in the shoot-out on Main Street. The challenge to honor and the calculated response, the countdown occurring within rule-bound temporal duration, the drive toward satisfaction, often as simple retribution — all of this comes together to shape the climactic moment of the western. But the concerns that are so apparent in the intense action of the climax are also in control of the rest of the story. The escalation of challenge and response leads to the standoff at high noon.

"Agon" is a useful concept to represent patterned conflict. I would then propose a working definition of it as *the conflictual dimension in behavior or human interaction that corresponds to the patterns of narrative.* In life it is the structured engagement in conflict, often including violence. In narrative it concerns the constraints of plot, as it unfolds in the confrontation between protagonist and antagonist. Broader than either life or narrative, it includes the struggles experienced in both. I would use the term "script" to name the constraints of narrative, as they are experienced in our day-to-day living. While life offers dilemmas for narrative to work through, narrative offers scripts for life.

## The Narrative Outlook

As mesmerizing as the action may seem, L'Amour's story world has more than action. In addition to his plot, he has his argument to make. Not only does he depict violent interaction as that which saves, ennobles, and civilizes, but he also defends that view explicitly in speeches among the characters. Insofar as the gunslinger defends his actions he is serving as apologist for the narrator's plot, and thus the narrator. He articulates the narrator's outlook. In literary studies this outlook is generally called "point of view." In L'Amour's stories differences in point of view among characters fall along ideological lines, though we are never left in doubt as to where the narrator's sympathies lie. To see this we must go beyond the agon to other relationships among the characters in L'Amour's novels.

## Civilizing Violence

### Men, Women, and Violence

In these western stories, the men and women are more sharply differentiated than the good and bad men. L'Amour's world is almost exclusively male. Females enter it by sufferance. Women perform a function, but it is passive and symbolic. They stand for a certain set of values — values that the men act to preserve. The great divide between men and women helps to keep questions about any contradiction of values from surfacing.

Two stories about the taming of a mining town in the Old West serve to illustrate. *The Empty Land* (1969) has Matt Coburn as its gunslinging hero, and *Sackett* (1961) features Tell Sackett. Both of these tales are distilled versions of the Sackett saga. In these two stories, the raw western town serves as synecdoche for the untamed frontier. The stories are parables about the civilizing work of subduing the North American continent.

The lesson in the mining-town stories is that *only violence civilizes.* In L'Amour's story world, violence is an unfortunate necessity. This conviction is frequently presented by way of a contrasting foil, a character who is unconvinced of the need for violent action on behalf of a good cause. These characters, though sympathetically portrayed, are shown to be suffering from overprotection. Unfortunately, their benign views do not account for the existence of bad men, who give no quarter, exhibit no mercy, and respond to kindness with opportunism, and always will.

Ange, Tell Sackett's love interest in *Sackett,* is something of an exception in that she is more of a rounded character than is usual with L'Amour's women. Tell has a disagreement with Ange. Matter-of-fact about his need for killing before he gets killed, Tell alienates her by his brutality. During the course of the story she realizes his enemies are bad men, and she converts to his point of view — after discovering how tough he really is during a midwinter descent of a mountain where the two of them have been stranded. On the ideological plane of conflict, *conversion* is possible and frequently occurs. The conversion consists in a shift from idealistic and therefore honorable — albeit naive and unrealistic — views to views that are grounded in the experienced reality, which accept that there will always be intractable, bad men, men who can be controlled only with violence.

Female characters are allowed to be soft. They are, in fact, required to be soft if they are to be a part of the game. They represent the soft center of social value that requires the hard shell of unyielding protection. It is to be expected they may not appreciate the flinty virtues of masculine combat, since it is outside their realm. Hard females, on the other hand, are outside the game, and they are not approved. Similarly, soft men are seen as outside. They, too, are anomalous. In biblical terms, they are an abomination.

## Menace of Nonviolence

The men who cross that line are not "real" men. This distinction between real men and unreal, "soft" men is also a part of the western genre's rigid world and codified character sets. Dick Felton, the first town marshal in *The Empty Land,* is such an anomaly. As the ideological foil to the hero, the gunfighter Matt Coburn, Felton is a proponent of negotiation and nonviolence. His naive convictions about the basic reasonableness of human nature provide the occasion for the unruly town element to take over the town. As the threat of chaos looms, Coburn tries to convince Felton:

> "The trouble with most folks coming out here is that they've been protected so long they're no longer even conscious of it. Back where they come from there are rules and laws, curbstones and sidewalks, and policemen to handle violence. The result is that violence is no longer real for them; it is something you read about but that never happens to you."
>
> Matt paused for a moment, and went on. "You're a brave man, Felton, but you're a stubborn one. You will go down there tonight and get somebody killed. The only rule those men understand is force, or the threat of force.... Well, there...I've talked too much.
>
> Felton was silent. Despite his stubbornness, he had the feeling that what Matt Coburn had said was the truth.[9]

Felton finds himself in a narrowing corner until in chapter 14 he is trapped in the town's main street, surrounded by predatory gunmen poised for the kill. He is saved by Coburn and his skillful gun work. Coburn rescues Felton, takes over as the second marshal, and delivers the town more or less intact to its future citizens.

It would seem that the world of these stories is articulated by two important axes (see fig. 1).

|  | Good | Bad |
|---|---|---|
| hard-shelled | heroes | villains |
| soft-bellied | women | wimps (nonviolent men) |

Figure 1

One axis is the horizontal one of the hard-shelled, the agon — the central, "presenting" struggle between the protagonist and the antagonist. This is what we mean by the main plot. The second axis is the vertical one between hard and soft characters. The second pairing is entirely different from the first because it distinguishes those "in the game" from those "outside." It is marked by mutual misunderstanding, if not ill-disguised contempt. Here the division is more basic, more troublesome. It represents a debate about the terms of reality, the rules of the game. If the first conflict is that of the agon, conducted between the protagonist and the antagonist, the second concerns an ideological struggle over the best way to conduct the agon. And so in L'Amour's mining-town tales we see unfolding in the action a conviction that only violence can preserve civilization from the forces that threaten to destroy it. A further aspect of the conviction is that civilization, at least the American version of it, was built upon this fact of violent conflict, even if it is sometimes not recognized by those who have benefited from it.

The second axis involves a contrast between the views of the protagonist, as advocate of the narrator, and those of an opposing foil character. The dispute among the characters serves as a stand-in for the narrator's dispute with the reader's possible objections to his outlook. Presumably arguing the case in explicit dialogue will contribute to suspension of disbelief, though it is entirely conceivable that the strategy may backfire, as readers are reminded of doubts they had already suppressed.

Since it will recur in other contexts and other stories, this axis needs a name. A designation that reflects its ties to narrative point of view would be useful, so I propose to formalize a term I have been using. The word "outlook" not only evokes the positional metaphor behind point of view but also conveys the basic sense of mental view. As a sort of bonus it offers us a third kind of meaning concerning future "prospects," as when we speak of a favorable outlook. As I am using it here in relation to the agon, the term "narrative outlook" has certain consistent features. It belongs to the narrator. It generates a struggle among the characters specifically concerning the best way to carry out the agon. That is, it constitutes a set of contrasting interpretations of the agon. Behind this it is a disagreement about the *nature of authentic power* — about the best way to bring about the desired change in the action of the agon. As such it reflects contrasting ideologies.[10]

## Myth and the Narrative Quality of Violence

My purpose is not to caricature a popular and enjoyable writer, whose work is more varied than I have suggested, but rather to use his writing, and his popularity, as a door opening into a world largely hidden from us — the world of our own cultural myths. L'Amour is useful as a point of access because his writings present the matter clearly and repeatedly. His widespread and enduring popularity suggests that he has struck a chord deep in our cultural consciousness. I would suggest that this narrative pattern of life-producing violence is a basic form of L'Amour's work and that it well deserves a characterization as *myth*. I should probably forestall unnecessary misunderstanding by stating that I do not intend the popular meaning of myth as falsehood, for the myths of a culture are more like questions than like answers. They are prior to judgments of true and false. They set the conditions for such judgments by defining the social reality in which the truth takes shape.

Furthermore, we have seen that the stories of Louis L'Amour not only express the pattern but *defend* it, especially through the speeches of some characters that highlight the necessity of the action. Even more, I would say that L'Amour's intent, despite his disclaimers, is to identify this pattern as an American myth, a foundational myth that helps to make sense of our society and its sense of reality. I would say that this ideological message, carried through in speech and plot, is the dimension of L'Amour's work that earned for him the Medal of Freedom.

The story of civilizing violence meets the requirements of a number of recent theories of myth.

1. *It establishes a cultural world.* This is, of course, the point of a foundational myth. In John Dominic Crossan's schema of narrative genres, stories are arrayed on a five-point spectrum that ranges from *myth* at the right to *parable* on the left. Whereas myths are stories that "set up" shared worlds, parables are stories that "upset" such worlds.[11] In the center are action stories "set in" the shared worlds. These would simply make use of the cultural universe of discourse established by myths, with no ambition to support or subvert them. At first glance, the majority of L'Amour's western tales seem to belong in the center.

But when Tell Sackett or Matt Coburn begins to defend his version of the story with lectures to the reader, we have moved beyond action story to narrative designed to defend a shared world. This is Crossan's category of "apologue" (a narrative that defends a shared world), which is situated on the right of the spectrum between action story and myth. And when L'Amour makes the claim in his saga series that the American nation was founded on a particular story, he has moved beyond apologue to the end of the chart, for that is the same claim made by myth. Despite his disclaimers he has aggressively adopted the mythic program outlined by Crossan.

2. *It masks a cultural contradiction.* L'Amour's stories also fit comfortably into the well-known theory of myth promulgated in the works of Claude Lévi-Strauss.[12] For Lévi-Strauss the function of such stories is to mask a contradiction deep in the belief system that constitutes a culture. In this view the cultural function of myth is not unlike that envisioned by Crossan. It serves to establish a common social reality. Lévi-Strauss is even more specific in suggesting a mediating role for stories in their multitudinous versions and retellings.[13] Through concrete imagery, stories find surrogate terms to replace the raw elements in tension. These new terms are able to mediate and thereby soften the harsh contradictions that divide values in a cultural fabric. Eventually, the dissonance caused by the edge of contradiction is dulled, and the adherent no longer feels so uneasy.

In the yarns of L'Amour we can see likewise a contradiction in the need to assert that the world of violent men can be overcome only by introducing more violent men into it, this time making sure that they are on our side. The stories cover this contradiction so well that we do not often see it as such — although it frequently troubles us without making it clear to us why it should. In fact, the stories are more apt to persuade us when they lack the lectures, which tend to arouse our suspicions. The stories in themselves serve to accomplish their mythic purpose, without our explicit awareness. One of the objectives of this book is to look behind the veil of the myth of civilizing violence and attempt to bring the intricacies of that cultural knot out into the light for examination.

3. *It has a narrative quality.* In the classic study mentioned earlier, Stephen Crites has suggested that we think of human experience as having the quality of narrative.[14] Many of Crites's proposals would seem to fit our cultural story of violence, as illuminated by the writings of Louis L'Amour. Our faith in violence as the answer to certain kinds of problems is sustained by stories. In fact it forms the kind of story we call a myth, despite L'Amour's claims to the contrary. On the analogy of Noam Chomsky's grammatical distinction between deep and surface structures, Crites distinguishes sacred stories and mundane stories. Sacred stories are the deep structures that underlie all actual expressions of narrative — the mundane stories. The sacred stories are the deep narratives that give identity to a culture. The mundane stories not only express but also reinforce by their repetition the sacred stories. Crites does not use the word "myth" in connection with his topic,

but it would seem that he has the mythic world in mind, especially the classic notion of myths as "stories of the gods."

In the thought of Crites, as I understand it, the narrative form of experience is given by nature, but the mythic content of the sacred stories is culturally determined. We must remember, of course, that the sacred stories are uttered only by way of mundane stories. Here again we are reminded that the function of myth is to set up a shared world. The effect of myth is to present a cultural reality as if it were a natural reality. This is occasion for intercultural misunderstanding insofar as I am tempted to see my own culture as natural and others as artificial, while those of other cultures view me and mine in the same way.

## Gospel: An Alternative Story?

*Two Versions of Reality*

But L'Amour's stories are not the only ones with claims to foundational status in the American experience. The Christian gospel also has its deserved place. As a continent explored by missionaries and colonized by religious refugees, North America was shaped by the gospel story. Its inhabitants of European descent understood their presence here in terms of the gospel's claims of ultimacy. Patriotic hymns such as "America" (1771) describe the millennial peace promised in the New Testament as to be achieved in the United States. "Such peace, of course, could only come through violence."[15] Even the midwestern cities — St. Louis and St. Paul — that served as launching stations for the westward drive chronicled in L'Amour's stories bear names testifying to the influence of the Christian story.

And yet this is the story about one whom Mahatma Gandhi, neither a Christian nor an American, said, "Jesus was the most active resister known perhaps to history. This was non-violence par excellence."[16] This is the gospel of nonviolent resistance that Martin Luther King, Jr., brought inside the American Christian experience decisively and unforgettably. Clearly this story and the myth of civilizing violence cannot coexist without tension and some adjustments.

And Christian thinkers, caught between two versions of reality, have been willing to make adjustments. Consider the legacy of Reinhold Niebuhr's "Christian realism." Niebuhr's social ethics have decisively influenced ethical thinking about war and peace in America for the last fifty years. Alarmed by the rise of Hitler and the Third

Reich, Niebuhr wrote as a convert from pacifism, a transformation he seems to have experienced as a deliverance from naïveté. With his popular essays, collected in *Christianity and Power Politics,* and their more technical elaboration in *An Interpretation of Christian Ethics,* he set the terms of theological discourse on political power for Cold War America.[17]

Niebuhr was at pains to assist those who were passionately engaged in the struggle for justice but who rejected nonviolence. For them, the avoidance of violence on principle seemed a breach of responsibility, a willful denial of a very powerful form of redress. In his essay "Why the Christian Church Is Not Pacifist," Niebuhr explicitly rejected nonviolent resistance, such as Gandhi admired in the gospel:

> There is not the slightest support in Scripture for this doctrine of non-violence. Nothing could be plainer than that the ethic uncompromisingly enjoins non-resistance and not non-violent resistance.[18]

Focusing on Jesus' words and teaching in lieu of his deeds, Niebuhr wished to remove Jesus' nonviolence from consideration as a model for Christian action. He did not dispute Jesus' adherence to an ideal of nonviolence, which he saw in terms of nonresistance. Instead he questioned its practicality, its contact with "reality." Niebuhr's reluctance to admit to the existence of any such entity as nonviolent resistance conforms to the spirit of the myth of violence. There can be no middle ground — either we resist evil and are therefore implicated in violence, or we are nonviolent and therefore fail to resist evil.

A second example: J. G. Davies, writing on the ethics of revolution, literally in moral support of those Christians whose activity in opposition to corrupt or unjust political regimes brings them into violent actions, questions the value of imitation of Christ when it comes to political action. For many if not most Christians in such circumstances, ethical nonviolence seems a dangerously irresponsible social policy. For Christian ethicists and political theorists, who must address these matters squarely, the example of Jesus seems to present a particular obstacle. Arguing that we should not imitate the life and work of Jesus too literally, Davies writes:

> Jesus was a carpenter, but this does not require all christians to be workers in wood. Jesus was not an industrial worker, but this does not mean that we may not earn our living as

such.... The imitation of Christ is not to be interpreted as demanding reproduction of the details of Jesus' life.[19]

And so, lest we be enticed by Gandhi's remark, we learn that determining whether nonviolence is an aspect of Jesus' life we ought to emulate is problematic. Christian defenders of political revolution such as Davies would insist that Jesus' apparent nonpolitical stance — especially as seen in his abstention from the use of armed "force" — does not require similar behavior on the part of his followers. Here Davies's theology converges with that of his opponents on the political right who would prefer that Christian piety take expression in devotional practices that do not threaten the status quo rather than in demands for social change. In this instance too, violence, in the form of a strong defensive military force, is felt to be entirely compatible with Christian discipleship. Here too the *imitatio Christi* is better expressed in the pilgrim's way of the cross than in the practice of nonviolent action.

A third example is the U.S. Catholic bishops' 1983 peace pastoral, *The Challenge of Peace: God's Promise and Our Response*.[20] A testament to the growing public recognition, even respectability, of the peace movement was the quasi-establishment it enjoyed in 1982, in the second draft of the pastoral letter. Here for the first time in memory a major Roman Catholic church document recommended nonviolence as a properly Christian response to war. When Vatican spokesperson Monsignor Jan Schott reminded the delegation of U.S. bishops that the teaching of the Catholic Church remains the just-war tradition, he was responding to a remarkable departure in official Catholic church documents.[21] The advocacy of nonviolence, as shown in the second draft of the peace pastoral, was unprecedented among official Catholic documents.

The opposing view was edited into the third draft. As dissenting voices among the bishops and in the larger church made themselves heard, the treatment of nonviolence was muted, though not erased. In response to critics such as Schott, the bishops lowered the profile of nonviolence in the letter, even while retaining it. They gave the just-war doctrine greater prominence and restricted nonviolence to the role of an option for individuals, not nations. And the section on the New Testament was recast. In general, their efforts further removed them from gospel nonviolence in two steps: Jesus was distanced from nonviolence, and Christian disciples were distanced from the example of Jesus. Jesus' disengagement from nonviolence is signaled by the number of caveats introduced against applying the New Testament in too literal or detailed a fashion (pars. 28, 32, 39, 55). That intention is followed through with more decisive steps, namely, removing the two passages that speak of Jesus as nonviolent.[22]

The needed distance between Jesus and his followers was reached by an ingenious stratagem. Replacing a running account of Jesus' practice (read "narrative"), the Gospel section of the new draft was constructed around certain virtues of which Jesus was exemplar — justice, forgiveness, love. These are shown both in his words (pars. 45–47 in the final draft) and in his actions (pars. 48–49). In effect the center of gravity shifts from allegiance to a person to adherence to a set of abstract values, with Jesus as a premier illustration.

These changes are condensed in the fate of one key sentence. The sentence that opened the section on Jesus in the second draft — which originally read, "As Christians we believe that in Jesus, who is our peace, that reign [of God] was inaugurated and *the ways of peace became visible*" — was dropped. It was replaced with another toward the end of the section, very much like it: "As disciples and as children of God it is our task to *seek the ways* in which to make the justice, forgiveness, mercy, and love of God visible in a world where violence and enmity are too often the norm."[23] And so Jesus is no longer presented as showing the "way" of peace, but rather the way is something that needs to be rediscovered in each age, just as Jesus did in his. The story that Jesus gives us is not the way, for each age needs to find its own way.

The bishops, like many Christians, are caught between two stories. Here we see that the narrative, which presents the activity of Jesus to the reader, is the datum that needs to be overcome. It is the "story" that threatens, in this view, the responsible use of power; it is the story that presents the danger to serious Christian action.

*A Thesis*

The signs indicate that we look to the story. If we are to address the nonviolence of the Gospel, it is to the narrative we must turn. Which leads to a thesis: Mark, as the biblical critics' candidate as the first evangelist, is the first to portray Jesus of Nazareth as the protagonist of a sustained written narrative. Narrative typically involves the literary features of conflict development and resolution. But here the conflict is a violent one, ending in a legally disguised murder. Meanwhile the protagonist is an acclaimed nonviolent hero. Under these circumstances a literary study of Mark's Gospel promises to yield elements of understanding about nonviolent conflict resolution.

Whether or not Mark's motivation was to display Jesus in conflict, his project entailed doing so. Mark portrays Jesus as one who actively resists the evil of his day. His activity of resistance brings him into opposition with the religious authorities, which in turn culminates in arrangements for his death. The conflict is indeed violent: as early in the story as Mk 3:6, Jesus' opponents resolve to "destroy him." Without withdrawing his resistance, the protagonist, Jesus, refuses to adopt the violent methods of his opponents. This deliberate combination of active resistance with the refusal to use violence in the resistance is a succinct description of what theorists mean by "nonviolent resistance."

Mark's decision to place Jesus into the world of narrative allows a portrayal of Jesus acting among relationships of deadly power. It shows Jesus responding to life-threatening conflict. We can think of it as a study of Jesus' behavior in the context of serious power relations, producing a "meaning" in terms of the demands of conflict. The more clearly it is shown that Mark's narrative is indeed a unified and organized story, the more likely it is that this is part of the writer's purpose. Put another way, the Christian mandate to "love one another" takes on weight and import precisely in conflict situations. The rest of the time it is a promissory note, an uncashed check. Mark contrives to address the reality of Christian love by the trajectory of his narrative.

# Chapter Two

## ON READING ANCIENT TEXTS

Myths, like reputations or careers, are made and broken at the level of storytelling. We have learned that the myth of constructive violence takes the form of a story. That is, it does its work in its capacity as story. If Mark's Gospel, as I hope to show, breaks the myth, it does so at that same storytelling level. Our attention will be fixed more closely on Mark's story than on the events of the historical Jesus. The nonviolent resistance that Mark's narrative attributes to Jesus will interest us more than the historical practice of Jesus himself, some forty years prior.

We do well to adopt procedures of analysis that fit the object of our study. Literary criticism is the proper methodology for studying narrative. It also is an appropriate tool for appraising nonviolent resistance in the Gospel, for the simple reason that stories typically involve conflict and conflict resolution. This dynamic interplay of struggle and its resolution is the mainspring of the narrative's plot, the action at the heart of its illumination of life, and is a dominant practical concern for any storyteller. If Mark's story has the shape and literary unity of a plotted narrative, then we can anticipate that what Mark gives us, not available elsewhere until his efforts, is a picture of Jesus as he was involved in conflict over extended time. In placing Jesus into the sustained narrative we call a Gospel, Mark has situated him in a framework of conflict and resolution. In effect, "Mark" is the name we have given the decision to take Jesus beyond narrative episodes and place him within a longer account.

Mark's is generally agreed to be the first of the canonical Gospels, written sometime around the cataclysmic events of 66–70 C.E. that brought about the Roman destruction of the Jerusalem temple. Because Mark was the first evangelist, we might assume that his creative effort was spent in fashioning that larger narrative. Supposing it constituted his primary concern, we might conclude that it fittingly constitutes ours as well. Before we come to our theological judgments, therefore, we might interpose a literary moment.

Granting the author's narrative interests, we are still left with a problem. How are we to approach this text? Should we read it like any other story, or are there special first-century rules of which we should be aware? My presumption in citing the works of Louis L'Amour in discussing the narrative possibilities of the Gospel evokes the potential pitfalls of reading ancient documents. The procedure needs to be defended, at least in principle. How do we guard against anachronisms? Is it legitimate to make comparisons with our own literature? And if not, how can we read the Gospel? The hazards of reading ancient literature cannot be ignored.

## The Absent Writer

The image of narrative discourse as a "delivery system," frequently encountered among literary critics today, evokes a communication model of *sender-message-receiver* as a framework for literary works, in the form of *author-text-reader*.[1] Thomas Pynchon, in his novel *The Crying of Lot 49*, exploits this critical model to explore writing's rich possibilities for misdirected discourse. The book is an expression of Pynchon's fascination with the fragility of human communication.

The heroine, Oedipa Maas, exhibits those paranoid qualities common among Pynchon's characters (a rock band in the novel is called "The Paranoids"). Which is to say she is continually interpreting signals in her environment as personally significant, usually with sinister import. In the third chapter of the novel a Jacobean play called *The Courier's Tragedy*, by a certain Richard Wharfinger, attracts her obsessive attention. Taking advantage of the chance to attend a university players' production, she discovers a line that jumps out at her, full of personal reference. Consequently she researches the play extensively. She finds many variant editions, each with a different version of the line, and the differences are radical, though never without a strong suggestion of personal meaning.

Anne Mangel has shown how Pynchon develops the theme of the tenuous linkage of communication by his use of Claude Shannon's information theory.[2] Mangel remarks:

> The notion of information being altered and lost in the process of transmission is found throughout *The Crying of Lot 49*. Messages are frequently distorted while being transferred, and Oedipa's disc jockey husband, Mucho, must take this into

consideration in his broadcasts. After he has interviewed his wife, Oedipa, who is an eyewitness to Dr. Hilarius's burst of insanity at the Hilarius Psychiatric Clinic, he says, "Thank you, Mrs. Edna Mosh." To the bewildered Oedipa, he explains, "It'll come out the right way. I was allowing for the distortion on these rigs, and then when they put it on tape..."[3]

In Pynchon's novel, the text of the play, *The Courier's Tragedy,* is a "rig." On the analogy of a radio transmitter it is a device or medium of communication. More specifically, it is the written text of the play that acts like a communication device. Because it is written it endures and is able to carry its message beyond the historical moment of "Wharfinger." It is, then, the problem of writing that is presented for our instruction in the novel. Because writing bridges a temporal gap between the sender and the receiver, the playwright's dilemma is that of his play. It is the tragedy of the courier, whose message is never unambiguously delivered. It is the problem of the absent author who cannot be consulted for confirmation, as the elusive Pynchon himself demonstrates.

## An Urgent Message from the Evangelist

Traces in the Gospel text give evidence that similar problems of distance plague our communication from Mark. Consider Mk 13:14. In this passage the need for clear communication is so urgently felt that the narrator's voice breaks through the surface of narrative conventions and buttonholes the reader:

> But when you see the desolating sacrilege set up where it ought not to be (let the reader understand), then let those who are in Judea flee to the mountains.

At this point of the unfolding account, we might note, Jesus is pictured on the Mount of Olives taking leave of his disciples. His speech takes the form of a farewell speech. It is his last word before the irreversible momentum of the passion account begins in the next chapter. His speech alerts the disciples to events that are to occur *after* chapter 16, beyond the horizon of the story being told here. But the future time outside the story that is the occasion of warning is not just *any* time of crisis. It is the end time, making its first appearance in the events of the fall of Jerusalem and the second temple, around 70 C.E. This means, of course, that the future of which Jesus speaks is nothing other than the present time for Mark's narrator. In fine apocalyptic fashion a voice from the past warns of a troubled future that just happens to be — God deliver us — the reader's present moment.

*"Let the reader understand."* Who is this "reader"? The commentaries agree in assuming it refers to a first-century Christian reader, presumably one with some knowledge of the crisis agitating the text. On the other hand, the commentaries agree that they themselves do *not* share this knowledge. True, the "desolating sacrilege" is a well-known phrase. It is familiar to us as the traditional "abomination of desolation" borrowed from the book of Daniel (9:27; 11:31; 12:11), where it refers to the effrontery of the Seleucid emperor, Antioches IV Epiphanes, in erecting a statue of Zeus in the Holy Place of the temple.

But what does it mean in Mark's text? D. E. Nineham admits to the text having exegetical difficulties "as great as any in the gospel." Wilfred Harrington agrees, and both offer some possible interpretations.[4] While they would prefer to be able to supply more definite information, neither seems unduly disturbed that he cannot. And certainly they do not feel their lack of data in this instance invalidates the rest of their reading of the Gospel. Despite the fact that the narrator seems to regard this part of the message with special urgency, taking the case right to the reader, commentators today feel unimplicated by the text. Indeed, even though they themselves are the only "readers" of whom they have certain and immediate knowledge, neither of the commentators mentioned above feels himself to be addressed. Each takes the commonsense position that Mark was writing for his own contemporaries, and this passage simply does not apply outside that context.

For us today this original reader has the status of what narrative critics call the implied reader. As we will see, the implied reader is one that reaches us only through the text; it is the reader implied by the text. It might be thought of as the typical reader that the writer had in mind, insofar as that can be determined by reading the text. If our task as living readers is to put ourselves in the role of the implied reader, as critics claim, we can surmise that the personal detachment of the commentators is peculiar.[5] It would suggest that a serious gap has opened up between the ancient sender and the modern receiver of Mark's message. The very moment the text gives strongest evidence of a need to establish immediate contact with the reader, tearing away the narrator's mask of anonymity, today's readers, the only real readers the text still has, experience the strongest sense of remoteness.

And here the commentators are entirely representative of modern readers. We simply cannot imagine including ourselves and our reading within the possible implications of Mk 13:14. When we read the Gospel, we read it as a distant text, written for others who are entirely removed in time and space. That is, we read it as written *not for us*. And yet we continue to read it because we believe it pertinent to ourselves. We are in the situation of Oedipa Maas, trying to interpret a message seemingly of urgent personal import, but one that finds its way to us across the ages, full of noise and riddled with referential holes. But whereas Oedipa, in the manner of a paranoid, sees urgent personal messages where they ought not be, we disregard evident urgent personal messages as addressed to someone else.

## Opaque Texts

Noise and dead space are not good for delivering messages. Claude Shannon's information theory presupposes a communication function that places a high premium on the *transparency* of the medium. If the device that carries the signal draws attention to itself, it is failing its purpose. A radio or telephone that produces static or a TV screen with the jitters interferes with the message entrusted to it for delivery. As "noise" enters the picture, transparency is lost; the medium becomes opaque. In discussing the communication model of literature, Robert Scholes makes the interesting observation that poetry differs from other forms of writing in the way it thickens language by emphasizing patterns of sound, rhythm, and imagery.[6] Poetic language encourages a shift of reader attention away from referential significance and toward formal properties of language itself. This opacity of poetry stands at the opposite extreme from Shannon's perfectly transparent information medium.

If we then consider a text to be a communication device of sorts, we might conclude that any text needing or inviting analysis is no longer serving its original function. It is no longer transparent. Like poetry, it is *opaque,* thickened. In this thickening of the text we have both the necessity and the possibility of interpretation. In such thickening we have not only the basis for the stability of a message through time but also the foundation of its instability, as "noise" enters the medium. In its opacity we encounter a text that needs accounting for. When, as Scholes says, "in a written act the message is all that we have,"[7] coming to us across the abyss of time, and when it is a message we believe to be of some consequence, we subject the text to methods of interpretation. It becomes the focal point of our vision, less a lens than a locus of interest in itself. We examine it for every clue. The referential dimension is attenuated, present for us only to the extent that we can find it in the configurations of the writing.

A Gospel is, of course, such a thickened text. It is "the word" commonly treated as an object for interpretation. We reflect this attitude when we present it as an object, as in liturgical display, or read it as if it were an oracle without origin or history. But the character of the objectified word, in the sense I have been discussing here, is in great part a consequence of the remoteness of its writer. It comes to us across distances of time as well as space. It is the work of hermeneutics to interpret this message from the past; it is the work of poetics to interpret it as narrative. And so here is our first rule of thumb: *examine the text itself for any evidence of purpose.* The text is our center of gravity, our court of appeal, and our lifeline. Examining it will be our first preoccupation.[8] In the pages below I will be using various strategies for studying the narrative of Mark's Gospel. The idea is to examine the formal properties of this writing in order to see how it works. By seeing what it does, we get a sense of its purpose.

## Genre

Biblical exegetes can get uneasy when we pay attention exclusively to the text, without anchoring our understanding in the events it talks about. When the activity of reading is imagined to involve only the reader and the text, a natural fear surfaces that we are in danger of *reading into* the text whatever we want to find there.

When faced with this threat of misreading ancient texts, critics almost invariably have recourse to the study of genres or literary forms.[9] In so doing a modern reader hopes to escape the ethnocentric tendency to impose one's own ways on persons of another time and place. A literalist reading of the Bible, without due attention to these differences in cultural styles, can constitute a form of cultural imperialism. Indeed, Bruce Malina has compared reading an ancient text with traveling to another land. It can be thought of as time-travel, with a potential as great as any chartered tourist excursion for culture shock or culture blindness:

> It takes only the ability to read to find out what these foreigners are saying, but it takes far more to find out what they mean.

> If meaning derives from a social system, while wording (e.g.,
> speaking or writing) simply embodies meanings from the social
> system, then any adequate understanding of the Bible requires
> some understanding of the social system embodied in the words
> that make up our sacred Scripture.[10]

The wise traveler will be careful to come equipped with a sense of
the customs of the destination culture. Genres and literary forms are
literary aspects of this cultural fabric.

We might compare literary forms to the body language that accom-
panies spoken communication. Each provides a vehicle for a large part
of the communication that is transpiring. Like body language, literary forms are for the most part used accurately and unconsciously
by the members of that culture. And as a result, they can likewise
be a rich source of misunderstanding in the encounter between cultures. For such reasons biblical critics can get very uneasy when
they encounter the use of modern examples, such as in my opening
chapter on Louis L'Amour. Used uncritically, such examples can be
instances of the cultural imperialism I mentioned above. They flat-
ten the variations among cultures and naively find in the texts what
they are disposed to expect there. Since all reading, in a way, is a
process of verifying expectations of a text — finding or not finding
what we expect to see there — a use of modern genres needs critical
demonstration.

Genres or literary forms are concerned with the meaning associated with context. Exegetical handbooks define genres in terms of
two features — their characteristic internal structure and their typical
functions.[11] Both aspects contribute to meaning. The *structure* is conventional — it is a device that is "commonly used, one that is found
elsewhere in the literature of the period." And since the structure is a
social convention, we can say that the words of a literary work find
part of their meaning in relation to their cultural context. Reading
them "out of context" impairs their meaning.

The second aspect of genre is the typical *function* it serves in communication. Certain forms are called upon to do certain tasks. In
order to situate the genre, and thus the act of reading, properly, we
must be aware of this task. In reading ancient genres this is especially
important. James L. Bailey and Lyle D. Vander Broek give a New Testament example of the diatribe, which in the ancient world was used
by teachers to instruct students about an error.[12] In itself the structure
does not suggest this specialized use. Here too the social context is the

key to meaning. Just as the words find their place inside the literary structure, so the structure finds its place within the literary culture.

## The Historical versus the Literary Projects

Most biblical critics understand the uses of literary genres along these general lines. They welcome genre theory as one more tool in their effort to clarify the original meaning of the text. While this approach alerts us to the risks of cross-cultural blindness, it does not fully solve the problem it raises. To see this more clearly, it is important to notice that genre theory is a historical project. It is quite different from what the literary critics are up to. The historical project is a part of the historical-critical approach to biblical meaning. It commonly uses the "author's intent" as a guide to reading. Authorial intent is at the center of historical criticism's interpretation of meaning.[13] In this approach, the key to meaning is to be found outside and beyond the text, in the mind of the author — as extrapolated from the text. Equipped with the interpretive key it provides, we can return to the text to unlock its secrets. In the genre project of historical criticism, identification of literary forms helps to refine our notion of the author's intent because the genres selected narrow possible options to those suitable for such genres. But literary genre theory has come to think of historical criticism's attempt to arrive at a standard existing outside the text for the purpose of interpreting the text as a ploy, a detour, and it has labeled this ploy the "intentional fallacy." Proponents of the theory hold that, in fact, all the information is derived from the text itself, and the detour is hence unnecessary.

The genre project of literary criticism, then, is more concerned with the process of reading than with establishing the intent of the author. Its focus is on the reader and the reader's end of the line of communication. How genres situate the act of reading demands more attention than how they situate the act of writing. In this spirit, Frank Kermode calls genre "a consensus, a set of fore-understandings exterior to a text which enable us to follow that text, whether it is a sentence, a book, or a life."[14] When we read a work, we bring to it a repertory of genres that we try out in our act of reading as possible models for what is before us. Competent reading involves a running assessment, proposals, rejections, adjustments, qualifications, by which we place the text inside or alongside the categories available to us.

To be clear about this, we might enumerate some of the implications of the literary genre project.

1. It concerns the reader and the reader's activity more than the author and the activity of writing. Genre assessments are invoked for interpreting the text rather than for clarifying the author's intent as the guide for interpreting the text. The repertory of genres relevant to the literary analysis is that of the reader, more than that of the author.

2. The reader at issue is the real reader, not the implied reader. This is the import of Kermode's notion of conventions external to the text. The real reader is external; the implied reader is not. Blurbs are printed on the covers of books and bookstores are arranged in genre categories for the real reader. The real reader is today's reader; the original reader exists today only in the text as the implied reader.

3. Genre assessment is a component of all competent reading. Without genre precedents to place the texts we read, they are "unreadable."[15] A corollary of this point is that all writing has its genre or literary form. Even a modest form like that of road signs has its genre rules. They are abbreviated for rapid comprehension. As a result of their extreme conciseness a great deal of the message must be conveyed by the conventions proper to the form. We know quite well that "No Passing" is a command and not an item of information. And "Eat" is an invitation to a relaxed respite away from the dust and tensions of the road, even though in its one-word abruptness it may evoke the parental imperatives of our childhood.

4. Genres are evolving, flexible forms. They come and go; they build on prior examples in order to move in new directions. What Kermode says of new genres — that they are "formed from realignments of existing genres"[16] — is true to some extent of all writing. Old forms are continually renewed. New forms are combinations of old forms, or they do not speak to us.

5. Genres, in contemporary genre theory, are components of a larger culture, which can itself be seen as a "text." It is in this spirit that Jonathan Culler defines genre as "a conventional function of language, a particular relation to the world which serves as norm or expectation to guide the reader in his encounter with the text." The interpretive role of genre — Culler calls this "naturalization" — places a text within the set of possibilities defined by our culture. "To assimilate or interpret something is to bring it within the modes of order which culture makes available, and this is usually done by talking about it in a mode of discourse which culture takes as natural."[17] Genres work as "natural" expressions because they are living components of a cultural text, which we take for reality, part of the given world.

The cultural component introduces an aspect of irreducible social subjectivity, by which I mean that some of the text's content remains unknowable outside that culture. A "feel" for a genre that is carried by the culture is part of what Culler and Tzvetan Todorov mean by *genre competence,* an aspect of reading competence. It is analogous to Noam Chomsky's language competence. When grammarians such as Chomsky appeal to the utterances of native speakers of the language as a criterion for correct usage, they are referring to a prereflective "feel" for the language. It is a way of knowing that can be fastidiously accurate without always being able to articulate the rules it uses.[18] This innate knowing can perhaps be simulated by someone living in a strange culture until it is no longer as strange. But ancient texts from ancient cultures, which we cannot visit and physically inhabit, permanently remain a problem.

### The Problem of Unshared Cultural Contexts

And here is the problem: literary genre theory assumes that the author and reader share basically the same cultural context. They are thought to agree on the assumptions behind the conventions of genre. When Kermode discusses the "fore-understandings exterior to the text," as mentioned earlier, he is thinking of cases where readers "share those fore-understandings rather exactly with the author of the text."[19] But in the case of Mark and other ancient writings, we clearly do not share the same cultural context, nor the same set of genre assumptions. This is what prompted the historical project in the first place.

When biblical critics who are attempting the shift to literary analysis begin to examine the shared world implied by genre conventions, they easily run aground, reverting to the historical project even while imagining themselves still in the vicinity of literary criticism. Knowing that the readers with whom the author shared such assumptions could only be the original readers, critics start to examine the possible ancient genres for clues. But in so doing, they have returned to the task of identifying the author's intent. The "original reader" is invoked to further specify that intent, just as the "original genre" is.[20] And, most telling, this original reader is no longer the real reader. In fact, this original reader is imaginary, constructed from implications in the text. Again, the original readers exist for us today only as implied readers. We are the real readers, and the only task of interpretation going forward is that undertaken by today's readers.

In cases where the author and the reader are separated by the gulf of centuries, two cultural contexts, two sets of genre possibilities, are involved in the text, the writer's and the reader's. But the repertory of genres that counts in the act of reading is that brought to the text by the reader. If all reading involves performing an ongoing series of genre judgments, if this is a necessary part of reading, then drawing from our own genre pool is inevitable. And although the historical critics may imagine it to be otherwise, the relevant primary repertory for reading Mark is inevitably our own. This is true, I think, even for the historians of genre.

On the other hand, the original collection of genres available to the author is of secondary importance in reading. What does it contribute to my reading? In the best of circumstances it acts as a control on the choice of relevant genres to use as models for the text before me. If the genres I bring to the text as models are like filters, then the ancient genres are filters of the filters. The active role of proposing options for reading the text belongs to the living genres of our own "native" set. In this sense first-century genres act as second-order controls. Negatively they may rule out some of today's options — *bildungsroman* may be eliminated as lacking early precedents, but biography not necessarily so. On the positive side, ancient genres may suggest modern analogues. Popular narrative is a very pertinent example. The western stories of Louis L'Amour turn out to be more than simply acceptable examples. In my discussion of the narrative myth of violence in relation to the Gospel of Mark, the models I bring to the Gospel must be shown to fit. Proper genre selection is confirmed by the text. The text, to a greater or lesser degree, meets the conventions of the genre, and the various points can be argued. I will be doing this in the next chapter. A proposed genre's appropriateness to the text is indicated by how well it illuminates that text. When it fits, it generates meaning. And this leads us to our second rule of thumb: *exploit analogies between modern and ancient genres.*

Because the discontinuity between author and reader is one of larger cultural texts, the distance between them can be addressed in another way. Anthropological studies can suggest analogies between components of the two cultures, as we have seen with the agon. In this case an apparent continuity between the ancient world and our own experience is supported by a continuity of narrative patterns. Later on, in chapter 6, we will see how Gene Sharp's nonviolent variation on our experience of conflict resolution suggests a parallel variation in narrative.[21] Our third rule of thumb follows from this: *cultural analogues can assist us in determining the purposes of analogous genres.*

*Popular Narrative*

When we say that a Gospel is a narrative, we are saying that we
profitably read it using narrative modes; it fits our expectations of
narrative. We bring our experience of reading narrative to the task
of making sense of the Gospel, whether we do it self-consciously and
critically or not. But what do we mean by our "experience of reading narrative"? For most of us this experience does not occur in the
company of the literary greats. We generally take our stories in a
much more commonplace form, whether on the beach or in the book
club. This reason alone is enough for us to turn to popular literature
like the stories of Louis L'Amour as analogues for reading the Gospel
narrative. But another consideration is involved. Popular genres are
particularly suited for defending and reinforcing shared social values,
and their popularity doubtlessly relates to this social function. The
comforting effect of much popular narrative certainly is a consequence
of its place in cultural reinforcement. In other words, the social role of
popular literature makes it an optimum site for exploring the narrative
myths of our cultures. The social impact of the Gospel finds a parallel
at this level as well. Popular literature, then, with its deep history and
wide audience, might well help us to situate the Markan narrative and
clarify our response to the reading.

As a primary candidate for the model we bring to reading a Gospel,
popular narrative seems to receive some confirmation from the use
of Koinē Greek in the New Testament. The fact that the Gospel of
Mark is couched in the language of the street rather than the academy
converges with other evidence to suggest that it displays a "popular
literary style."[22] Mary Ann Tolbert has proposed just such a cultural
and literary context for the writing of Mark's Gospel. Noting the rise
in the classical age of a popular culture and literature alongside the
culture of the elite,[23] she posits a popular genre, the prose novel, with
literary features that match many of those of the Gospel.

Popular literature is inherently ephemeral, being considered less
valuable and less worthy of retaining. The lack of historical evidence
occasioned by the fleeting nature of popular literature has delayed our
recognition of its influence in the first-century world. It seems to have
been more widespread than previously thought. Extrapolating from
what little has been preserved in the way of popular novels, along
with examples from similar works of greater literary pretension and
historical, biographical interest, such as the *Cyropaedia* of Xenophon
of Athens, Tolbert is able to propose a popular form very much like

the Gospel. At the very least she has isolated a family of writings with genres both popular and stylistically similar to the Gospel.

Some of the features in Tolbert's proposed popular genre are found in the Gospel: the mythic motif of the wandering hero, religious interest in divine rescues, a conventional style with formulaic development and brief dramatic scenes, dialogue with narrative summaries, episodic development, openings that begin abruptly or *in medias res,* a central turning point, a final recognition scene.[24] Some of these are also similar to our own popular literature and, we might suspect, fit the requirements for the popular literature of any era. And some of it is of course peculiar to its own age. Nevertheless, Tolbert's investigations suggest we are on the right track in situating ourselves among the popular literary expressions of Mark's culture and our own.

In his text for aspiring playwrights, *Playwriting: The Structure of Action,* Sam Smiley looks at the popular form of drama we encounter in our pervasive exposure to movies and television. Smiley prefers the traditional name of "melodrama," and sees it as a third, distinct form, as old as the art of storytelling, rather than "tragicomedy," frequently conceived as a combination of tragedy and comedy.[25] Since we associate melodrama with the oversentimentalized nineteenth-century stage, with its mustachioed villains, the term is open to misconstruction. What Smiley invokes is a genre as ancient as Euripides and as current as the movies. In fact, "Two modern entertainment industries depend upon melodrama as their basic material — television and cinema."[26]

Since he views it as a distinct, third form, Smiley distinguishes melodrama from tragedy and comedy. His views contribute to our sense of popular literature. Melodrama is more easily constructed than tragedy or comedy. Furthermore, it is easier to pull off. A poorly constructed melodrama is more likely to engage an audience than an equally poor tragedy or comedy. Also, it involves serious action. Usually the seriousness arises from a threat posed by an unsympathetic character to the well-being of a sympathetic one. The threat is genuine, though usually not permanent:

> Such a temporarily serious play comes into being through the use of an action formulated to move from happiness to unhappiness and back to happiness, materials selected to generate suspense in the whole, style controlled to express dislike and terror, and purpose applied to demonstrate life's potential for good and man's inventive vitality.[27]

Good and evil are more clearly distinguished than in tragedy or comedy, and this distinction centers in the characters. The protagonist is "a good hero who suffers but finally wins" in competition with a bad antagonist, properly called a villain, who deserves the punishment usually meted out for him or her. These characters tend to be static, having made their fundamental moral choices before the action starts. The characters do not change during the action as they do in tragedy. Instead of Aristotle's tragic emotions of pity and terror, the emotive powers appropriate to popular drama are fear for the hero and hate for the villain. Thus the more satisfying ending will not only reward the hero, for whom we wish happiness, but also punish the villain, for whom we fervently desire disaster.[28]

Popular narrative commonly comes to us in subgenres. The typical novel of Louis L'Amour belongs to the subgenre of the western. This form joins a cluster of others in the general popular group sometimes called "genre literature." Examples include science fiction, fantasy, romance novels, mysteries, spy stories, and thrillers. And more. These are the subcategories of popular literature. Popular literature differs from high literature by its stricter adherence to conventions. It is self-admitted formula writing and offers the consolations of familiar patterns. It foregrounds the plot at the expense of character depiction and stylistic virtuosity. The virtues of popular literature are those of expectation met and (threatened) values reaffirmed. Not only does the plot formula become an old friend, but the conflict involves a threat to culturally shared values that is inevitably turned back.

## Narrative Criticism and the Gospel

### Story and Discourse

The power of narrative concepts for dealing with the text of Mark's Gospel has been illustrated in a flurry of studies in recent years.[29] One of the services of this critical development has been to stir us from the doze in which narrative had been all but forgotten. This history of forgetfulness can be accounted for. The Christian community was convinced that the Gospels were written to guide and instruct us, and certainly not just to divert, entertain, and amuse. In William Beardslee's terms, they would seem to belong to Aristotle's *Rhetoric* rather than his *Poetics*.[30] The rhetorical category was better able to account for the teaching function of the Gospels but found it difficult to do justice to the narrative form. It reduced the story to little more than illustration for propositional truths or, even more trivially, appealing packaging. Narrative criticism, by contrast, understands the work to achieve its effects by way of the narrative itself. The story that Mark labored to shape does the text's work. It becomes a theological text by way of being a theological narrative.

In addition to waking us from our forgetfulness, narrative criticism has developed precise categories for it.[31] A consensus has emerged among these studies that the main parts of the narrative structure are *story* and *discourse*. In a brief survey of narrative studies on the international scene, Jonathan Culler concludes that this division of the field between story and discourse is irreducible. Culler articulates this distinction as one "between a sequence of events and a discourse that orders and presents events."[32]

In the critical literature, "discourse" is a term with many meanings. As I am using it here, it contrasts with story. Narratives, whether verbal or scenic, reach their audience by way of a discourse. While these two modes of discourse share an interest in presenting stories, they go about the matter in divergent ways. Dramas show; novels tell. Yet both are discourses. Both order and present events for an audience. But in the case of verbal discourse we have the further mediation of a narrating voice.

The *narrator* who tells the story controls the delivery of the account, disclosing and withholding information, rearranging the sequence of events, elaborating some and abbreviating others to suggest their relative importance. Narrators can double as characters, either in a central role, like Huck Finn in his story or Holden Caulfield in *Catcher in the Rye,* or a peripheral one, like Ishmael in *Moby Dick* or Benjy in *The Sound and the Fury.* As the peripheral character narrating moves further away from the center of the action, he or she approaches the status of the narrator outside the story. The narrator inside the story can only relate what he or she knows. This gives rise to certain effects, as in the withholding of key information from the reader in mystery novels or the more seriously conceived but similar play of perspectives in works like Lawrence Durrell's *Alexandria Quartet.*

The "omniscient" narrator outside the story also offers some characteristic effects. We recognize matters of tone (skeptical, buoyant, fatalistic, matter-of-fact), an "eye" for a certain kind of detail, and so forth. One overwhelming advantage of the omniscient narrator is its apparent modesty. We may not recognize when the omniscient narrator is in fact at work. Its presence should not be confused with the absence of a narrator. Because it draws no attention to itself it can do its work all the more quietly and effectively. Another advantage, paradoxically, is its Godlike omnipotence. The reader, realizing the omniscient narrator is in full control of all the circumstances of the narrative, trusts its total possession of the "facts" and its apparent objectivity.

The literary notion of the narrator clarifies some otherwise troublesome aspects of the Gospel account. In short, the narrative voice recounting the Gospel story knows all manner of things that Mark, as an ordinary though talented mortal, could not. The voice tells us what people are thinking. It tells us what motivates their actions. It knows about Jesus when he is alone, in the garden or at the baptism. While we might, if pushed, decide the evangelist conducted extensive interviews in order to verify all these private scenes, a simpler and more elegant solution is that he has adopted the time-honored convention of the omniscient narrator. The Godlike quality of the omniscient narrator lends a subtle authority to the statements — a matter of no small moment considering that the protagonist, a carpenter from a small town in Galilee and a theological nonprofessional, has the entire religious establishment to overcome.[33]

We can categorize narrators by the quality of their *point of view,* and the omniscient narrator is the most comprehensive in its outlook. "Point of view is a feature of narrative inextricably linked with the narrator," David Rhoads and Donald Michie remind us. Citing the work of Boris Uspensky, they note that point of view in narrative is expressed on four planes: "the ideological system of values and beliefs of the narrator and each of the characters; the characteristic style of speech which identifies a speaker; the physical place or point in time from which a narrator or character views something; and the mental actions or emotional states of mind such as thinking, feeling, or experiencing."[34] The aspect that most claims our attention is that of the ideological point of view of the narrator. Our working notion of narrative outlook concerns the ideological point of view, especially insofar as it is consciously defended.

Narrative studies now see that the narrator is one part of a larger system of discourse. We are already acquainted with this system since it is essentially a version of the communication model of *author-text-reader* that we encountered earlier during the discussion of the absent writer.[35] At the receiving end of the structure of discourse is the notion of the *implied reader,* a component of the text that has proven useful in studying the Gospels. This idea, most commonly associated with reader-response theory, is disputed in its formulations and can be surprisingly complex. In its simplest formulation it refers to the reader implied in the text. For instance, as mentioned above, the reader named in Mk 13:14, in the famous phrase that breaks into Jesus' speech ("let the reader understand"), is the implied reader. Insofar as the implied reader represents the "ideal reader" of the text — the reader envisioned by the writer as having the proper set of competencies to interpret it correctly — then the implied reader is a model for actual readers. I want to adopt, at least for the duration of the reading, a position as close to the implied reader as possible.[36] An allied notion that has as yet not proven as productive for Gospel criticism has been the parallel idea of the *implied author,* derived from the theories of the critic Wayne Booth.[37] In both cases the implied author and implied reader are to be distinguished from the real author and real reader. The former are implied in the text; the latter are outside the text in the real world.

In narrative theory, *story* refers to discourse as the string of events in their natural, chronological order, before they are arranged by the art of the storyteller. Though not as unprocessed as we might suppose, Holinshed's chronicles provided the "raw" data for Shakespeare's history plays. Event is plotted, and in the plotting we perceive a claim to purpose. More properly, the event of the "story" exists prior to any telling, even the minimal narrative of chronicling. Since the only access to this "natural" condition of the story is through the narrative as told, in discourse, this original chronology is purely hypothetical. We reconstruct it from what we hear or read. But the story as we encounter it is always mediated by a discourse that "orders and presents these events." This ordering of the events is called the plot.

*Plot,* then, is a step removed from "story." Plot can be called the artful arrangement of the events, for plotted action is seldom presented in its simple chronological form. Events are omitted or elaborately developed, and they frequently are transposed in time, as in the "flashback." The nature of the events of the story shaped by the discourse may be factual or fictional. The storytelling art is by no means restricted to fictional materials, as the evening news teaches us nightly with its stories. The presentation of the story is always important. Even the most naive of storytellers must be careful with the plotting, as the experience of joke telling instructs us. Our interest in plot centers on the one form we have called the agon. We will return to it in the later chapters.

Besides adding precision to our thinking about narrative, the categories of story and discourse have pointed implications for our study of Mark's Gospel, as well as the myth of constructive violence. As naming the events mediated by discourse, "story" points to what Mark's Gospel is "about" — the events in Jesus' life some forty years prior to the writing of the Gospel. While most New Testament studies of nonviolence focus on the historical events in the life of Jesus of Nazareth, we are placing our attention elsewhere. As an ordering and presenting of the events, the discourse of the Gospel narrative is the focus of our interest. Rather than viewing Mark's Gospel as a lens for observing the historical Jesus of Nazareth, we wish to examine Mark's portrait of Jesus for clues toward the evangelist's theory about the meaning of Jesus' action.

## Plot and Conflict

Insofar as Mark can be called a narrative text, we gain by examining it with the tools of literary criticism. Insofar as the Gospel can be seen as popular narrative, it invites us to focus our attention on the plot of the narrative. Reliance upon conventional style with a formulaic plot is a consistent feature of popular narrative, whether modern or ancient. Plots are commonly thought to occur around conflict, and the conflict is usually between characters.[38] In the pattern we have called the agon, both forces are personal: the protagonist and the antagonist. In Mark's Gospel the conflict between the characters conforms to the situation in popular narrative insofar as the characters enjoy fixed roles that do not change. The terms of opposition are clear and unvarying. Furthermore, in Mark the characterization privileges the plot, in particular the conflict at the heart of the plot. This can be seen in two ways. First, the character traits of the personages in the Gospel are selected for their value in delineating the line of conflict in the plot. Second, the characters are grouped so as to simplify the forces of conflict.

That character traits primarily reflect lines of conflict can be seen in even the most "complex" of the characters, the protagonist, Jesus of Nazareth. While we might agree with Rhoads and Michie that "the narrator creates a very complex characterization of Jesus,"[39] this complexity stems more from the multiple conflicts he enters and the need to clarify the terms of conflict than from any inclination on the narrator's part to share interesting biographical information toward providing a character portrait of Jesus. The complexity derives from the complexity of the action. The narrator is very concerned to tell the plot of the story clearly and not at all interested in telling us what Jesus looked like. This can be put briefly by saying that the real Gospel portrait of Jesus is to be found in the action of the plot, rather than in the characterization.

An example of how characters are grouped to delineate the forces of conflict in the plot can be found in the merging of the Judean authorities into one body of opposition to Jesus. The components of the group already form groups in themselves. Six main groups are mentioned: scribes, Pharisees, Herodians, chief priests, elders, and, perhaps surprisingly, Jesus' family. The Sadducees make a cameo appearance in this group (12:18–27), and the council, or Sanhedrin, functions as an official version of the chief priests' and elders' group.[40] Historically and sociologically, the Pharisees and the temple priests were quite distinct and frequently in opposition to one another.[41] Their religious commitment was rooted in different institutions of Judaism, the synagogue and the temple, respectively, and their theologies differed accordingly.

And so a second narrative impulse seems to be at work here. First of all, the narrative wants to cluster the diverse groups into a single opposition movement. But it also needs to bridge the gap between the earlier opposition, mainly pharisaic in composition, and the later, mainly priestly. In bridging this gap the narrative provides continuity over a major hiatus in the oppositional role. In addition to these two groups, the "scribes" serve as an important line of continuity. The scribal group begins the opposition (1:21–28) and maintains a prominent place in it through to the trial of Jesus before the council and his handing over to Pilate (15:1). In this narrative "scribes" seem to provide a third term for linking the temporally distinct groups of Pharisees and chief priests. The clustering of the oppositional groups into a single role is the pattern with other personae in the story. The disciples are more vivid as a group than as individuals; the sick persons repeat the same narrative pattern in story after story, as if belonging to the same club.

In this focus on the action of the plot, Mark's Gospel seems to conform to the description of popular narrative, early and late. More pertinently, in the action of the plot we find the narrative conflict developed and resolved. If we are to pursue this study further, we must investigate this dimension more closely. And so we turn next to the plot of Mark's Gospel.

Apart from putting on display some of the main aspects of narrative criticism, the purpose of this chapter was to justify the narrative approach in Gospel interpretation as one proper to the text, though neglected in the course of tradition due to other concerns. The narrative focus dictates the methodology. And while the first determination of genre study on the Gospel of Mark affirms its narrative character, this can be specified further by classing the Gospel text with those narratives we call "popular." As a popular narrative, it adopts a certain relation to popular social attitudes. While we might assume this relation is one of support, since popular literature has to sell, this is not necessarily the case. In fact, our supposition is that the Gospel confronts and opposes certain accepted social attitudes, including those that favor violence. In terms of Crossan's categories, delineated in the previous chapter, Mark's Gospel is a parable opposed to the cultural myth of violence.

*Chapter Three* _____

# THE GOSPEL AS AGON

One of the satisfactions offered by popular literature is the security of an unvarying plot formula. We permit ourselves to worry as we witness a serious threat mounted against the hero, who stands as the image and guardian of social values. But in the course of a narrowly averted disaster the hero undoes the villain, and the world is restored to its proper frame, all the more securely for having been tested. This happens in the struggle we have called the agon, which depicts the determined resistance against the threat of evil that is the narrative's image of social conflict. In the agon we can locate the development and resolution of conflict that justify the literary focus of our investigation.

This already gives us two reasons for investigating Mark's narrative plot. First, insofar as Mark's story works within the frame of popular literature, it depends upon the formula plot. And this needs some clarification in the case of the Gospel. Second, if we are to perceive the development and resolution of conflict in the Gospel, we need to isolate the plot features in which the conflict is to be found.

But there is a third reason as well. As a part of our exploration of nonviolence in the Gospel it is important to see that Mark depicts Jesus as an active resister. In the first chapter we saw that Reinhold Niebuhr rejected this side of Jesus' activity in the name of "Christian realism." Jesus was thought to preach "an ethic of pure nonresistance," undiluted by aggressive action. And yet, while he may have been nonviolent, Jesus was also determinedly confrontational. In showing this I want to respond to those appraisals of the Gospel that depict Jesus as a compliant victim whose simple goodness aroused opposition from a malevolent set of demonic men. Jesus' goodness in Mark's story is not passive and private. It is a goodness that brings him to initiate a challenge against certain practices of his day. He provokes and disturbs. It is the burden of this chapter to show how Mark presents his story plot as narrative conflict.

And finally, there is a fourth reason. Mark's text does not easily

yield its plot to today's readers. Just as the message may get miscon-
strued over the distance of the ages, so may its form be mistaken. And
so, before we chart the plot, we need to defend it.


## A Case for Mark's Plot

In plots, discourse and story intersect. The rearrangement of the story
events is a consequence of their presentation in the discourse. The only
access we have to the events of the story is through the discourse.
The story is mediated by the discourse, and none of it is unmediated.
Verbal narrative, stories that are told, differ in many important ways
from scenic narratives, stories that are acted in the theater or on TV.
But what they have in common is the mediation of a discourse that
arranges the action for presentation to an "audience" in the ordering
we call plot. For this reason, literary critics of the novel, a relatively
recent genre in canonical Western literature, have been able to draw
on the long tradition of dramatic theory. And a primary contribution
of this tradition is the classic plot.

The classic plot displays a unity of action. Complications that develop, moving the plot into what is frequently called the rising action,
are directed by actions and choices made at the beginning. Typically
they lead to certain anticipated forms of opposition and raise the question of the protagonist's ability to sustain the course of action in the
face of the implied conflict. These lead the action to a major turning
point, the climax, which is a result of previous actions. The climax is a
primary cause of the falling action, bringing the plot to its conclusion,
or dénouement. The unity of action is one of causality, and as such
it imitates an experience of a reality that is tied together by decisions
and actions with anticipated consequences.

Aristotle, who offered the tragic plot as the model of dramatic
unity, contrasted its logical unity of causality with the temporal unity
of mere chronology. In a chronological period of time, a person or set
of persons can be involved in a number of actions that are unrelated.
But in the logic of plotted action the multiple actions are pared down
to a single action with a beginning, a middle, and an end. Aristotle
takes the single action as a principle of order to place this simple plot
in contrast with episodic plots.[1]

Unfortunately, Aristotle's notion of *episodic plot,* "in which the episodes follow one another in no probable or inevitable sequence,"[2]
seems to describe, accurately enough, Mark's text. First of all, the

Gospel is episodic in the simple sense that its individual episodes are clearly defined, whereas the larger pattern they describe is not. Norman Petersen has noted that the conspicuous agreement among biblical critics of all schools concerning the "boundaries of the minimal units" of Mark's text is matched only by "the conspicuous lack of agreement among these same critics about the boundaries of larger units comprised of two of more minimal units."[3] The only undisputed segments in the Gospel are the individual episodes.

But the inability to agree on larger segments of the text points to another way in which the episodic texture reveals itself. Mark's Gospel is *paratactic,* insofar as its episodes are presented democratically with minimal connectives, in simple coordinate, rather than subordinate, constructions. Usually a simple "and" (*kai*) introduces a new event or sentence in Mark's Gospel.[4] Between episodes the narration neglects the kind of connections that could provide transition and a sense of causality between events. Lacking apparent commitment to the larger whole, each episode seems to stand alone, in arbitrary association with its neighbors.

All in all, Mark's Gospel appears to provide a vivid example of Aristotle's episodic plot. The result is a situation in which no one can claim to have discovered the undisputed overarching pattern of the Gospel. In homage to Henry James's famous story about a perpetually elusive narrative pattern, Robert Fowler notes, "In different ways, many have sought the figure of Mark's carpet, and no one has ever failed to find it. That no two versions of the figure are ever identical simply makes critics try harder."[5] When Fowler himself attempts to determine the features of Mark's text, his skepticism about the "figure in the carpet" prompts him to fall back upon those features of the text that are undisputed. He accepts only two as meeting this criterion. The feature of episodic style, as I have been discussing, is one. The other is Mark's penchant for double structures. *Dualities* or doublets are pervasive in the Gospel. Frans Neirynck has shown that duality appears at every level of the text,[6] from repeated major narrative movements at the macroscale, down to microelements of the sentence structure. Neirynck argues that the omnipresence of this trait shows a degree of control over the materials that can be explained only by a unity of authorship. But authorial unity does not necessarily imply a unified written work, though it allows us to raise the question more legitimately. The plot of Mark still remains a disputed question.

However, the more certain features of the text may guide us to the answer. Using its combination of episodic texture and pervasive use of dualities, it seems possible to make a case for its overall narrative pattern. Among the many levels displaying narrative duality is the macroscopic level of the major movements. Actions are repeated not only as individual incidents but also in the context of larger sequences that relate to similar sequences elsewhere. Pairing these sequences is not difficult, and it offers us an approach to the larger shape of the story.

We can accept the encouragement of Walter Ong in seeking a more unified dramatic structure for the Gospel since he points out that typically the historical shift from oral to written narrative in a culture is marked by a corresponding shift from episodic sequences toward "tight, Freytag-pyramid" literary structures. "Because of increased conscious control, the story line develops tighter and tighter climactic structures in place of the old oral episodic plot."[7] Insofar as Mark's work occupies a transitional place between the oral traditions about Jesus and the written Gospels, re-creating in its production the historical journey of narrative from spoken to written forms, we are invited to seek signs of centered literary unity amid the episodic strings.

The diagram of Gustav Freytag (see fig. 2), originally devised to explicate the structure of five-act tragedies, has been widely accepted for presenting the plot structures of many kinds of story other than tragedy, including those of most narratives and plays. It will help us as well in our efforts to determine the plotting in Mark's story.[8]

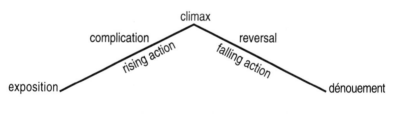

Figure 2

The constituent parts are well understood. The *exposition* sets the tone, gives the setting, introduces the characters, and supplies other facts necessary to the understanding of the play; the *complication* continues through successive stages of conflict up to the climax; the *climax* is the main turning point in the plot; the *reversal* stresses the activity of the forces opposing the hero, leading logically to the closing events; the *dénouement* is the outcome of events, the "unknotting." The relations among these various parts are graphically represented by Freytag's diagram, with "the rising slope suggesting the rising action or tying of the knot, the falling slope the falling action or resolution, the apex representing the climax."[9]

## The Main Form: Blocking the Action

Prominent among the differences between the Synoptic Gospels' order of events — which originates with Mark — and the quite distinct sequence found in the Gospel of John is the climactic event that precipitates the passion account. In John's Gospel the raising of Lazarus from the dead, in chapter 11, proves to be the final intolerable act of Jesus that pushes the Judean authorities into decisive action. One must die to save the nation (Jn 11:50).

By contrast, Mark assigns this narrative role to another event, namely, *the cleansing of the temple.* It is the final and most extreme of Jesus' actions challenging the deadly social structures of his day. In the account of the cleansing, at Mk 11:18, we learn the authorities are resolved to "destroy" him. In shaping his narrative Mark is clearly conscious of the prophetic precedent of Jeremiah. The prophet's famous temple confrontation, reported in chapters 7 and 26 of his book, is cited by Jesus tellingly in his similar action (Mk 11:18; Jer 7:11). Jeremiah was arrested and threatened with execution. He refused to defend himself. The reenactment of this pattern by Jesus, along with the somewhat garbled charges of threatening the temple issued at his trial, reinforce the climactic role of the temple action in Mark's narrative arrangement. The moment extends into the temple debates of chapter 12, at which time the authorities attempt to stop Jesus. Despite their failures at this time they are clearly resolved to succeed.

Freytag's pyramid, the diagram that we have borrowed to visualize this dramatic form, clarifies the plan of the narrative. The first thirteen chapters of Mark's plot belong to the rising action and the last three chapters to the falling action (see fig. 3).

In this reading of Mark's narrative form, three developments reinforce one another in the climactic rise and fall: the buildup and release of *dramatic intensity* of the conflict; the *control of events* taken and lost by the protagonist, Jesus; and the rising and descending *fortunes* of the protagonist. Each of these peaks in the temple episodes, to be

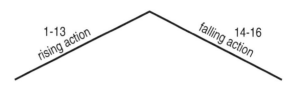

Figure 3

followed by an opposite movement. First, the rise and fall of dramatic
intensity is seen in the mounting conflict. Jesus' refusal to be dissuaded
by the premonitions about the probable consequences of the road he
is traveling leads him to a confrontation that puts him in mortal jeopardy. After the climax in the temple, the passion account in chapters
14–15 follows with a sense of numb inevitability.

Second, Jesus is shown in the rising action to be in control of the
successive events. His initiative dominates the action, to be succeeded
by the counterinitiative of his opponents in the falling action. Following the pattern of challenge and response, he persistently raises
the stakes, keeping the pressure on and maintaining the initiative. In
the passion account, this initiative passes to the opposition, and Jesus
becomes a passive target of their reaction.

The third pattern is that of the waxing and waning fortunes of the
protagonist. In the rising action Jesus is the bearer of possibility, the
vehicle on which people's dreams and hopes ride. In the falling action
the dream is shattered and the hope lost among patterns of betrayal
and abandonment. This pattern is probably the most striking and apparent to the reader, an image that can remain even when the story is
adapted to the pageantry of liturgy or folk drama.

This initial perception of the main form of Mark's plot gets further support from the dual patterns in the episodic structure. Thus the
more certain features of the text confirm our sense of the larger form.
When mounting a play, a theater director groups and positions the actors so as to clarify the dramatic action. Something similar happens
in Mark, as the dual forms articulate the action of the plot by defining its dimensions. This work of "blocking the action" is performed
primarily by framing structures. The dual segments give us two major
movements in Mark, corresponding to the rising and falling actions
of traditional plot theory.

## Two Beginnings

Anyone who has seen the musical *Godspell* will recall that in its depiction of the Gospel story only two characters are readily identifiable. Along with the "Jesus character" there is another who takes the dual role of John the Baptist at the beginning of the show and the role of Judas at the end. In both roles he is in charge of the action — getting it moving and then bringing it to a close. This surprising double role points up something in Mark's story. John the Baptist and Judas are similar catalysts of action. The one opens the conflict; the other closes it. In each case, the character introduces a sequence of events, and the parallels between the two sequences underline the similarity of their roles.

First of all, both the Baptist (1:2–8) and the Betrayer (14:1–11) are *catalytic figures:* in Mark, each is given a title that identifies his characteristic activity. What is more, the action named in the title is not simply associated with the character but in fact contributes directly to the plot. The baptism and the betrayal, when directed to the protagonist, Jesus, are the specific catalyzing activities. The *symbolic actions* of the baptism (1:9–11) and the cup (14:12–31) encapsulate these two moments, as John performs the baptism and Judas violates the solidarity implied by the cup. In Mk 10:35–40 the baptism finds a parallel in the cup, and the cup then emerges as a symbol of Jesus' ordeal (see 14:23, 36). The *temptations* in the desert (1:12–13) and the garden (14:32–42) follow. These frame the full, elapsed time of Jesus' struggle. The internal conflict of Jesus is not elaborated as one of the conflicts in the story, but neither is it ignored. The *arrests of John* (1:14) *and of Jesus* (14:43–52) conclude the series. Mark's arrangement suggests a motivation for Jesus' decision to go public. With John no longer active, someone must take up the task. John precedes Jesus, and his arrest becomes a premonition of Jesus' own. At 14:41–42, the initiating activity of John is completed, and that of Judas takes over.

Something of an exception to the prevailing pattern established by the other paired dualities in Mark, the Baptist and the Betrayer are not so much a frame for the intervening material as they are similar starting points (see fig. 4).

While in some ways Judas can be said to conclude a sequence of actions begun by John, he does this by beginning a fresh sequence of actions, the passion account. It is this sequence of actions that closes off the main action of the plot begun by the Baptist. Both figures are initiators, and what they initiate are the rising and falling actions of

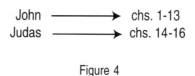

Figure 4

the plot. Chapters 1–13 contain the rising action, while the passion account in chapters 14–16 presents the falling action. John triggers the rising action in chapters 1–13 while Judas performs the equivalent function for the falling action in chapters 14–16 (see fig. 5).

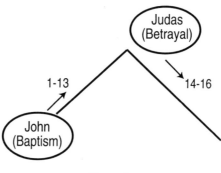

Figure 5

The literary manuals call these two motives in the dramatic structure the "exciting force" and the "tragic force," respectively.[10] The language reflects the habit of the handbooks to use tragedy as the paradigm for dramatic form, though they intend the application to be broader. An example of the exciting force setting into motion a rising action is the ghost's revelation to Hamlet in act 1 of Shakespeare's play. Later in the play, the blind stabbing of Polonius is the tragic force that causes Hamlet to be sent away just as he seems on the verge of success.[11]

In Mark's Gospel these moments are personified, as I have shown. The baptism is the exciting force that places Jesus in the moment of receiving the mandate for carrying out the story project. John the Baptist is the personal catalyst for the action of the plot. In relation to the plot he is the exciting force personified — he is "the Baptist." Similarly Judas, "the betrayer," personifies the action that generates the downward motion of the plot.

*Cleansing Actions: Synagogue and Temple*

The rising action is itself reinforced by another pair of events, which serve to frame the action as its point of departure and climactic terminus. In the exorcism in the Capernaum synagogue (1:21–28), Jesus engages the opposition. He rids the synagogue of an "unclean" spirit, outdoing the scribes. This rather outrageous initiative of Jesus finds its counterpart in the even more disturbing cleansing of the temple in chapter 11, which culminates his increasingly confrontative program of action. In these two "cleansing" moments we find a suitable symbol for the reforming work of Jesus. The parallels between the two moments are ample enough to force the conclusion that a parallel is being elaborated (see fig. 6).

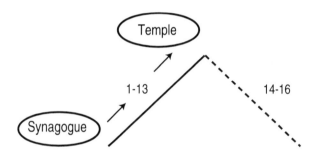

Figure 6

Some of the pertinent parallels deserve to be cited: both actions are *cleansings of holy places,* at the center of their respective localities. Both are *evictions,* though the verbs used are switched, in the sense that each uses the verb expected in the other context. The merchants of 11:15 are "cast out," with a verb otherwise reserved for demons (*ekballo*). Meanwhile the demons of 1:25–26 are evicted with the command to "come out," in an almost physical manner. Both powerful actions raise *questions about Jesus' authority* (1:22, 27; 2:10; 11:28–33). These questions are aired in the following *debates,* giving us the two clusters of "controversy stories" in Mark, in 2:1–3:6 and 12:1–37. In both cases, the action is imaged as the rejection of *the old as "withered"* (3:1–5; 11:20–22), to be replaced by *the new as "wine"* (2:22; 12:1–12). Finally, and most importantly, the *key terminology of conflict* is found in the word "destroy," which appears twice in each location, aimed symmetrically in each direction, against

Jesus (3:6; 11:18) and against his professed opponents (1:24; 12:9).[12]
Destruction is unquestionably at issue in this conflict; violence is an
indisputable concern of Mark's plot.

The events of the synagogue and the temple mark off a stretch of
narrative that features the confrontational initiative of Jesus. By their
privileged positions at the beginning and the end of it, they serve to
characterize this time of rising action. As violations of significant sites
they represent a challenge to honor in the manner of the agon. They
demand a response. And insofar as they bracket the full time of Jesus'
initiative, they warn us that the entire trajectory of the rising action
requires a response. We find that response characterized by the key
phrase "destroy him." This language puts us on notice to anticipate
the quality of Jesus' counterresponse to his violent opponents.

While these framing actions can thus be read as key moments in
the pattern of the agon, they also point to the ideological outlook of
Mark's narrative conflict (something we will explore more completely
in the next chapter). We know this because these significant sites are
"holy places" and Jesus' actions are "cleansings." This evokes the ritual language of the holy and the unclean, which sets the terms for the
worldview that would find its center in Jerusalem. These framing actions show Jesus adopting a stance of trenchant criticism against the
expression of the holy in his day, as epitomized by its holy places. The
implied charge is extreme: they have become havens for the demonic.

Furthermore, insofar as many of the actions of Jesus bracketed by
these events express God's compassion for the suffering and marginal
people of the land, a definite continuity between challenge and compassion emerges. Jesus' critique of the holy is balanced by actions of
liberation and renewal in God's name. The release of the holy places
is to be seen as a release of the liberating God restored to a needful
people.

*Anointing Actions*

Like the rising action, the falling action of the narrative is bracketed
by parallel events — the anointing attempts at the beginning and end
of the passion (14:1–11; 15:42–16:8) — in a framing pattern unique
to Mark. In Mark, the pair operate as a frame, in each case set apart
from the intervening action (see fig. 7).[13]

The Bethany anointing (14:3–9) is sandwiched between a pair of
passages that some critics see as originally forming one unit (14:1–
2, 10–11). It has to do with the council's conspiracy against Jesus and

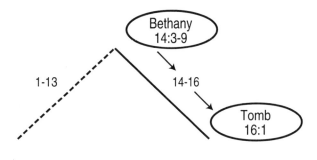

Figure 7

Judas's instrumental role in that conspiracy. The anointing is identified by Jesus as a burial anointing, by anticipation (14:8). Like the burial anointing at the end of the Gospel, it is untimely. This is too early; the later anointing is too late. This effort succeeds in anointing Jesus' body, though his body is not dead; the later anointing fails because his body is gone from the tomb: although he has died, he is apparently not dead. Together the two anointing attempts work to make a whole. At opposite ends of the passion account, prior and subsequent to the appropriate moment, they strive to supply the necessary ritual of burial. Neither succeeds since they are shut off from access to the body of Jesus during the crucial time of his death and burial, by the Sabbath prohibition and by the hostile forces that have crucified him. They can only do homage from the edges of the arena of narrative action.

Like the cleansings of the holy places characterizing Jesus' initiative in the rising action, the anointings of his body provide a powerful symbolism for the falling action of the fallen hero. Like cleansing, anointing is a ritual action we still use. At Bethany it is Jesus' head that is anointed (14:3), which signals that Jesus dies as Messiah, as D. E. Nineham recognizes.[14] "Messiah" literally means "Anointed One" and refers to the practice of anointing the head of a new king.

The political dimension of the symbol speaks to the agon — Jesus dies as Messiah, the anticipated king, the threat to the usurpers in present control (like Herod, in Matthew's infancy narrative [Mt 2:1–11]). Jesus' claims, backed by his actions, have resulted in his execution. Furthermore, the only anointing given the Anointed One is burial anointing. The meanings of "Messiah" are condensed in this narrative symbol. And while it brings to mind ideas of the "suffering Messiah," the phrase is not to be confused with certain pious extrap-

olations of this theme. We ought not put aside its narrative context.
We do not have here an "innocent victim" ambushed by the unpro-
voked malice of wicked enemies unable to stomach the prospect of
sharing the planet with virtuous persons. Rather Jesus is experiencing
the consequences of his deliberate, sustained challenge to the standing
social arrangement through the first thirteen chapters of the Gospel.
Any piety here is political and confrontational.

## The Dramatic Movement of the Plot

So far I have used Mark's penchant for doublets to support my sense
that the temple cleansing is the climax of the Gospel narrative, giving
the authorities a reason to remove Jesus from the scene. Although I
can thus trace the possible outlines of a plot structure, I need to fill
it out. I need to show it at work, especially in the time of rising action, where the forward movement of narrative typically runs through
a series of minor crises, thwarted at first and then regaining momentum, until at last the major crisis is reached. I want to propose such a
pattern for Mark's narrative.

In this task I will depend on two other studies. The Gospel outline devised by Eduard Schweizer will provide the basis for identifying
six dramatic "acts" in the Gospel narrative.[15] Although Gospel exegetes in their forgetfulness of the narrative tend to produce thematic
outlines more suitable to expository prose, Schweizer's outline, which
has been well received, has certain features more suggestive of narrative than most.[16] (See Appendix A for a fuller treatment of Schweizer's
outline and its narrative possibilities.)

While Schweizer's outline allows us to segment the Gospel into acts,
it fails to recognize the framing dual episodes that bracket each of
the segments, similar to those that we have seen to define the major
movements of the plot. Once we have located these dual episodes it
will be useful to take some clues from Tzvetan Todorov to see them
at work. Todorov's theory of narrative transformations[17] determines
the movement in a narrative sequence by comparing two statements,
one describing the situation at the beginning of the sequence and another describing the new situation at the end of it. When properly
done, each of the two statements is a grammatical transformation
of the other, hence the narrative "transformation" (see Appendix B).
The theory is precise and nuanced. Todorov catalogues only twelve
possible modes of transformation.

While each episode of the Gospel is theoretically open to dem-onstration of narrative transformation, I am interested here in the framing episodes of the various stretches of text I have called "acts." In these the text itself seems to provide statements of its purpose, marking out the movement in the sequence in the Todorovian man-ner. One difference is that the Gospel (or my explication of it) seems to favor antithetical pairs, or contrary statements. This is only one of Todorov's twelve options. In the section below I will try to show how each act of the Gospel plot moves forward in terms of these bracket-ing episodes, repeating on a smaller scale the pattern seen in the larger movements of the plot.

### Act 1: The First Week (1:14–3:6)

After an expository prologue (1:1–13) that includes the baptismal mandate of Jesus, the first full "act" of the Gospel presents the conflict that generates the action of the story. Beginning with Jesus' initia-tive — calling followers and healing the sick and possessed — the action moves from cure stories to debates in which the scribes and Pharisees emerge in opposition to his efforts. The act concludes with the Pharisees joining with the followers of Herod Antipas in Galilee, in a conspiracy against Jesus.

Two synagogue events frame this part of the action. The Ca-pernaum synagogue that houses the opening confrontation with the demons (1:21–28) parallels the synagogue that is the setting for the cure of the withered hand (3:1–6). The two Sabbath accounts describe an opening "week." In the framing episodes the terms of this section's movement are given in the verb "destroy." The fearful demons intro-duce this language, and it is later picked up by the narrator to describe the key decision taken against Jesus by his opponents (see fig. 8).

Will you destroy us? (1:24) → Let us destroy him! (3:6)

Figure 8

The agreement between King Herod's people and the Pharisees is an unusual consolidation of forces, the first of many in the Gospel.

It creates a situation that demands a response. What options does it leave open to Jesus? If we eliminate the option of no response, as ruled out by the dynamics of the agon, three remain available. He can back off from the challenge and end the move toward confrontation; he can respond in kind; or he can intensify the original program.

In the first scenario, Jesus could retreat from his challenge, explaining that matters are getting out of hand. He could tell his followers that he had not intended to place them in jeopardy and that now he feels he has no choice but to terminate the program. In this scenario the story would stop here.

Again, he could respond in kind, destruction for destruction. This is a possible story, but not the one we find in the Gospel. This is the story I imagine as "Rambo Jesus."

The third option, the one chosen, is to continue his original program, but at a heightened level. In response to the opponents' consolidation of forces, Jesus consolidates his own following. He names twelve "to be with him and to be sent out" (3:14). He organizes his movement. This leads into the second act, in which this newly organized group is contrasted with the family of Jesus.

The dramatic connection proposed here, like those that follow, is not spelled out in the text in terms of cause and effect. In Mark's episodic style the narrative simply presents us with one event after another. We are left to draw our own conclusions, making our own connections. This readerly activity of supplying meaningful connectives is already seen as early as the synoptic revisions of Mark. For instance, in Mt 12:15, in the passage parallel to Mark's, we see Mark's suggestion completed. The causal connection not expressed in Mark's text, namely, that Jesus was aware of his opponents' secret conspiracy, is spelled out in Mt 12:15 (although Matthew's redaction will take the narrative in another direction: "When Jesus became aware of this [the conspiracy], he departed"). Here, as one of Mark's earliest readers, Matthew demonstrates any reader's tendency to close the gap in the action by inferring the necessary information to supply the causal linkages of narrative plot.[18]

### Act 2: The New Family (3:7–6:6)

The second "act" of the Markan narrative begins with the consolidation of Jesus' movement by naming "the twelve" as a cadre, here placed in contrast to Jesus' birth family, who have come to fetch him. These events are followed by a cluster of parables (4:1–34) that read like inaugural teachings for the newly consolidated disciples. This represents a period when his disciples are "with him" (3:14) in a period of apprenticeship. The episode on the lake follows the parables. This and other occasions for crossing the lake show the disciples to be confused. It is as if they repeatedly are given an opportunity to "cross over" to new insight, which they repeatedly fail to reach. In chapter 5, after the crossing, three miracles are recounted: the story of the Gerasene demoniac, called "Legion," and the interpolated stories of the daughter of Jairus and the woman with the hemorrhage.

In this section, Jesus' "new family" replaces his natural family, which represents the cultural matrix of Jesus' upbringing and which will stand in opposition to his new message. The two "family" episodes (3:20–35; 6:1–6) are the only instances in which Jesus' relatives enter the Gospel story. In the first instance his family comes to take him home, fearing he is deranged. Apparently he is too much of an embarrassment to them. The scribes use the occasion to interpret his estrangement as demon possession. Jesus uses the occasion to interpret his group of disciples as a new "family" that does his "Father's" will. This moment points ahead to the Nazareth synagogue (at 6:1–6), when his own people will finally reject him.

The terms of the framing language, then, have to do with his homecoming: he is requested to return home, but in the end he is refused asylum there (see fig. 9).

Come home! (3:20-21) → Leave home! (6:1-6)

Figure 9

They reject him in response to what they fear is his rejection of them. In bringing the good news to Nazareth he has the temerity to imply that they are in need of it. Yet he is one of their own, a local product. Apparently the upbringing he received at their hands does not seem adequate to him. He has been listening to other mentors, other "parents." As one result of the consolidation of his movement, he is in effect cut loose from his home moorings.

*Act 3: Feeding the Multitude and Other Stories (6:7–8:30)*

The episode at Nazareth that concludes the second act closes a door. Following this, Jesus sends the twelve out on mission (they were called "to be sent out"), knocking on other doors. This account of mission, which raises a question about Jesus' identity (6:14–16), initiates a section that concludes with Peter's identification of Jesus as Messiah (8:27–30). The third act moves beyond the previous, insofar as the disciples move beyond apprenticeship to delegated ministry. The question of identity proves to be a seed of conflict since the disciples' delegated action depends upon the answer to that question.

The miracles of loaves in this section in particular heighten the question of identity. "Bread" language dominates this act.[19] The section shows a period of desultory movement as though Jesus, shut out from his home place, had not as yet received a clear signal for the next direction to take. The movement will take on a sense of purpose in act 4, in the march on Jerusalem. In act 3 the ministry of Jesus is provisionally expanded beyond the confines of Galilee to include a few, apparently representative, gentiles.

Two "identity" sayings that frame the third act are verbally parallel and outline a sequence in which the problem of Jesus' identity is raised. The episode of Peter's recognition at 8:27–30 has a counterpart earlier, at 6:14–16. In both cases there are reports regarding popular speculation about Jesus. The candidates listed in each instance are John the Baptist, Elijah, or one of the prophets. At 6:16, Herod identifies Jesus as the Baptist, the one who had "come first" (9:12). But in 8:29, in response to the same question, Peter identifies Jesus as the Messiah. So the third act of the plot is similarly framed by parallel episodes (see fig. 10).[20]

| The king identifies Jesus as the Baptist: the forerunner (6:14-16) | → | The followers identify Jesus as Messiah: king (8:27-30) |

Figure 10

The third act charts the political content of the plot. The king of Galilee, concerned about Jesus' identity, unknowingly has his concerns justified because the Messiah, God's king, has appeared on the scene. This is the narrative strand that Matthew's infancy narrative develops as regards the original Herod, concerned about a possible rival in Mt 2:1–12. Here the signal for directed action is Peter's recognition of the Messiah. Now they can move toward the city, where the Messiah belongs. The king moves on to the capital. The political implications of this move suggest the dynamic of popular uprising, which is a familiar pattern for the Judeans of the day, as we will notice later.

### Act 4: The Road to the City (8:31–10:52)

The fourth act is bracketed by the accounts of two blind men, one at Bethsaida (Mk 8:22–26) and another, named Bartimaeus, at Jericho (10:46–52). Jesus heals the Bethsaida blind man with a second attempt at a cure, since after the first attempt human figures still appear to him "like trees walking." This initially inadequate healing seems to represent the as-yet partial insight of the disciples, witnessed in the following episode. The healing of Bartimaeus also has implications for discipleship insofar as he "followed him on the way," which leads, of course, to Jerusalem in the next episode (see fig. 11). Whereas the first blind man compares with Peter, the second contrasts with the ambitious brothers, James and John. Matthew elaborates the comparison by redoubling the number of blind men (Mt 20:29–34).

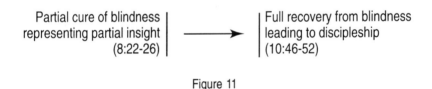

Figure 11

These episodes mark out the time of Jesus' major teaching, and the insight to be gained in the teaching is symbolized by the acquired sight of these framing figures. Three times along the way Jesus previews what they are to expect in the city (8:31; 9:30–31; 10:33–34). In each case his teaching meets with misunderstanding on the part of the disciples, first by Peter, then by the twelve as a group, and then by James and John. While they accept the messianic role of Jesus, they consistently misinterpret the nature of his power. Their misunderstanding expresses itself in an interest in personal ambition and special privileges and in the rejection of Jesus' "servant" methods for effecting change. The sense that the group is moving on Jerusalem in order to take it over, which implies violent revolt, generates the teachings of this section about servant discipleship. Jesus counters the implications of violent takeover with his teaching, even while he continues his rather aggressive march on the city.

Upon arrival at Jerusalem, in chapter 11, there is indeed a triumphal entry into the city, but it is defined by the reference to Zec 9:9–10. This passage pictures a commander without an army. He triumphantly enters the conquered city but without the usual accompanying military forces. We are to imagine a conquering hero without an army. Immediately afterward he initiates a program of disarmament.

### Recapitulation: The Time of Rising Action in Mark's Gospel

Once we realize that Mark's plot is shaped to describe a time of rising action followed by a time of falling action, we can better appreciate how the Gospel presents Jesus as entering into conflict in a deliberate, purposeful way. If Jesus is nonviolent, he is not passively so. His nonviolence is one of active resistance. The opening "week" of activity sets an intense level of confrontation, as it moves from the initial healing actions by Jesus to the antagonistic responses of his opponents, disputing his actions. In the episode of the cure of the withered hand at 3:1–6 the narrative arrives at its first crisis, as Jesus' opponents conspire to "destroy" him. With this conspiracy and Jesus' response to it, the rising action is off and running. When Jesus and his party finally reach the temple, the violent language of destruction recurs (11:18), and the promise engendered by the first crisis finds fulfillment in the main crisis and climax of the plot.

As the occasion for the initial crisis in the rising action, the story of the man with the paralyzed hand gives us an entry point into the meaning of conflict in Mark's Gospel. The story introduces language for the final crisis in Jerusalem. By situating the episode on the Sabbath and in the synagogue, God's time and place, the narrative has Jesus asking what it is that God would want. What kind of activity would God desire to occur on this privileged time, in this dedicated place? What kind of activity in fact best characterizes God? What worship?

Jesus' opponents prefer a species of worship uncluttered by concerns for suffering humans. They experience no contradiction between their passion for pure worship and their indifference to human pain. Presumably God, in their view, shares the same outlook. The God who is not troubled by the suffering of others conceivably might even require it. The enemies of Jesus, here called Herodians and Pharisees, may have room in their theology for a God who would require someone to suffer and die. But this is not Jesus' God. Events confirm this later in Jerusalem, during the debate about the Great Commandment following upon the temple incident, including the scribe's comment on worship (12:33).

Nor is this harsh God the God of Mark. At his baptism, despite what we tend to suspect, Jesus is not given a divine mandate to march to his death. In this narrative God does not demand the death of Jesus. That demand is the determined policy of his opponents, who do not share his faith in the God of possibility but in fact are characterized as in league with the demonic.[21] The story of the withered hand, which expressly poses the questions of life and death (3:4), shows us clearly that the God for whom Jesus is advocate favors life. Jesus' God in this Gospel is assertively and polemically *against* death in all its guises and is *for* life in its fullness — *for* restoring the disabled man to full ability. Jesus and his opponents vote by their actions: life and death. Jesus renews the man; his opponents decide to destroy Jesus (3:6). Here in the first crisis of the unfolding narrative, the lines are drawn. From this way station the road leads to Jerusalem, as each side acts out the terms of its faith convictions.

Why then does Jesus go to Jerusalem? Not to step out a divinely pre-scripted ritual unto death. True, he goes in response to a mandate from God. But this mandate is not that Jesus die but instead that he struggle to overcome those who promote death, who cultivate its structures, whose allegiance to it is seen in their willingness to kill when to their advantage. Jesus is liquidated by the lieutenants of death, but they do not, this narrative asserts, prevail. And so, when we imagine that the baptismal mandate of Jesus demands his death and requires him to march as if in procession upon Jerusalem in order to die there, we must understand we work against the grain of the Gospel.

### Act 5: The Temple Action as the Narrative Climax (11:1–13:37)

The confrontation that begins in the synagogues of Galilee reaches a pitch of high tension in the Jerusalem temple.[22] The plot to destroy Jesus, presented to the reader in 3:6 as a proposal for the future development of the narrative, reaches its fulfillment in 11:18, as the temple demonstration prompts the authorities to act on their earlier resolve. But moving from the cure stories of the early Galilee sections of the Gospel to the sterner moment of the temple cleansing, a different Jesus seems to take over the story. As Jesus travels from the edge to the center of the Judean social topography, his actions shift from the compassionate to the wrathful. The cleansing of the temple, which follows almost immediately upon Jesus' arrival in Jerusalem, stands as the high point of the rising action. It is the sharp edge of the crisis that precipitates his fall. In this action, Jesus gives every evidence of being angry. This has proven to be troublesome for anyone who conceives Jesus as unflappably mild-mannered or who would understand wrath to be incompatible with compassion.

A frequent part of this picture is the specter of Jesus coming upon the temple and "losing his temper," surprised by the venality of the Holy (market) Place. His anger is then excused as unpremeditated (and then serves to excuse the Christian's ill-controlled temper): as if Jesus were angry despite his principles. Ched Myers reminds us that those who engage in this interesting daydream forget that temples were known to be commercial centers, and no one expected them to be otherwise.[23] It would be most unlikely that Jesus would have been surprised. In fact, the text portrays his actions as very deliberate. Having entered the temple on his arrival (11:10), he retires to the house in Bethany where he would stay during his time in Jerusalem, and he returns to the city on the next day (11:11) to carry out his action. It is presented as a carefully conceived act of disruption. As I have suggested, it stands as the concluding dramatic development of his initial confrontation at Capernaum (1:21–28) and the outcome of its narrative logic. It is a deliberate and integral part of the story, the climax of its plot.[24]

That compassion and wrath are not of necessity mutually exclusive can be observed in many instances. For one, Dorothy Day, who began her work in the Catholic Worker movement by providing shelter and sustenance to anyone needing it, eventually found herself moving toward confrontational acts of civil disobedience. In the 1950s she participated in protesting the civil defense programs of the time. While she experienced a continuity between the works of hospitality and the acts of civil disobedience, most of her supporters in the first could not follow her to the second. She could claim that the compassion addressed the effects of social dysfunction, while confrontation addressed the causes. But her critics saw her as abandoning good works to turn to troublemaking. For one reason or another, they did not share her analysis of the causes of social inequity.

## Prophetic Dismantling

The popular characterization of the temple action as a "cleansing" is more profound than we might suspect. More is happening here than clearing away abuses in order to restore a prayerful decorum. The prophetic actions and texts surrounding the central climactic action of the cleansing show it to be a judgment on the temple itself (see Appendix C). As I will discuss in the following chapter, the unclean and the holy, as determined by the temple, stand as two extremes of one social system — the Judean purity system. In the temple action the Judean social system itself is rhetorically dismantled. Pronouncing judgment on the central shrine, the "tabernacle" of stone, like a latter-day Samson in the temple of Dagon, Jesus in effect pulls out the central tent pole holding up the web of social conventions that converge on the "Holy Place."

The language of destruction, which announced the beginning of the main conflict in Capernaum (1:24; 3:6), returns with the temple events (11:18; 12:9). It is the key motif of the plot's conflict. But whereas Jesus' opponents wish to destroy him (3:6; 11:18), and he is seen as a threat to the demons (1:24), he himself leaves the fate of his opponents to God (12:9). Jesus does not "destroy" persons in this story.

And yet their fear of his destroying power does hover around him, always pointing to the temple. They charge him with intending to destroy the temple (14:58; 15:29), and he has indeed predicted its fall (13:2), a physical destruction that occurs as Mark is writing this account around 70 C.E. Yet the only action within the story that can account for the rumor of temple destruction is the temple cleansing at 11:15–19, with its implications of judgment. In fact, in the story as Mark tells it Jesus does "destroy" the temple, but not as a physical building. Rather, it is the temple in its role as capstone of the holiness system of purity that is dismantled. The climax of the plot is the "symbolic" destruction of the temple. But the reality of the temple is not the building — the reality is the symbolic world of which the temple is the central axis. Jesus' caustic judgment at Mk 11:15–19 constitutes this destruction. This is the end. The razing in 70 C.E., as Mark is writing his Gospel, is merely the clearing away of the empty hulk, the debris of its demise.

In this narrative climax and its subsequent events the programmatic nonviolence of the Gospel is presented at the level of Mark's narrative rather than of Jesus' historical activity. In the Gospel as Mark narrates it, the temple is targeted because it is the center of the ideological world. Nonviolence is neither an arbitrary nor a tactically chosen method for Jesus; it is the mode of his resistance from the very beginning of the story.[25] In Mark, of course, the political system targeted from the opening of the account is the sociological world of the purity system — the ideological world administered by the Sanhedrin from the temple as base, with the approval of the Romans. The political position of the temple, the political posture of the religious authorities in Judea, and their role in maintaining the conditions of Roman imperialism have all been amply demonstrated by the sociohistorical literature. The purity system served the objectives of the dominant orders.

This can be put quite simply by saying that any dispute as to whether Jesus' action at the temple was an attempt at religious reform or one of humanitarian liberation is a false dilemma. It is false because the God of Israel is the God of the exodus and the prophets, and any religious reform would also "restore" the divine zeal for humanitarian liberation. Conversely, any human liberation movement in Israel would certainly take the route of restoring the God of the exodus and the prophets. So it is not surprising that at the time of Jesus' death the temple veil is reported torn; God's authentic presence is no longer obscured. The God of bondage is replaced by a God of freedom for whom human well-being is a clear concern. As for Israel, by removing the bindings on their worship and their minds, Jesus makes it possible for them to clear away their other impediments.

*Act 6: Within the Times of Anointing (14:1–16:8)*

Jesus' confrontational performance has its consequences, and so we come in act 6 to the time of falling action. The movement of this part is characterized by a sense of inevitability and a growing remoteness that places Jesus far outside the safe circle of his own party. Connected with the anointing episodes that begin and end the falling action are two Janus-like characters, Judas Iscariot and Joseph of Arimathea. These two dramatize the action of the section. Each is tellingly identified by his membership in his respective group. At this stage in the narrative the groups have evolved into opposing camps. We read: "Judas Iscariot, who was one of the twelve" (14:10), and "Joseph of Arimathea, a respected member of the council" (15:43). The narrative makes these identifications for a reason. Despite their membership in one of the opposing parties, each of these figures is now seen to be consorting with the "enemy." Judas "went to the chief priests, in order to betray him to them." Meanwhile, Joseph "was also himself looking for the kingdom of God."

The two are symmetrical mediating figures whose destiny is to mediate, in effect, the body of Jesus (see fig. 12). Judas hands him over to the chief priests; Joseph retrieves him. Judas's action — in whose case the verb *paradidomai*, "hand over," comes to mean "betray" — sets off a chain of "handings over" that culminate in the death of Jesus. Through the drumbeat of its repetitions, at 15:1, at 15:15, the verb echoes into the precarious distance to which they lose Jesus. Once he moves out of the comparative security of his own group he is passed on into greater and greater jeopardy: from the Judean council to Pilate, who has the authority to condemn him to death; from Pilate to the soldiers, who have the practical capability to carry through the order. In this dance of distance, Jesus' isolation is palpable and powerfully felt by the reader.

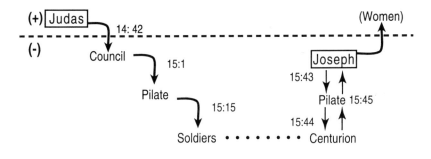

Figure 12

It is worth noting how, in this Gospel, Joseph's efforts to recover the body of Jesus initiate a movement that retraces all of the previous steps. Joseph, like a messenger into the underworld, must act out a social image of Jesus' descent into death, and return.

The falling action of the Gospel is shown here as an X-ray of the chain of events that Judas has precipitated. Like the Baptist on behalf of the rising action, Judas is the catalyst for the falling action. The transformations between the framing situations of the sequence are complex, for the sequence moves in a double stride: from life to death, but then back to life again — from the presence of Jesus to his loss, but then again his presence in a new and puzzling way. The last moment is posited, but not clearly realized. No resurrection

appearances conclude Mark's work as it is usually critically recon-
structed. And yet the ending certainly moves us beyond the first
transformation into death and loss. However, that moment remains
inaccessible to the reader as it is to the disciples, and so the narrative
moves on.

*Chapter Four* ———————————————————————

# THE SYMBOLISM OF POWER

In addition to the agon, we have the narrative outlook. While the first term names the struggle between protagonist and antagonist in the narrative plot, the second identifies an understanding of power promoted as the best way to pursue the objectives of the agon. Every genre has a tacit theory about the kind of power best suited for bringing its plots to satisfactory resolution, but most are not as frank about the need for violence as are the stories of Louis L'Amour. Others may avoid violence or may be unclear about their own tacit support of it. To see this larger picture, which has implications for the Gospel narrative, it will be useful to take a welcome break from the western stories and jump across the borderlines of geography and genre to the narrative world of Sherlock Holmes.

In Holmes, Arthur Conan Doyle would incarnate the nineteenth century's confidence in the power of reason to deliver us from peril through its application in the scientific method. In the story "The Five Orange Pips," Holmes articulates his credo:

> "The ideal reasoner," he remarked, "would, when he had once been shown a single fact in all its bearings, deduce from it not only all the chain of events which led up to it but also all the results which would follow from it. As Georges Cuvier could correctly describe a whole animal by the contemplation of a single bone, so the observer who has thoroughly understood one link in a series of incidents should be able to accurately state all the other ones, both before and after. We have not yet grasped the results which the reason alone can attain to."[1]

The exemplar of reason unencumbered by emotion, Holmes finds the ideal foil in Dr. John Watson, the narrator of his exploits. Watson's sentimental nature not only screens the narration against too many clues, so as to set the reader up for Holmes's deductive surprises; it also situates Watson as a suitable debating partner for their ongoing dispute about the relative merits of their two views of reality. In these stories, knowledge is power, and Holmes's version of technological reason inevitably evokes Watson's awe as the eeriest of mysteries answers to the mundane facts of scientific explanation. For, as Robert Paul notes, "In all cases where the supernatural was in question, the evidence turns out to be entirely factual and the agencies material."[2] An example is when the fantastic turns out to be phosphorous paint in *The Hound of the Baskervilles.*

As to "the results which the reason alone can attain to," the twentieth century would submit its own report, qualifying for many the promise of Holmes's credo. From the ovens of Auschwitz to the video marketing of Desert Storm, the power of technical reason unencumbered by emotion has received doubtful support. And while Holmes's vision retains a strong cultural grip on our beliefs, we have definitely noticed erosion in the structure of confidence. The myth once taken for granted has become visible to us.

Whereas in the stories of Louis L'Amour the narrative disputes directly advocate violent means, the violence in the Sherlock Holmes stories is indirect. The logic of technology, supposedly unleavened by enfeebling emotion but actually committed to a strongly felt program of dominating the world of nature and circumstance, hides a complicity with violence that history has since brought to the surface. This complicity has been uncovered in the commentary of other narratives as well — for example, early warnings such as Mary Shelley's *Doctor Frankenstein* and late apocalyptic scares such as Kurt Vonnegut's *Cat's Cradle.* Dr. Felix Hoenikker, the inventor of "ice-nine" in Vonnegut's novel, feels a commitment only to the project, not to the planet, which fails to survive his obsessions.

When we compare the stories of L'Amour and Conan Doyle, we begin to realize that allegiance to a certain kind of power is typical of many subgenres of popular literature. To the commitments to violent action of the western hero and to the scientific method of Holmes we could readily add others. The power of self-immolating love animates certain romance novels. Belief in the socially transforming power of scientific research helps to define a kind of science fiction. The prevalence of international conspiracies controlling our lives is characteristic of certain species of thrillers. And so forth. We begin to suspect, in fact, that decisions concerning the nature of authentic power contribute to the definition of popular genres. Each implies a belief system about the way the world works, and the form of power it advocates is what makes its kind of story work.

In the act of suspending disbelief the reader joins the narrator in allegiance to a certain theory of power, at least for the duration of the story. For this is the mainspring that loads the action of the story, the power behind the agon. The need to win the reader over may be one reason why a narrator might spend some time trying to convince the reader, typically through speeches among characters, of the validity of this outlook. In any case, it has given us the ideological debates in the L'Amour novels and Holmes's frequent methodological discussions with Watson, complete with dramatic demonstrations of Holmes's deductive powers as he describes the recent history of each person who walks in the door on the basis of subtle clues.

## Mark's Symbolic Vocabulary

Like most popular narratives, Mark's Gospel invokes a theory of power to situate the action of the agon. It too is a part of the narrator's agenda. It too develops a dispute about the nature of true power. In the Gospel, however, this power is questioned, not endorsed. We find it in the narrator's use of the ritual language of *holy and unclean*.

The language of Judean ritual provides a basis for interpreting the conflict of the agon and raises the question of the use and true nature of power. The question is put in the form of another: What is authentic holiness? The purity language of the Gospel does not raise the question of violence directly, and in this it resembles the Holmes stories. However, it also differs from the Holmes pattern — in order to discover the latter's implicit link with violence it was necessary to await the testimony of history and other writings. In Mark's Gospel the implication is part of the text itself, found in the violent language of destruction that characterizes the opponents of Jesus (e.g., 3:6; 11:18). In the Markan narrative, their language of power inclines them toward violence.

Both holy and unclean were seen in Judaism as powerful realities beyond the realm of normal life. Both were fenced off from normal life because of their potential for danger. In this threat they were alike, though one was the epitome of good and the other of evil. They came to be polar opposites, but they had not always been. In fact they imply two distinct systems, since the opposite of holy is profane or secular, whereas the opposite of unclean is clean. As dangerous powers, each finds its antithesis within normal, familiar reality. Together they offer a symbolic language of power, good, and evil.[3]

As Mary Douglas has convincingly shown, *dirt* is best understood from an anthropological point of view as "matter out of place." Mud in the garden is good, clean soil, but mud in the kitchen is dirt. To have such an awareness of dirt is to understand a system of proper places and also to see a violation of that system. "Where there is dirt there is system. Dirt is the by-product of a systematic ordering and classification of matter, insofar as ordering involves rejecting inappropriate elements. This idea of dirt takes us straight into the field of symbolism."[4] In many cultures the symbolic ordering of the environment in a purity system is a source of power, both in the orderliness and in the instances of disorder: "So many ideas about power are based on an idea of society as a series of forms contrasted with surrounding non-form. There is power in the forms and other power in the inarticulate area, margins, confused lines, and beyond the external boundaries."[5] Associated with the notion of dirt is that of contamination or pollution. Contact with dirt can make a person dirty. Boundaries guard against contagion and need to be carefully maintained. Openings in the boundaries, such as gates and thresholds, are potent and need particular vigilance.

As for the other side of things, one possible meaning for *holy* is "set apart." This seems to be the etymology of the Hebrew word for holy, *kadosh.* Consecrating someone or something is to set it apart as holy. Such a notion of holiness is symmetrical with uncleanness in that it lends itself to strategies of barrier erecting in order to contain the dangerous powers. The unclean pollutes; the holy is threatening and dangerous. In addition to the image of separation, holiness sometimes favors the image of *wholeness,* since physical integrity and completeness are required of those who work in the temple, and people with damaged bodies are forbidden to have active roles in the temple worship.[6]

In the hieratic society of postexilic Judaism the ritual principles of the holy and the unclean were opposed to describe a social topography that found its expressions in many areas of life. Jerome Neyrey, basing his work on the studies of Mary Douglas and their application by Bruce Malina to the New Testament world, has explored the sacred topography of Judaism as it is reflected in Mark's Gospel and in Judean writings contemporary to the narrative of the Gospel.[7] Neyrey shows how the religious imagination of the day had fenced the world of Judaism off into ritual zones, ordering all areas of Jewish life. A sacred *topography* rippled out in concentric zones from the Holy of Holies in the temple, through the courts of the temple to the Holy

City, and then out to the Holy Land and eventually to the unclean pagan nations. This might be suggested simplistically by a diagram of concentric circles (see fig. 13).

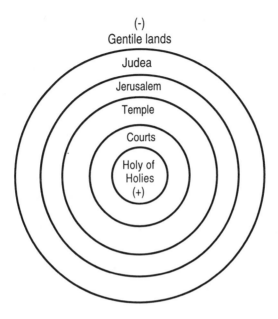

Figure 13

This pattern was repeated in other dimensions of Judean life. A ritual *calendar* distinguished holy days from profane, and they were rated on a scale of relative holiness. *Food* was designated as either fit for the altar, fit for the table, or unfit for consumption of any kind. And *persons* were scaled in a social ranking as to their "holiness" — not so much a moral standing as a status in relation to the holy places. The priests stood at the top, the physically damaged, such as eunuchs, were at the bottom, while the gentiles were off the map entirely. This sense of "holiness" had earlier prompted the various genealogies of the Old Testament, useful for calculating one's (or another's) proximity to the holiness of Judaism. In other words, the ranking of persons according to holiness has to do with one's standing in *relation to the temple*. In this regard, priests are counted as holier than ordinary Israelites; Israelites are holier than converts; and so forth. The map of persons replicates the map of places.

The topography of Palestine — with its towns and deserts, its synagogues and houses — and even the physical bodies of its inhabitants

provide Mark with a narrative arena in which the contest of powers is played out, almost as on a playing field or a game board. In
this chapter we will observe more closely the terms of holiness and
uncleanness as they appear in the Gospel. Mark presents the Judean
establishment's system of barriers and preventions as ineffectual. The
only effective opposition to the unclean power is the holy power invested in the protagonist Jesus. Jesus' critique is condensed in the
abrogation of food laws in Mk 7:15–19. For Mark, this would seem
to stand as the emblem of the work of Jesus throughout the Gospel.[8]

In brief, we will see that holiness understood in a system of opposition to the unclean is rejected for its inhumane qualities and therefore
rejected as an inadequate attribute or image of the compassionate
God. Jesus will replace this image of holiness with one that privileges
compassion and, concomitantly, displays a nondestructive expression
of wrath as response to the violations of compassion.

Mark's Gospel makes use of this set of social maps in its own distinctive way. The zones are clearly articulated. *Times* are carefully
marked. The Sabbath and the following day, probably "the Lord's
Day," are carefully distinguished. These two kinds of days are superimposed upon two ages, by way of the Sabbath law. The new era of
freedom overtakes the former age of the law. The timeframe of the
Sabbath is treated almost like a physical enclosure or container, inside
of which certain things are not possible, outside of which they are
(1:32–34). Other more explicit enclosures are the *places* and *buildings* mentioned. On that first Sabbath, Jesus went into the synagogue
(1:21), came out of the synagogue (1:24), and entered the house of Simon (1:29). On the next day, he left the house (1:35) to go to a desert
place. This Sabbath was spent in Capernaum, which seems to represent the "social" site of this part of the narrative, in contrast to the
deserted wilderness.[9]

Neyrey makes the point that in Mark's Gospel, Jesus violates nearly
every kind of boundary that Judaism had set up. This alone suggests a concerted attack upon the received social system, for a simple
blindness to its customs could never manage to be so comprehensive.
According to Douglas,[10] fundamental security is at stake in the boundaries that typify a purity system. The social ordering, though often
enough seeming purely arbitrary from an outsider's point of view, is
taken for granted by members of that society as a given datum — a
part of the natural order established by God. This order is thoroughly
internalized, and any violation of it is felt with the intensity that is
commonly called, with good reason, a gut reaction. The unclean must

be warded off, guarded against, and any breach of its barriers makes us queasy. When holiness is defined as purity, the threat of contamination is one of radical blight, insofar as it involves the very root and foundation of ordered existence.

An important and related aspect of Mark's spatial symbolism besides the patterns of place and time is the enclosure symbol of the *human body*. When Jesus is in the town, in the synagogue, on the Sabbath, he encounters a man with an "unclean spirit." He instructs the spirit to "come out" (1:25), and the spirit "came out" (1:26). As mentioned above, the connotation is almost physical, as the verb departs from the narrator's usual choice (*ekballo*) for expelling demons. It is frequently noted that Jesus casts out demons, as in the Capernaum synagogue (1:21–28), as if they are being evicted from a dwelling they have made their home: "Come out of him!" (1:25). And the Gerasene: "Come out of the man, you unclean spirit!" (5:8). And the spirits who are Legion come out of the man and go into the pigs. And on being accused of being able to cast out demons through collusion with Beelzebub: "No one can enter a strong man's house and plunder his goods unless he first binds the strong man" (3:27).

The symbolism that would imagine the human body as an enclosure for possible holy or unclean powers to inhabit, with that body's key points of contact being the hand and mouth, is found in the Markan narrative primarily in the healings and the debates. In these two kinds of stories, Jesus is engaged in a struggle with the Judean authorities. In the healings we witness a competition of power over the unclean, with Jesus winning the contest. In the debates the two sides enter into direct dispute.

The notion of the human body as an enclosure is consonant with the purity studies of Douglas, in her identification of a metaphorical relation in ritual between the human social enclosure, whether it be house or temple, and the human body. Social orders, reinforced by ritual, protect us from pollution and contamination by guarding the gates in the walls between zones. In ritual's obsessive regard for the bodily apertures, especially as regards the effluence of bodily fluids (fluids are intrinsically symbolic of the anomalous and unstructured), steps are taken to ensure the safety of the body social and politic. At the time of Passover, the Israelites smeared the blood of slaughtered lambs on the doorposts against the entry of the Angel of Death, but

the structure of living organisms is better able to reflect complex social forms than door posts and lintels. So we find that the rituals of sacrifice specify what kind of animal shall be used, young or old, male, female, or neutered, and that these roles signify various aspects of the situation which calls for sacrifice. ... Even more direct is the symbolism worked upon the human body. The body is a complex structure. The functions of its different parts and their relation afford a source of symbols for other complex structures. We cannot possibly interpret rituals concerning excreta, breast milk, saliva and the rest unless we are prepared to see in the body a symbol of society and to see the powers and dangers credited to social structure reproduced in small on the human body.[11]

Mark's stories of the cure of the deaf-mute (7:31–37) and the blind man at Bethsaida (8:22–26) spring to mind. Jesus spat to make mud, which he smeared upon the tongue of the one and the eyes of the other. The uneasiness we feel about this behavior testifies to our own investment in the purity system. But it is not simply the bodily concerns of ritual that are sounded in this text. For the metaphorical substitution of building and body seems to be at work at every level.

This symbolic world, set up in the first act, the initial week of Mark's Gospel, is further extended in acts 2 and 3. In act 2, Jesus' holy power is shown reaching out to the "untouchables" who are outlawed by the purity system of Judea. In act 3, Jesus' mission briefly but explicitly extends to the unclean lands of the gentiles. Thus his ministry of holy power has increasingly opened to all those shut out by the Judean system of purity and pollution. At this point he is uniquely positioned to begin his move toward Jerusalem and its temple, moving from edge to center of the social topography of purity, symbolically inverting the purity map as he does so.

## Act 1: Holy and Unclean Power in Mark

### Dangerous Language

The word "holy" appears the first time in Mark in 1:8, in reference to the Holy Spirit. The word appears in the second part of an antithetical sentence that serves as a pivotal statement, at the very center of the introduction to the Gospel (1:1–15), separating the part about John from the next part, about Jesus. At this point, John is speaking:

> I baptized with water,
> but he will baptize with the *Holy Spirit.* (1:8)

The ensuing episodes concerning Jesus take him to the water of the Jordan for the baptism and to the desert for temptation. The "Spirit" comes upon him at the Jordan and "drives him" into the desert. After these events, once John is arrested and taken out of the narrative action, Jesus himself enters public life with a summary statement of his message (1:14–15) and the enlistment of the first four disciples. The word "holy" is not repeated in all of these dealings. Only when we reach the spectacular opening event of the public mission of Jesus, the demon-expulsion in the Capernaum synagogue, does the word "holy" recur. It is used by the demon addressing Jesus through the mouth of the possessed man:

> What have you to do with us, Jesus of Nazareth?
> Have you come to destroy us?
> I know who you are — the *Holy One* of God! (1:24)

We have encountered this verse before, as the passage that introduces the theme of destruction to the Gospel. We see that the theme is brought to the narrative by the demons. We also see that they define Jesus at the opposite extreme — as the Holy One. We are given to understand that he is filled with the power of the Holy Spirit that came upon him at the Jordan. The demons unquestionably recognize this.

But the narrator does not use the word "demon" in this opening story (although it will appear shortly, at 1:37). Instead, we read:

> There was a man with an *unclean spirit.*

On the face of it, "unclean spirit" is a paradoxical term. If dirt is "matter out of place," we have a very material notion here. Dirt is so irredeemably material it even lacks the form and order that would give it some mental or spiritual reality. Instead, it is drifted, inappropriate physical matter. So when Mark brings the two worlds of matter and spirit together in the unlikely phrase "unclean spirit," there occurs a collision we ought not fail to notice.[12]

This language is conceivable, and its incongruity may even go unnoticed, because it belongs to the wider symbolic realm of Judaic ritual where the unclean is posed as an opposite to holiness, and not simply to cleanliness. As long as the holy and the unclean are socially accepted as polar opposites, cleanliness (or cleanness) can be equated with holiness under the rubric of *purity,* as the cleansing image of baptism in the mandating events of the story already suggests. This is the language Mark adopts, fitted to his own purposes, to portray the dramatic conflict of the Gospel narrative. In so doing he draws upon a vocabulary that interprets the entire social world with its elaborate discriminations.

## Dangerous Gates

In light of the violations performed by Jesus' activity in the narrative, it is striking how the doorways, both of bodies and of places, are vigilantly guarded in the world of the Gospel narrative. The doorways of buildings are blocked, preventing crowds or supplicants from getting to Jesus or preventing Jesus' access to them. In 1:32–33, the Sabbath that has kept them away from him is now past, and so they flock to him at Peter's house. Here the town is gathered outside the door. Conversely, in 1:45, after the leper's cure, Jesus is blocked from entering the town. In 2:2, the paralytic is blocked from entering the doorway to the house in which Jesus is teaching. The cumulative effect of these various preventions is an impression of frustrated communication and commerce. In fact, added together, they sketch a *system of preventions,* isolating one area from another:

desert | town | house | sick person

Access is controlled — the "gates" can strategically be opened or shut. But they exist to allow "closed-ness." The gates activate the discrete zones of the social landscape by drawing out the implications of their existence. The zones make prevention possible. And when their gates are closed, the sick cannot be cured. The ailing body of the supplicant becomes a metaphor for the social condition — something we have usually recognized vaguely with certain supplicants, like the paralytic. In the Gospel, the gates Jesus encounters are consistently closed.

More telling is how in these opening chapters the same is true of the apertures of the human bodies, of Jesus, of his friends, and of his enemies. In the Galilee confrontation section of act 1 in Mark, the bodily gates of *mouth* and *hand* are featured, with symmetrical regularity.[13] Four cures, presenting Jesus' initial program, are followed by four debate stories that present the official reaction against him. They are arranged in pairs (see fig. 14). The first pair of episodes (the

| Sabbath | Capernaum Demoniac | word | mouth (out) |
| | Simon's Mother-in-Law | touch | hand |
| | Leper | touch | hand |
| | Paralytic | word | mouth (out) |
| | Eating with Sinners | touch | (hand) |
| | Fasting Question | meal | mouth (in) |
| Sabbath | Grain on the Sabbath | meal | mouth (in) |
| | Withered Hand | touch | hand |

Figure 14

Capernaum demoniac and Simon's mother-in-law) and the last pair (grain on the Sabbath and the withered hand) have action set on the *Sabbath,* and this setting affects the meaning. The stories of the paralyzed man and the paralyzed hand, which conclude the two sets of four, are similar in many respects, including their merging of cure and debate stories.

In the four cures that begin the activity of Jesus, the first and fourth contrast Jesus' *word* with that of the scribes, those supposedly the custodians of the word: "He taught with authority, unlike the scribes!" (1:22). And later, to the silent scribes watching him: "Which is easier, to say to the paralytic, 'Your sins are forgiven,' or to say, 'Pick up your mat and walk'?" (2:9). For one with the authority of the word, either is equally easy. In contrast, the scribes are mute, speechless "authorities" on the word. Their mouths are closed, and Jesus must read their minds in order to register their three-part objection: "Why does this man speak thus? It is blasphemy! Who can forgive sins but God alone?" (2:7). This muteness recurs at 3:1–6, in the story of the withered hand. Again they oppose him in silence. Jesus has the word of power; they are impotent. Advocates of barriers, they find themselves blocked, able neither to offer help nor to allow it.

When in chapter 2 the cures give way to debates, the "mouth" language shifts its symbolism from *word* to *meals,* and the application moves from Jesus to his disciples. The same contrast between the two parties remains, but now fasters are pitted against feasters. The disciples feast; the Pharisees and their disciples fast. Historical studies have

commented upon Jesus' reputation for eating and drinking.[14] In the
present instance the text evokes this memory, fitting it into the framework of the ritual symbolism controlling the narration. In addition to
the body code, the text connects the fasting to the social system: Why
are they doing what is not lawful on the Sabbath? What seems as perhaps overly schematic language ("mouth: out; mouth: in") is validated
in the section in 7:1–23 on food laws. There it is established that it is
not what goes into a person that makes the difference but rather what
comes out.

In addition to the mouth, a "gate" of the body, the cure stories feature the *hand,* as a symbol of touch or contact. The cure of Simon's
mother-in-law (1:29–31), the single healing story without dialogue,
features the helping hand of Jesus. No words are given in this episode, which follows immediately upon the celebration of his powerful
word in the synagogue. The following cure, of the leper, has no short-
age of dialogue, but here we are surprised by the manner in which
Jesus effects the cure: "He stretched out his hand and touched him"
(1:41). The leper, the most prominent victim of the system of preventions in these early chapters, typifies the untouchable. Touching the
leper is Jesus' risk and the leper's greatest need. The risk is worth taking. While power flows out from one to the other, it is not the unclean
power contaminating Jesus, but rather the power of wholeness healing the leper. Ironically, Jesus, though not contaminated, contracts the
leper's social isolation at the end of the story (1:45).

Contamination remains a concern in the following debates. In the
episode showing Jesus "eating with sinners" (1:15–17) his "hand"
is not mentioned, but the bone of contention is unregulated contact
with the unclean (especially during eating). It is not without significance that the party opposing Jesus shifts from the "scribes," whose
domain is the word, to the Pharisees, by way of the transitional phrase
"scribes of the Pharisees" (2:16).[15] The Pharisees and their disciples,
who dominate chapter 2, are those "set apart," who do not make contact. While the "hand" is underplayed in 1:15–17, in the final story of
the section it is overdetermined. In 3:1–6, Jesus restores the hand of
a man. The story combines a number of motifs, but one thing that it
establishes is that Jesus not only touches those who need it but also
enables others to touch.

At stake in all of these configurations of the body-enclosure, whatever form it takes, is *power,* holy and unclean. A consistent pattern
emerges of Jesus and his friends consistently adopting strategies that
favor openness, while his opponents stay closed. Mark's use of ritual

language has its own consistent features and can be considered as a "code." In this case the "body code" displays a remarkable regularity (see fig. 15).

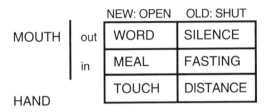

Figure 15

Thus the formal arrangement of Mark's opening "week" sets up the narrative conflict of the Gospel. Its balanced form follows Jesus' cures with an account of the Pharisees' debates, in a sequence representing situation and response, initiative and rebuttal. It positions the beginning and ending synagogue episodes as the frame for the narrative transformation around the term "destroy." And most usefully it sets up a system of symbolic containers: time, place, house, and body. Among these, the house and the body have especially attracted our interest due to the narrative's attention to the guarded "gates" of these enclosures. Gates can be closed. At the level of conflict symbolism, Jesus' opponents are shown to be defending a social system that preserves itself by prevention mechanisms. Jesus, by contrast, is the advocate of open gates. His power opposes his opponents' impotence.

## Act 2: Faith and Fear

The second act includes most of chapter 3 and all of chapters 4 and 5 of Mark and concludes with the Nazareth episode in 6:1–6. The cures in chapter 5 nicely illustrate the continuing world of the polarized values, holy/unclean, open/closed, demonstrating both the consistency of the narrative and its flexibility toward new possibilities. In chapter 5 of the Gospel a series of healings show Jesus extending holy power to the rejected or untouchables in his world. Frank Kermode has remarked on the prevailing imagery of uncleanness in these cures, relating to an "excess of maleness" on the part of the Gerasene demoniac (5:1–20) and an "excess of femaleness" on the part of the woman with the hemorrhage (5:25–34).[16] The latter account is sandwiched within another female story, that of Jairus's daughter, a seeming (unclean) corpse. Jesus' trust in holy power throughout this part of the story is expressed in his repeated injunctions for them to respond with faith, not fear. The plea is appropriate in the face of the menace of the power of the unclean.

In the first of these stories, Mk 5:1–20, the wild man among the tombs harbors a multitude of demons, the "Legion." He is a walking, unpredictable extension of the open door of death and the underworld, the tombs. Through him the militant unclean spirits — "Legion" is a military self-identification — have invaded the daily world, and they are drawing people down. The storm threat of the previous episode (4:35–41) with its exorcist overtones remains vivid in this story. The man's demonic strength, his uncontrolled violence, is chaotic and "flowing" like a flood rampaging through the area. In him the demons have emerged from the underworld and have established a beachhead in the region. They are recruiting, and they claim victims.

The man cannot be bound. All attempts at containment have been worthless, whether walls or gates. But to the astonishment of all, holy power tames him. Jesus does not bind him or harm him. He delivers him from the binding spirits. The demons released into the swine descend into the sea. They reenter the underworld through the door of the abyss. The possessed man's deliverance consists in providing the unclean powers an avenue of escape, a return to place. By taking the swine with them, they prevent unclean eating as a threat to the door of the mouth. Jesus closes the gates of death and the underworld by annulling a process of entry. The man is "cleansed"; the threat is closed off.

The meaning of violence is central to the story. The man's violence is demonic. Anticipating the objection that the problem dramatized by "Legion" is not violence in itself but rather uncontrolled violence, the story shows that violence is not given to self-control. The narrator finds violence to be appropriate for characterizing the demonic, which is uncontrolled because no one is stronger. The stronger would bind and then plunder (3:27). Here we see opening a vista of greater and greater strength and further plundering. What can end it? This is the question raised by the story.

As an amplification of strength, violence is contrasted with power.[17] Unlike the passion account, in which Jesus appears to be completely powerless (though this ought not be simply assumed), here he is entirely powerful. Nevertheless, his method of effecting change is not that of violence. In fact, the options of violence have not worked. No one is stronger than the demoniac, just as no army is mightier than the Roman Empire's. The metaphor of "Legion" cuts both ways. Jesus' holy power, perceived as a greater power, is not violent in its expression. No one is destroyed. They are only placed, replaced, and empowered. If holy power is not violent, we are given to wonder, What is it?

The woman with the discharge is in a situation parallel to that of the leper (Lev 13–14; 15). In contrast to the tombs of the wild man, the womb is the birth door. Here too the door is open and cannot be closed as it should be. The story treats of the matter as a disease, for it notes that the doctors have all failed. But it is also an uncleanness, since like leprosy the disease was considered to make one ritually impure. It was viewed as an excess, an emission of unclean power. It required her to be quarantined for the safety of the greater society (Lev 15:31).

Just as the social regulations treat the woman's body like a container, so in this story the body of Jesus is treated in the same way, but out of him flows holy power:

And Jesus, perceiving in himself that power had gone forth from him, immediately turned about in the crowd and said, "Who touched my garments?" (Mk 5:30)

The hand of the woman and the garment of Jesus have symbolic significance. Here the woman, rather than Jesus, violates the purity rules. Jesus delivers holy power but not by his own hand. His garment somehow participates in his power (and the body code), and this participation will later be made visible on the Mountain of Transfiguration (9:2–7). Conversely, the stripping of Jesus in the passion account would seem to be a part of this symbol system as well, since it coincides with the advent of his time of powerlessness. The taunting of the soldiers includes investing him with the false robes of power (15:16–20).

In the woman's story, following the Gerasene's account of promiscuous violence, threatening death, we have a disorder that threatens the possibility of giving birth. The consequence is equivalent: a deadly serious threat to society. The law finds no other recourse but that of quarantine, as with the leper. In other words, like the doctors the law is impotent. Jesus' healing power once again closes a dangerously open door, one that in its anomaly threatens the life of the community.

The story of the twelve-year-old girl, Jairus's daughter (5:21–24, 36–45), brackets the story of the woman with the hemorrhage and has other textual links to that story — the female gender of the sufferer, the cited duration of twelve years, the title "daughter." The legally marriageable age of the girl puts her at the threshold of fertility. Most noticeable at first glance is the convergence of the two themes: birth threatened, death threatening. The death of the girl is a hopeless waste and a threat to Jairus's family's future. As in the woman's story, fertility is attacked, but here by the unclean power of death. Until now death has delivered its threat; birth has been threatened by disorder. But in this episode, with the girl cut off from life as she enters into her time of fertility, death threatens the very possibility of birth-giving. The social threat of the unclean power is dramatized by the convergence of death and birth. Again we read of doors, as Jesus and the disciples enter inside, shutting out the crowd. He takes the girl by the hand, as with Simon's mother-in-law (1:29–31). The girl is given food — an action that contrasts with the end of the Gerasene story, in which the demise of the swine ends unclean food. Here the holy food signals the same thing: a return and a closing of an open door to death.

In effect, Jesus' practice is a critique of the purity system as impotently prohibiting life, rather than furthering it. The system is dysfunctional, oppressive. Advancing beyond the systematic openness shown in the first two chapters comprising act 1 of Mark, holy power in the current sequence effectively closes off the threat of the unclean emerging through various doors into the common world. A threat to life — which occurs when an unclean power is let loose by a door left open — is averted as Jesus closes the door.

The sequence of cure stories ends with the foiled cures of the crisis episode that concludes act 2: the Nazareth synagogue story (6:1–6). Successful elsewhere, Jesus performs no cures, here frustrated by the crowd's "unbelief." Thus, in this concluding scene, we are alerted to a thematic thread that unites this act: the opposed terms "fear" and "faith" recur throughout act 2 of Mark (4:40; 5:15, 33–34, 36; 6:6).[18] In light of this sequence, the Nazarenes' lack of faith is attributable to their fear. Fear closes doors, in the manner of the Judean authorities who oppose Jesus. And so his own people close the door on him.

An inner relation ties the opposition motif of *fear* and *faith* in act 2 to the *destruction* motif of act 1. The response of Jesus' opponents has included both their fear of being destroyed (1:24) and their willingness to destroy (3:6). Throughout this narrative, a preoccupation with the theme of destruction identifies the antagonists. Their fear of destruction and their willingness to inflict it on others constitute a dynamic that underlies much recourse to violence. In this scenario, those who live by fear tend to inflict it. Those who understand destruction as the ultimate threat are inclined to answer its threat by returning it. As loss of being or identity, destruction promises the final means of removal and as such offers the ultimate weapon. From my fear I learn that this is the most certain way to remove opposition. My fear of destruction impresses me with its value as an instrument of conflict.

In Mark fear finds its contrary in faith, rather than in an act of courage as we might have expected. Faith as confidence in God replaces confidence in the usual "realistic" answer to fear, namely, courageous strength. In faith God is not only the "rock" of true defense, as the ancient biblical theme would have it, but also the liberator of an enslaved people, as in the foundational experience of the exodus. A God who cares truly for this people, a realization perhaps obscured by the Judean purity system, is a God who deserves trust in the program Jesus is pursuing. A God who loves them makes possible compassionate action that appears to be fearless. "Faith" then names the necessary confidence that would act decisively with compassion, that would confront without destroying, that would trust in God for the ability to carry opposition forward in a context of love.

## Act 3: Opening a Door to the Gentiles

The third act of the Gospel, running from the middle of the sixth chapter to nearly the end of the eighth, presents a third set of cures (Mk 7:24–30, 31–37). But these are introduced by a major debating moment (7:1–23), which shifts the narrator's attention to those persons outside the Judean social universe, the unclean gentiles.

In chapter 7, the differences between Jesus and the authorities, about matters of the unclean, reach a crisis. The dispute in 7:1–23 builds on the story about eating with sinners (2:15–17). In the latter story, the "scribes of the Pharisees" contested the practice of Jesus' disciples eating food under unclean circumstances. A body code of "closed hands" was implied. In the present case, the Pharisees and the "scribes from Jerusalem" object to the practice of Jesus' disciples eating without washing their hands. A code language of "guarded hands" is now explicit. The debate in Mk 7:1–23 also confirms the "mouth" language of the body symbolism as well, inasmuch as what goes into a person's mouth is contrasted with that which comes out.

Certainly the handwashing incident is crucial to the meaning of the move toward the gentile world in this part of the text, and it has been explored extensively by the commentators.[19] But our attention is irresistibly drawn to the obscure little healing story that follows it, a story that seems to embody the changes announced in the debate account. The strangeness of this story about a stranger in a strange land teases our attention and seems to offer keys to the meaning of this rather obscure part of Mark. It invites fuller consideration.

This story of a Greek woman (7:24–30) exploits the principles newly articulated by Jesus. The story is essentially an exorcism. Its action is narrated in such a way as to repeat motifs encountered earlier.[20] While the story has an air of recapitulation, if not déjà vu, there is one aspect that receives unusual elaboration, and that is the gentile connection. Wilfred Harrington notes that while Mark's Gospel does not elaborate much in the way of a mission to the gentiles, this story along with a few others are enough to show "that the door had been opened for them."[21] The recapitulative sense of this story suggests that it brings together many of the earlier motifs in order to place them in a gentile setting. As a matter of fact, it is second in a series of four stories that seem to have been told with a view toward the gentiles, if we count the preceding account that overruled the food laws to remove a barrier to gentile conversion, reminiscent of Acts 10 or Acts 15. The following story of the deaf-mute (7:31–37) is set, rather awkwardly, in gentile territory. And the second loaves-miracle (8:1–11), which follows the story of the deaf-mute, is widely believed to differ from the first loaves-miracle (6:31–44) in its gentile interest, as represented by vocabulary and symbolism.[22]

Clues to the gentile emphasis in the exorcism story are given by the detailed identification of the woman by religion (Greek) and by birth (a Phoenician from Syria). A further clue is to be found in the inordinate amount of comment about the *setting* (fully two of the seven verses). And it is the setting that points to the aspects of the story that interest us. The *changes of place* are strongly marked. Jesus leaves Galilee; he enters a house. And then he hopes no one else will enter it (a blocked door).[23] The woman manages an entry and falls at his feet. The action of the cure reflects this set of terms. She begs Jesus to evict ("chase out") a demon from her daughter, who is at a distance. The strange dialogue about not giving to dogs the food of the children seems to echo her action. If dogs are generally fed outside, sometimes they come inside the house and beg scraps at the family's feet, as, for instance, she is currently doing at the feet of Jesus. Here the system of preventions is operating at full force, attuned to the danger of pollution.

The threat of pollution enters the story at three levels, at least: the territorial threat of sojourning in gentile territory, the demonic threat to the possessed daughter, and the less obvious threat concerning kosher food laws, implied in the language of the dialogue. The relation between the first two levels, the territorial setting and the action of the exorcism — if indeed the woman comes into the narrative as a representative of the gentiles — is one of "cleansing" the gentile lands. We can suspect a convergence here between demons and pagan idols. In this sense, the exorcism reinstates the gentiles into the Jewish world metonymically.

The dialogue about dogs represents the third level of the unclean threat — that of the food laws. This supposedly witty exchange seldom fails to irritate readers. But that which provokes us often stimulates further consideration. At this point in the conversation between Jesus and the woman the issue under discussion is whether Jesus should move ahead with the exorcism. The obstacle presenting itself is not any difficulty with exorcism as such, but rather whether exorcism ought to be worked among gentiles. At issue, then, is the *gentile mission itself.* If the door is to be opened to the gentiles in this story, the woman is the one who must give the password.

The verbal exchange between Jesus and the woman has to do with food laws in the sense that it turns around the terms of the previous episode, which declared all foods clean (7:19). From texts like Ex 22:31, we know that unclean food can be characterized as fit for dogs:

> You shall be a people consecrated to me; therefore you shall not eat any flesh that is torn by beasts in the field; you shall cast it to the dogs.

If the kosher food laws maintained that humans should not eat food that is fit for dogs, that is, unclean, then Jesus' saying at 7:27 ("Let the children be fed first, since it isn't good to take bread out of children's mouths and throw it to the dogs") articulates the converse principle: no dogs should eat food that is fit for humans, that is, clean. And so the situation between Jesus and the woman is imaginatively dramatized as a family meal. As seen earlier, the woman reminds him that the family "pets" frequently succeed in begging a meal.

Notably our focus has shifted from the problem of unclean food, something eaten, to the problem of unclean *eaters* of the food. And the family meal that is evoked, while it is ostensibly that of the house of Israel, is shown to be understood as applying more widely in Judea: "clean" food is that which is proper for any *human* consumption; those who fail to observe these regulations are acting as less than human. Whatever else Jesus is doing with this harsh saying, he is reminding the woman (as the narrator reminds the reader) what is culturally at stake in her request. In agreeing with her request, Jesus is conceding *full humanity to the gentiles,* despite the Judean purity maps. We shall see later that denying humanity to those outside our own tribe is concomitant with the use of violence.

### Gentile Mission, or Last Chance for Purity Rules?

We need to take one more step. We need to determine what this episode is doing here, in this part of the Gospel. Harrington represents the prevailing opinion in his view that this story and those following (up to 8:26) were "planned to meet the needs of gentile-christian readers. Mark wanted to show that the concern of Jesus was not limited to Jews but reached to non-Jewish peoples, beyond the confines of Galilee."[24] Yet we might be excused in thinking that the dialogue about dogs feeding under the table offers dubious consolation to gentile Christians, offering as much insult as invitation. Mark, it would seem, might do better than this in selecting his stories.

Equally puzzling is the sporadic interest the narrator displays in this theme of including the gentiles in the kingdom: first, briefly, in 5:1–20, then here, in 7:1–8:26. Then there is nothing until the temple action, when Jesus declares, quoting Isa 56:7, "My house shall be a house of prayer *for all peoples* [gentiles]" (Mk 11:14 — only Mark includes the prepositional phrase). Mark's Gospel does not show any of the sustained interest in the gentiles that is so prominent a feature of Luke's Gospel, where the gentile mission of the early church is an undisputed theme. At the same time, Mark alone stresses the gentile inclusion at the temple action.

These apparent discrepancies are clarified immensely if we take a clue from the narrative positions of the gentile woman and the temple action. The two episodes stand at opposite ends of the long journey to Jerusalem. For just after the gentile-related events of Mark 7–8, of which the woman's story is so prominent a part, Jesus will begin his trek to the city (8:31). But more importantly, the two episodes also stand at the far extremes of the Judean social map. In the symbolic maps, the gentiles are off the edge in the zone of the absolutely unclean. Meanwhile the temple, as site of the Holy of Holies, stands at dead center. Certainly, this positioning of the so-called gentile mission in relation to the journey to Jerusalem makes narrative sense if the journey is interpreted as a deliberate, almost processional, march from edge to center.

In this regard, the gentile mission represents the extreme case of Jesus' attack on the unclean powers. His ministry to the expendable population that is marked by Judean uncleanness includes the sick, the hungry, the hopelessly marginalized. But his mission to the marginal is not complete until the gentiles too are reached. The dynamic of recovery by recapitulation of that which is lost is a pattern we have already encountered in the discussion above regarding the story of Joseph of Arimathea reclaiming the body of Jesus. The pattern dictates that all required steps are taken and narrated. Nothing thought to be "untouchable" is left untouched; nothing presumed unmentionable is left unmentioned.

With this change of focus a new image of completeness in the ministry of Jesus replaces the former impression of an occasional, incomplete ministry to the gentiles. We need only posit that ministry as a part of Mark's narrative program of Jesus overcoming the unclean powers. In this case, Mark is not abrogating the purity rules (7:1–23) in order to make room in the kingdom for the gentiles, but rather he is extending the invitation to the gentiles in order to complete his abrogation of the purity rules.

## The Climactic Event

Mark's priorities relate to his narrative program. That program shows Jesus expanding his assault on the unclean powers through the first eight chapters. Toward the end of chapter 8 he turns his attention toward Jerusalem, moving from the periphery to the center. It is as if he brings a retinue of the various victims of the purity system with him, right to the center. There he turns the purity system inside out.

Upon arriving at the city, at the conclusion of this journey, Jesus arranges an action of protest and prophetic judgment that we popularly call the *temple cleansing*. The intensity of this paradoxical gesture is difficult to appreciate adequately. After all, the Holy of Holies is categorically least in need of cleansing. It escapes the threat of uncleanness by definition. Its role is to define the unclean as that which is opposed

to or removed from it as the center of holiness. It is the standard by
which the relative diminishments of purity, graduating into uncleanness, are to be determined. To put the temple under judgment is to
place in question the standard itself. Cleansing the temple is no re-
formist gesture but a deep judgment on the system it represents. In
repudiating the central principle of the purity system, Jesus repudiates
its entirety.

In citing Isa 56:7 in the temple precincts (Mk 11:17), Jesus alludes
to the fuller prophecy of Isa 56:1–8. In this passage the eunuchs and
the gentiles are imagined as offering sacrifice in the temple when the
future messianic time should arrive. These two figures represent the
two extremely unclean classes of the maimed and the non-Judean —
the population of the second and third acts of the Gospel brought
in proxy to the temple by Jesus. When he arrives at the temple, in
chapter 11, he pronounces judgment on the central shrine, pulling the
props out from under the purity system.

The paradox of cleansing the Holy of Holies is further expressed in
the language of *curse and blessing*. The cursed fig tree is an emblem
of the temple action. The account of the fig tree is given in two parts
(11:12–14, 20–23), positioned on either side of the cleansing episode
to provide a narrative frame in the manner that has become familiar to us in this Gospel. The withering of the tree is interpreted in a
short dialogue (11:23–26). To the startled disciples Jesus once again
urges faith. Whoever enjoins "this mountain" (the Temple Mount of
Zion) to be cast into the sea will succeed if faith overrules doubt.
The curse on the tree is then equivalent to a curse on the Temple
Mount, the Holy Place thought to be the very fount of blessing,
the source of life.[25] In cursing the fig tree as being fruitless, Jesus
is condemning the temple as unholy, as cursed. But this has already
been shown in the sickness in the land. The social healing of Jesus
had encountered the social disabling of the pollution system represented by the temple. The temple is treated as the source of the blight
upon the land, not its blessing. In Mark's Gospel, this is the meaning of the temple: the system of sickness, impotence, privilege, and
destitution.

In the text, the symbolic "gate" for this is the temple veil. At its
rending at the moment of Jesus' death (15:38) a door is opened. The
holy is once again made accessible. There is deep convergence between
the opening of holy power here and the Holy One's control over unclean power, with its gates and pollutions, in the early chapters of the
Gospel. But now the moment is one of utter seriousness, for the prin-

ciple of the unclean, the system itself, is overcome in order to release holy power. The cause, not merely the effects, is addressed.

## Bodily Healing as Social Metaphor

The sickness in the land that Jesus addresses by disabling the source of the blight in the temple cleansing has been previously disclosed in the numerous stories of healing described by the narrator, stories couched in terms of a contest between the holy and the unclean. The metaphor that relates *body* and *house* as equivalent enclosures with gates, used by the law as a method of prevention, is also seen in Mark's Gospel as an avenue of *healing*. The doors that can be closed can also be opened. In depicting the healing of the sick, the cure stories show a power of restoring wholeness to those who are fragmented that contrasts diametrically with the destructive power proper to violence. Healing power cannot be controlled; it cannot be used as a threat to coerce and control the behavior of others.

The symbolic character of the healings is easy to misconstrue, and so it is worth a further word. We commonly exploit the homiletic value of these stories, thinking of them as depicting physical cures with symbolic overtones — the leper as the social outcast, the paralytic as the spiritually stifled, the blind man as lacking faith's insight. But this approach turns the narrative's intent upside down. In the narration the symbolism lies at the very center of the healing actions. When Ched Myers calls the healing stories in Mark "symbolic actions,"[26] he is not claiming them to be cures with symbolic overtones. Rather, he recognizes them as symbolic actions with healing intent and effects.

To see this we need to appreciate the distinction some anthropologists make between disease and illness. They understand *disease* as an interpretation of sickness according to a "biomedical" model that views wholeness, or health, in terms of the individual human body as a discrete organic system. It pays attention to biological symptoms and microbes. It is the prevailing model of sickness in our culture. But another model stands alongside it and challenges its hegemony. *Illness* is a reading of sickness according to an "ethnomedical" model that views wholeness in terms of an individual's location in and relation to a social system as his or her bodily context. It emphasizes "culturally construed causes of illness." John Pilch describes illness as "a socio-cultural perspective that is concerned with personal perception and experience of certain socially disvalued states, including, but not limited to, disease."[27]

An example of this distinction can be found in our attitudes toward physical disability. For us, some conditions such as nearsightedness may be physical impairments from a biomedical perspective, but because of optical devices such as contact lenses, myopic persons are not prevented from leading "normal" lives. Although at one time such people were stigmatized with names like "four-eyes" and discouraged from strenuous activities, they are no longer seen as anything other than "normal." They are no longer prohibited from activities by reason of their poor eyesight — as indicated by the corrective lenses worn even by racing drivers moving in excess of two hundred miles per hour.

Compare this visual impairment with paralysis of the lower limbs. When persons with this particular affliction (an organic "disease") manage to have a healthy outlook and self-image — that is, when they perceive themselves as normal on the illness scale — they encounter reactions of amazement and disbelief from the rest of us who faithfully embody our cultural attitudes. But this situation is changing, as we redesign our environment to be wheel-chair accessible. Such an enterprise is often claimed to be unfeasible or politically impossible, but it is a relatively small task for a nation that has redesigned itself to accommodate the automobile at every level. With public policy changes like the Americans with Disabilities Act of 1990,[28] people now considered disabled might increasingly move away from the margins of social life. They may well be culturally perceived as normal and with less and less difficulty will see themselves in the same light.

A symptomatic phrase we use in this regard is "functioning in society." The phrase indicates how the criterion for health in certain frameworks is *social,* rather than organic. As a matter of fact, few of us beyond the age of twenty-five do not cope with some form of organic disability. Which of these should exclude a person from the normal population and which should not is a matter of social convention. In this discussion "wholeness" refers to a certain mode of relating to one's social context, rather than referring to a condition of the individual organism. Furthermore, we should carefully note that the changing boundary of what is considered the "normal" population is frankly accepted as a *political* issue, as seen in the disabilities act — it is a matter of public debates and government definition.

And the debate engages at least two notions about what constitutes a workable society. On one side are those who believe that the healthy society requires exclusion of those who deviate from the norm. This is a standard model of purity that asks how we can realistically continue to countenance pluralism. It senses that standards are eroding and that with that erosion society itself is undercut. On the other side are those who view the healthy society as inclusive of these populations, along with their resulting tensions. This model implies access to a nondestructive mode of conflict resolution. It sees the society that needs a portion of its population excluded as the price required to feel good about itself as a dysfunctional society, like the family that needs its "black sheep" in order to define its identity against it.[29] The inclusive impulse that would widen the circle that encloses us is one that humanizes in the literal sense that it extends the list of those who are normal, hence fully human. It continually strives to reduce the number of categories that society sees as expendable populations, that is, not fully human. Here again we can locate an important link with *violence,* which depends upon the ability to dehumanize the victims of its work.

## Jesus' Symbolic Acts

These remarks have consequence for the Gospel narrative insofar as Jesus' restorative acts are performed within the framework of healing rather than curing. He addresses illness within its social meaning and does not focus on it as disease. As Pilch writes:

> Jesus and all healers of that period could only perceive illness and not disease.... Notice in each healing instance the almost total disregard of symptoms (something very essential to disease). Instead there is constant concern for meaning.... Jesus' activity is best described as healing, not curing. He provides social meaning for the life problems resulting from the sickness.[30]

A sensitivity to the distinction between disease and illness, between curing and healing, is necessary to prevent us from imposing today's prevailing model of sickness as disease on Mark's narrative. Although the biomedical model prevails in today's world, it is under revision, as noted. We need to see past our preoccupation with cures in order to see Jesus' involvement in healing.

Once we set aside the biomedical model of disease and enter the meaning-oriented world of illness and healing, we enter a new level of appreciation of Mark's portrayal of the dispute between Jesus and the Judean authorities concerning the appropriateness of Jesus' healing activity. It is a debate about definitions. It is a dispute conducted in first-century terms, within the symbolic universe of meaning that defines illness and healing. Because illness is a symbolic condition, that is, a dislocation in the symbolic net that comprises society, Jesus' actions are correspondingly symbolic. They operate in an essential manner at the level of the symbolism that creates a shared world.

Placing in doubt this shared world, the protagonist, Jesus, disputes by his healings the adequacy of the prevailing symbolic universe of the purity system. In rejecting the system he is implicitly criticizing those who maintain it. As Myers puts it, "In sum, Jesus' acts were powerful not because they challenged the laws of nature, but because they challenged the very structure of social existence."[31] Their power, then, lay not in their ability to cure disease, a matter that would not have been clearly perceived by the people in the first century, including Jesus, but rather in their role of confronting the structures that promoted and sustained illness. In this sense, the healings were not simply a series of metaphors for the social healing that was needed in Judea, but in fact an active part of that social healing. In bringing the isolated ones back into social existence, the healings restored both the larger society and the excluded ones. The cure was metonymy as much as metaphor: the healed body was a part of the whole as well as surrogate for it. In healing the part, Jesus restored the whole.

Insofar as healing restores wholeness, the meaning of health coincides with one of the meanings of holiness. By privileging the image of holiness-as-wholeness over that of holiness-as-separation it exposes the latter as a form of social mutilation. By restoring health, as inclusion, Jesus redesigns boundaries, bringing in those who previously needed to be left out for the society to succeed. In other words, he *resymbolizes society* by reimaging its members, who are invited to reimagine themselves. This is the equivalent of what Richard Horsley calls a social revolution.[32] In the former system, the wholeness of the individual replicated that of the larger whole of society, in the manner of ritual symbolism. Accordingly, in Jesus' healing activity the repairing of the maimed members implies the repair of the mutilated society. In the new reality, society is "defined" by caring and by the impulse to reach and include. That is, it is defined by the activity of Jesus. It is defined as indefinite in terms of the old categories, being open to all. Its new criterion is the work of compassion.

## Nonviolent Action

All of this can be restated in the language of *social consent*. Ched Myers draws a parallel between Jesus' miraculous cures and the shamanistic cures of many primitive societies, as described by Mary Douglas. Both kinds of curing action require belief. Jesus repeatedly demands faith as a requirement for healing. Similarly, the shaman's work cannot succeed without belief. Douglas writes:

> Magicality is an instrument of mutual coercion, which only works when common consent upholds the system. It is useless for a witch doctor to invest a fetish with magic power by the sole authority of his charisma. Magic derives its potency from the legitimacy of the system in which this kind of communication is made.[33]

There are no wonder-workers without a believing clientele. It is the system that is effective — or else dysfunctional. Compare this to the words of Gene Sharp, on the nonviolent use of power:

> Throughout history, under a variety of political systems, people in every part of the world have waged conflict and wielded undeniable power by using a very different technique of struggle — one which does not kill and destroy. That technique is nonviolent action. Although it has been known by a variety of names, its basis has always been the same: the belief that the exercise of power depends on the consent of the ruled who, by withdrawing that consent, can control and even destroy the power of their opponent.[34]

Withdrawal of consent is at the center of nonviolent action, just as conferral of consent is essential to healing activity.

In the earlier healing stories, where Jesus violates the purity rules on all sides, even requiring "faith" against them, we already see his consent withdrawn from the pollution system. Now, in the deliberate action in the temple cleansing he formally withholds his consent and invites others to do so as well. At this point, the authorities necessarily must formulate a response. Their solution is the violent one of arranging for his death.

Jesus' death brings to a conclusion any attempt to elicit his consent to their system. He withholds his consent even until he is killed, and his refusal stands. In failing to elicit a retraction from him, they fail — for the judgment stands. In killing him they may remove the immediate source of their difficulties, but they have not managed to provide a convincing rebuttal. They have lost the "battle of myths,"[35] the dispute over ideological outlooks. The charge against the system is still alive, unanswered, to be picked up by others whom he has gathered and prepared. He succeeds; his opponents fail. The essence of nonviolent power is *publicly withholding consent* from the dominant political system, and this has been Jesus' pattern from the first healings of chapter 1 — even while he invites consent to his rival program.

In presenting the rising action that builds to the confrontation in the temple, Mark shows that Jesus' culminating protest is the conclusion of a consistent history of activity. The temple action, the proximate cause of the crucifixion, does not appear on the scene unanticipated, without context. The resistance activity of Jesus begins on the first page of the Gospel. The narrative sketches a dynamic of resistance in which that first small step of refusal to acquiesce in diminishing behavior has its consequences. It begins with the daily activities of touching, speaking, and eating and moves into the unforeseen. For the consequences build as each decision presents a new occasion of decision making: I am given the repeated opportunity to decide whether to abandon the principles that brought me thus far or to continue them onto the next level. Once I begin, I set out on a course of daunting action that is as far as can be imagined from the manipulative foot-dragging typical of passive resistance. In active nonviolent resistance I am called out of my comfort into risk. Insofar as this dynamic draws on principle it calls me into authenticity. It summons me to clarity of purpose and away from the muddled motivations that would combine principle with personal resentments. It is, if you will, a spiral of nonviolence moving from edge to center.

One more open door remains to the story, and that is the one that ends it, in chapter 16 — the open door of the tomb. Jesus' commitment to life is expressed as new life. Death does not "close" his story. Death is not final (closed) for him; nor is his narrative closed. Instead it returns to the site of its beginning, Galilee, to be told again. What the symbolic vocabulary of holy and unclean allows us to see is that Jesus pursues his challenge from the very beginning in a nonviolent manner. In the final chapters of this book we will see how the conflict is resolved nonviolently. But here we have seen that the conflict is also mounted and intensified along the lines of nonviolent confrontation. Healing names a power contrary to destructive force. And withholding consent, of course, is a primary nonviolent strategy. It struggles at the level of outlook, of ideological control, rather than that of military enforcement.

But the ideological struggle between Jesus and the Judean authorities inside the story plot reminds us that the narrative outlook is the site of a similar struggle between the narrator and the reader. That the symbolism of holy/unclean is operating at the level of narrative ideology is indicated in at least two ways. First, as a language, as a vocabulary of conflict, it is the property of the teller of the story, the narrator. It is a principle of the discourse insofar as it guides the selection and arrangement of incidents in the plot and the language of presentation in the telling. It offers us the narrative's interpretation of the events.

Second, it also shows us the ideological level of the narrative insofar as in presenting the question of true holiness — preventions or compassion — it raises the question of authentic power. The struggle between Jesus and the demons is in some ways a personification of the question of power. Settled in its own terms, it finds its application in the struggle between Jesus and the authorities, who are increasingly assimilated to the demonic through their adherence to destructive forms of power. In asking about power the narrative is asking about the proper conduct of conflict. And by putting Jesus in the conflict of sustained narrative it provides the occasion to test the question and its response.

# JESUS AND HIS DISCIPLES

In our earlier examination of *The Empty Land* by Louis L'Amour, we discovered that action novels have room for other kinds of conflict besides that of the basic agon: for example, when the quiet-loving town marshal, Dick Felton, was reported to have ideas different from Matt Coburn, the hired gun, about keeping the peace in the raw mining town of Confusion. When they were given some time in the dialogue to debate the various merits of their contrasting approaches, we knew that popular narrative would occasionally supplement its culturally supportive patterns of action with rhetoric. The ideological issues in the narrative can move from drama to verbal statement. And when their philosophical differences overflowed into the plot, as Coburn rescued Felton in the main street of town from an outlaw ambush Felton's own mistakenly benevolent views of human nature had allowed to develop, we knew that their ideological dispute could also have a piece of the action.

We have let L'Amour be our main guide as we peel off layers of supposedly simple narrative. Mark's Gospel is generally thought to be primitively organized, when it is conceded any organization at all. And when we add the suggestion that it belongs to the genre of popular narratives, we increase the prejudice against complexity. But then the supposedly simple stories of L'Amour also have proven more complex than expected. The Gospel agon is shown in the contest between Jesus and the Judean authorities. And this conflict has an ideological side to it as well, as we saw in the discussion of the holy and unclean in the last chapter. Now we will see that the ideological outlook, like the debate between Coburn and Fulton, has its verbal, rhetorical moments in the Gospel. In Mark the rhetorical argument is to be found in the teaching of Jesus. Which is to say, Jesus' teaching in the Gospel supports the narrative rather than the other way around.

## The Teaching of Jesus

Jesus' relation to his disciples is typically that of teacher to students. In Mark's narrative he spends much of his time instructing followers. His teaching concerns Christology and discipleship. Insofar as his teaching interprets his own identity, it is christological. Insofar as it concerns the mission and identity of his followers, it takes discipleship as its theme. Christology and discipleship are related themes, of course. Only disciples would think Christology a matter of interest. But there is more to it than this. To some extent disciples adopt the identity of the one they follow. The identity of the Christ becomes crucial for the identity of the Christian. Christology, it would seem, serves the needs of discipleship theology.

Currently commentators on Mark's Gospel are accustomed to see there a Christology of the "suffering Messiah."[1] This approach favors a language of destiny and directs attention to Jesus' cross as something that "happens to him." Jesus' suffering is mysteriously mandated by God, and the action of the narrative unfolds with a measured inevitability. In this reading the primary meaningful event is Jesus' death, interpreted as a sacrifice ("a ransom for many" [Mk 10:45]). The decisive action of a work of cosmic redemption takes place outside the narration of the Gospel, to heal a universal rupture in a salvation-history story beyond the boundaries of Mark's narrative. The redemption story may be one of our faith stories, but to assimilate Mark's account to it we must ignore much of the narrative in front of us.

Traditionally, exegetes have seen the christological titles of the Gospels as windows into the theology of the evangelists and the early church.[2] They are engaged in the formulation of Mark's theological concept of Christ as abstracted from the titles contained in the Gospel. The tacit assumption is that the purpose of Mark's Gospel is to define one or more concepts as the correct definition of Christ's being. In this approach the truth sought, and presumably the truth taught, resides in propositional statements for which the narrative exists as setting. The narrative serves the christological titles.

The approach has a firm grip on exegetical imaginations, as illustrated when Jack Dean Kingsbury turns his attention to the study of narrative in his *Conflict in Mark*. His sensitivity to the dramatic qualities of the narrative leads him to identify the two main conflicts in the Gospel — that of Jesus with the authorities and that of Jesus with the disciples.[3] However, in addition to these two plotlines, he adds a "story of Jesus" as a set of christological titles — Messiah, Son of David, and Son of God. These are interpreted as strategically placed in the narrative so as to represent a progressive disclosure of Jesus' identity. Here narrative does not provide the setting for the titles so much as it dissolves itself into the series of nominatives. Narrative movement is seen as little more than the progressive disclosure of truth, without drama, without conflict among the characters.

### Precedents in Scripture

The notion of the "suffering Messiah" turns on two Old Testament strands in Mark — that of the Messiah and that of the servant of Yahweh. They are structured right into the narrative, a fact that lends support to the views of those who argue that these themes are Mark's central interest. Mark's baptism account, the inaugural moment in the story of Jesus, reflects these themes. Among the symbols that interact to elaborate the meaning of this rich scene, the voice from heaven assumes a prominent role, as it delivers a message to Jesus at 1:11:

> You are my son, my beloved;
> in you I am well pleased.

Critics have long recognized that these words combine key scriptural passages.[4] In addition to a probable link with Genesis 22, prohibiting Abraham's sacrifice of his "beloved son" Isaac, two major references are at work here. The first is the classic messianic text of Ps 2:7; the second is Isa 42:1, about the servant of Yahweh. Together these two biblical figures suggest two quite different roles. Despite the strong contrast in content, the two passages are similar in form. Both are introductory in their respective locations. And more importantly, each has the task of identifying the figure concerned. Each indicates something and in fact could be accompanied by a designating gesture of the hand: "*You* are my son" (Ps 2:7); "*Behold* my servant" (Isa 42:1). Precisely in their indicative function the two texts serve Mark's narrative. Together they identify Jesus as called to combine two roles.

The baptism of Jesus fulfills the narrative function of *mandate,* commissioning the protagonist for the following action.[5] In the old television series *Mission Impossible,* still sometimes viewed on reruns, the mandate came to the protagonist on a taped recording that would "self-destruct" in a matter of seconds. The mandate sets the terms of the task for the following story, and Jesus' mandate combines the roles of Messiah and servant. The combination is unexpected, as seen in the disparity between their fundamental images as king and slave. The roles evoke historical periods briefly — the glory days of David's kingdom and the national humiliation of the Babylonian captivity.

Jesus is told, in effect, "You are the Messiah, but you are to pursue that role in the manner of the servant." In working out the implications of this unexpected combination, the Gospel finds its *narrative program.* The image of the Messiah, as incorporating dominating power in its conventionally acclaimed manifestations, contrasts with the servant, who personifies the power of patient, enduring love, faithful despite what the conventional views would deem powerlessness. We can restate this narrative mandate as the call for Jesus to mount a program of social and political resistance against the false leaders of Judea, but to carry out that resistance in a nonviolent manner.

In the unfolding narrative, the messianic identification is developed first, leading to Peter's statement at midpoint, in 8:29: "You are the Messiah." Upon making his identification, which Jesus neither denies nor asks to have advertised (8:30), Peter finds himself embroiled in a dispute with Jesus, presumably about what it means to be Messiah. Jesus expands Peter's narrower notion with words more appropriate to the servant (8:31–33). In terms of the baptismal message, Peter's knowledge is understandably partial, as he was not present at the Jordan to hear the voice from heaven. In response to the incompleteness of his response, Jesus adds the supplementary lessons on the servant as they make their way to Jerusalem. In this journey the program of the baptismal voice is carried through in two stages. During the Transfiguration episode the voice from heaven is heard again (9:7):

> This is my son, my beloved;
> *listen to him.*

This time the voice is speaking *about* Jesus, rather than speaking *to* him. That is, it is addressing the three apostles who have joined him on the mountaintop, especially Peter. Peter had objected to Jesus' interpretation of his mission (8:32–33). Now the voice decides their dispute in Jesus' favor.

One of the first things Jesus does after his baptism is to call others (1:16–20). Part of his own mandate is to mandate others, and teaching others becomes a prominent part of his activity. Given the original mandate of Jesus and the partial understanding of the disciples, it is no surprise that the movement toward Jerusalem begins with a re-negotiation of the disciples' lakeside call (8:34–35). If Jesus is to pass along the full mandate, it must include the servant's role. The theme of servant discipleship is explicit in two passages. At Mk 9:35, Jesus answers the disciples' concern about their relative importance and pecking order by saying the first shall be last and servant of all. In 10:43–44, he counters the ambitions of James and John by repeating the lesson about last and first and connecting it to the passage from Second Isaiah.

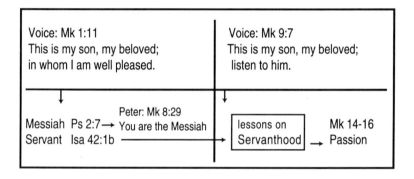

Figure 16

The pattern of teaching in the narrative suggests the relationship depicted in figure 16. What we see is that the titles Messiah and servant not only shape the teaching of Jesus but also shape the contours of Mark's account. Since the baptism of Jesus is his commissioning mandate, we can say that the two themes of his baptism, Messiah and servant, are directed to the narrative that unfolds the mandate.

### Messiah: Christological Lessons

When we think of these biblical roles as shaping the action, we need to see them more fully. How is the narrator using them to interest the reader? Translating this question into the language of narrative criticism, we would ask about the conformation and attitudes of the "implied reader" of Mark. As we saw in chapter 2, this is the reader implied in the text. We also saw, as in the example of Mk 13:14 ("let the reader understand"), that our appropriation of this partic-ular implied reader is partial and flawed. We can use outside help here. Fortunately such outside help is available in historical studies of the first-century Mediterranean sociological world.[6] These would allow us to say, for instance, that the messianic theme is defined by the first-century experience of "popular messiahs," while the servant texts speak to a profound fissure in the Judean collective psyche. Also, some of the language we generally tend to assign a ritual meaning (slave, cross, ransom) finds a likely context more closely related to the narrative.

Although the lessons in the first phase of Jesus' teaching are given more by example than through verbal lessons, some explicitly verbal instruction does take place, notably in the parables of 4:1–34 and the lessons on unclean food in 7:1–23. The practice of Jesus, however, dominates the "lessons" of this first part. If "Messiah" is a partially correct answer to the lessons of the first half, how are we to interpret those lessons? Since we see that Peter's answer is accepted as correct by Jesus, we can view the lessons as messianic. But since the answer is also incorrect, at least in some regards, we might guess that to name the lessons of the first half as simply messianic would be to repeat Peter's mistake.

The messianic theme comes to Mark's narrative already defined to a considerable extent. This prior meaning is not exclusively determined by the scriptural theme, since that theme reaches Mark's writing by way of its first-century interpretations. In this regard, studies in historical sociology investigating the turbulent happenings under Roman imperial control have turned up interesting evidence of numerous examples of "popular messiahs": "In contrast to the idealized branch of David hoped for by the learned Essenes and others, the popular leaders actually recognized as king by their followers led armed revolts against the Romans and their upper-class Jewish collaborators."[7]

Historical sociology does not raise the historical question in the very difficult terms of the historical person of Jesus so much as it studies the context of his times. For instance, as Richard Horsley and John Hanson remind us, a major revolt originated in Sepphoris, a city a few miles north of Nazareth, in 4 B.C.E., at about the time Jesus was born. In retaliation, Sepphoris was burned and its inhabitants sold into slavery.[8] As many have pointed out, the land of Palestine was the scene of intense social turbulence from the Maccabean revolt in 165 B.C.E. to the Bar Kokhba rebellion in 138 B.C.E. It is difficult to imagine Jesus living his life in a vacuum, unaffected by this social ferment. It is even more difficult to imagine his movement taking shape, even apart from Mark's account of it, without this sociohistorical background as its context, and perhaps its foil.

If the historical context of popular messiahs was such as Horsley and others have predicated, it would probably be part of the awareness of the author and the first readers. This might especially be true if Mark's narrative belongs to the genre of popular narrative, as I have discussed earlier. If this is what "Messiah" popularly meant in Mark's day, it is probably safe to assume that this meaning is reflected in his text. Nevertheless, it is useful to indicate some points of contact.

Aside from the plot of the story, we cannot forget that the Gospel is written around the time of the great revolt of 66–70 C.E. In the farewell speech of Mark 13, these events are moved to the foreground of reader attention. The speech includes warnings about "false messiahs" (13:21–22) that imply a similarity between the popular messiahs and Jesus. Presumably the similarity is sufficient to require vigilance, that the necessary distinctions be made.

In the world depicted by the plot, we see elements of a movement very much akin to the popular messiahs. The origins in Galilee, and among peasants, is typical. The movement from the hinterlands to Jerusalem is also a characteristic pattern. And finally the political context of Jesus' trial and execution is telling. Most striking here is the combination of bandit and Messiah in the charges leveled against Jesus in the closing chapters. Officially, the narrator and the high priest both claim Jesus to be "Messiah." For the one it is an authentic claim, for the other it is bogus. But a less official and less recognized undercurrent in the text keeps repeating the word "bandit" (*lestes* — 11:17; 14:48; 15:37). At the arrest of Jesus and at the crucifixion, the comparison is elaborated. In the episode concerning Barabbas, who "committed murder during the uprising" (15:7), it is dramatized.

Kingdom, Messiah, and the capital city of Jerusalem are all primary terms of the account. The large-scale movement upon the city, when juxtaposed with the messianic acclamation of Peter, powerfully suggests a political or social movement. Peter's remarks at 8:27–33, along with his vehement dispute with Jesus, are sometimes thought to reflect the disciples' political reading of "Messiah."

In a sense, then, the confrontational work of Jesus is aligned with the popular movements of resistance, called messianic. "Messiah" becomes almost a code word for conflict in the text. While it would be tempting to equate this with the rising action of the plot, such an equation would be misleading, for the falling action, as the movement of resolution, is also integral to the conflict. Conversely, the nonviolent character of Jesus' mode of "messianic" resistance is nonviolent from the very beginning.[9] It is the work of the servant.

## Servant: A Nonviolent Christology

The servant texts arose out of a situation of national *exile,* a saga of social dislocation. When Jerusalem was destroyed in 587 B.C.E. and its urban elite transported to Babylon, they received a blow of a severity hard to estimate. Such an impact is sustained at different levels. At an immediate level is the humiliation of defeat and the experience of moving from independence to political subjection. One of the main ways of acquiring slaves in the ancient world was through military conquest. In the Babylonian captivity an entire nation (at least its elite) was dragged into exile into the conquering country to experience a communal subjugation. The image of the captured slave is appropriate, and it is likely to have contributed to the prophet's image of the servant — the "Ebed Yahweh" or "slave of Yahweh."

But there are also deeper, more long-range effects. Involved in the power struggle between nations is a perception of the relative power of their national gods, and here Israel was vulnerable. Babylon's Marduk obviously proved stronger than Israel's Yahweh in battle. At stake for the Jerusalemites was the cultural construction of the worlds guarded by their respective divinities. In the language of the sociology of knowledge, cultures construct a meaningful world, a symbolic universe that is thought to provide an answer for every problem. And God's place in all of this is to give that universe an ultimate authority — Peter Berger's "sacred canopy." Putting it another way, if God is the author of reality, what is at stake is the untorn fabric of reality itself.[10]

Second Isaiah countered threat with theory and not with bigger threats, with words not swords. His was a mode of radicalized teaching that reenvisioned the role of Israel on the world stage. The new world the prophet preached was a new appropriation of reality or, if you will, a new reality. But it was a new reality that was grounded in the old. For the new reality described a possibility of power and did not attempt to glorify powerlessness. He does not succumb to our view that only strength is powerful; he manages not to confuse strength and power. The figure of the servant is at the center of this redefinition of power for Israel. As the slave of Yahweh, this figure is absolutely powerless on one scale of reference, and the image of the slave drives this point home, not to be escaped. But in the shell of this notion the prophet opens up new possibilities of power.

The image of power that the prophet presents is one perhaps accessible only after the easier approaches are denied. It is the notion of power as a social relationship or set of relationships. In her book *Powers of the Weak,* Elizabeth Janeway explores possibilities for empowerment among those outside the social "corridors of power."[11] While Janeway's view is not new, it is continually rediscovered as if new. And the reason is that the formal definition of power, the "myth" of power in her view, runs along contrary lines. In the official view, instead of power consisting in "the whole complicated structure of social relations in which, and by which, we live," power is seen as an attribute of certain persons in positions of command, whom we are accustomed to calling "the powerful." We live by one definition but give allegiance to the other. The allegiance blinds us to the reality, and it is this dynamic that constitutes Janeway's "myth." Those who gain by the myth are not likely to question it, of course, and so it remains unseen. Because power works as a network of relations, those on the bottom contribute as essentially as those on the top. This can be seen when those below withhold their consent, as in nonviolent resistance.

When Mark invokes the servant theme he is bringing this entire congeries of meanings to play in relationship to the kingdom of God. He does not shy from the notion of slavery, extending the language of servanthood explicitly at 10:44 to include the slave. Two related realities associated with the world of slaves — crucifixion and ransoming — also take on a meaningful character in Mark's text.

***Slave.*** Talk of servant and slave would be directly influenced by first-century experience and knowledge of the institution of slavery. Slaves were common, although apparently less so in Judea than in other parts of the empire. The symbol of the servant/slave in Mark is invested with firsthand knowledge of slavery. Although we can know some categorical facts about slavery in those days, we cannot share that era's experience of it.[12]

Even though we lack the first century's experiential knowledge of slavery, we do have some knowledge of the culture of subjugation, of which slavery is an extreme example. Both deference and a studied personification of dullness are useful for the slave to reinforce the master's sense of mastery and simple human superiority and to avoid implications of insubordination that might irritate the master and make life even more intolerable for the slave. The charade of subhumanness in a particular instance keeps the larger charade of a subhuman human class from any examination that might be detrimental to the vulnerable party in the relationship. Certainly this spirit is seen at a national level in Judea's chafing under imperialist Roman subjection. In this regard, "servant" makes an appropriate and dramatic contrast with "Messiah."

**Cross.** Mark's narrative makes two textual connections that reflect real aspects of slavery in the ancient Roman world. The first links "slave" and "cross."[13] Reinforcing the textual connection is the very real relationship between the two sociological institutions of crucifixion and slavery. Crucifixion was a punishment reserved for nonpersons — preeminently slaves but also vicious prisoners of war and troublesome political dissidents. Because of its unspeakably humiliating cruelty, it was valued as an effective deterrent. For this purpose it needed to be a public, highly visible act. Its public nature was a main cause of its intense degree of humiliation. As it was used against persons without rights, one could expect them to be already desperate. Hence drastic measures were justified as needed. In other words, what crucifixion served to deter was precisely acts of rebellion. Because of its very public nature it can be expected to have become an emblem of the consequences of revolt.[14]

It would seem that any reference to crucifixion in Jesus' day or Mark's day or for many years after would involve such associations. For early readers the symbol would have been invested with sociological content based on their very real experience of witnessing crucifixions. Ched Myers mentions the exegetical impulse to see in Mark the beginning of a spiritualizing tendency, which would define the cross as personal asceticism. While this indeed has happened, it would seem to have occurred much later. It is very difficult to imagine the cross being spiritualized while it still carried the overpowering political freight of deadly threat against political dissidents. The abolition of crucifixion as a historical practice would be the psychological requirement for any spiritualizing of the cross.

**Ransom.** A second textual link to slavery is that of the ransom (*lutron*) in 10:45. It is not coincidental that the two words, "slave" and "ransom," appear together. As regards this, Myers writes: "The term [ransom] referred to the price required to redeem captives or purchase freedom for indentured servants. Jesus promises that the way of 'servanthood' has been transformed by the Human One into the way of liberation."[15] In a society of fixed roles, "the most common and also the most dramatic rise in status came about in the manumission of slaves."[16] So it was not only a prominent image of release from subjugation or travail but also one of the few images of social mobility available in those times. All of this is supported by the traditions of Israel's release from slavery into freedom, contrasted with their present imperial domination.

The image in 10:45 is one of substitution. Losing a life to gain a life was a theme enunciated in 8:35, but now it is repeated in terms of benefiting others. Substitution is a recurrent theme in sacrificial contexts, although scholars insist it is not part of the biblical understanding of sacrifice.[17] But nonsacrificial substitution also has a place in Mark's framework, inasmuch as it appears at different moments. We have already noticed how the burden of the leper's isolation is taken on by Jesus (1:45). And even more clearly, the insurrectionist Barabbas is replaced in the dock by Jesus (15:6–15). Here the motif of substitution points to a pattern of "taking the place" of the socially punished.

Nonviolence is the political version of this substitutionary movement. At a first level it is a substitution of behaviors, one set for another. It occurs within a frame of antagonisms (agon) and with the set of expectations that go with it. Expected violent behavior is replaced by nonviolent behavior. This introduces what Gene Sharp calls an asymmetry into the relation. In this substitution it interrupts the threatened cycles of escalation of violence — the conventions of confrontation.[18] This liberates in the sense that it stops a line of violence by "absorbing" it, refusing to pay it back. The nonviolent actor's motivation is not to be a victim but to be a conspicuous noncombatant. The posture is a clear invitation to the opponent *not* to strike. It releases the future victims of this mounting dialectic of violence from its grip. It does this without losing its force as confrontation. In this sense, it releases from the history of harm, the past as well as the future. Here nonviolence is a "narrative" form of political ransom. In the narrative of Jesus it specifies further the nature of the "cross" that was proper to his movement. It is not simply the cross of resistance, although it is that, but it is also the cross of nonviolent response.

We see then an integral connection between the *cross* of 8:35 and the *slave* and *ransom* of 10:45. To gain one's self means to put one's self at risk, but to risk one's self in order to interrupt the flow of violence in its cycles is to ransom others. It is a ransom because it delivers others from the history and consequences of violence as force or as injustice, in this particular concrete instance.

The messianic and servant themes define the plot of Mark. What we see is that the rising action of Mark's narrative suggests the movement characteristic of popular messianic revolts, but with a difference. In Mark, the disciples fail to recognize Jesus' messianic mission, possibly because it lacks the usual militant features of the popular movements. When, however, they do come to this realization, Jesus must instruct them in the differences between their notions, based on the popular expectations, and his. He uses the servant typology to accomplish this task.

Two points need to be reaffirmed about Jesus' teaching as sketched in the previous description. First, Jesus takes as his topic his own identity; that is, his teaching is christological. Second, the Christology points to the plot. The Gospel Christology points to an action, and the action is recited in the narrative, not posited outside the contours of the narrative in a realm of cosmic redemption. In brief, the titles "Messiah" and "servant" work as the narrative program of the plot, not as a separate theology of the suffering Messiah.

## The Teaching of Jesus as Subplot

The relation between Jesus and his disciples is not shown in the narrative as simply an occasion of teaching. It is also a site of conflict. It is part of the plot. The disciples repeatedly fail to understand Jesus; he in turn is repeatedly impatient with them. "Understanding" is a key motif through the middle part of the narrative, and their failure is emphasized by three boat crossings that dramatize their lack of insight and three episodes on the road to Jerusalem that highlight their difficulties in receiving his teaching.

### Finding the Main Plot and the Subplot

In the dramatic plot of traditional drama, conflict arises between characters in the story. David Rhoads and Donald Michie have shown us that Mark's plot is structured around conflicts among characters in the traditional manner.[19] This is the dimension that builds suspense and tension. "Without conflict, most stories would only be a sequence of events strung together without tension or suspense or struggle on the part of the characters." In large part, it is the presence of conflicts in Mark that prompts us to think of the Gospel as a larger whole and not simply a collection of sermon-sized stories. It is also the development and resolution of these conflicts that constitute the main interest of this study.

According to Rhoads and Michie the structuring conflicts in Mark are threefold:

- Jesus against the demons,

- Jesus against the religious authorities, and

- Jesus and the disciples.

These generate the action and call for resolution. We see Jesus in action in the conflict among the characters in the Gospel story, and Mark underscores these conflicts in his treatment of characterization.

But the presence of multiple conflicts raises the question of their hierarchical order. In ordinary language, we must determine which is the main plot and which are subplots. For multiple conflicts indicate multiple plots. In Shakespeare's *Hamlet,* for instance, the conflict of Hamlet with Claudius identifies the main plot, while the conflict between Hamlet and Laertes identifies the subplot.[20] What are the equivalent patterns in Mark? We need to look at each of the three conflict areas in turn.

In one of the earliest studies of conflict in Mark, James Robinson showed how the conflict between Jesus and the demons, which he interpreted as part of the apocalyptic frame of the story, was essentially decided in the opening episodes of Jesus' baptism and his desert temptation.[21] Rhoads and Michie agree that this conflict is over before the Gospel story proper begins.[22] In light of the previous chapter, we can fill this picture in further. The symbolic vocabulary of holy and unclean is grounded in Mark's narrative in the cosmic conflict between the Holy Spirit and the unclean spirits. Filled with the power of the Holy Spirit, Jesus is recognized by the unclean spirits as "the Holy One of God." In the course of the narrative he invites others to join him. They are called out of the familiar daily reality into the charged and powerful world of the spirit conflict. Those invited are allowed no middle ground, and any who refuse him by questioning his credentials, as the scribes do, are in effect refusing access to holy power. This leaves them no recourse except the demonic, as we see in 3:29, where their refusal is described as the sin against the Holy Spirit.

The apocalyptic ultimacy of this level of the conflict underlies the struggle among the human characters playing itself out in the plot unfolding before our eyes. Two radically opposed kinds of power are pitted against each other in the Holy Spirit and unclean spirits, and the ultimacy they represent is that of the foundations of authentic power. The language of destruction finds its roots in the demonic and, in this Gospel, is the terminology chosen to characterize unclean power. Against it the holy power of Jesus contends. In other words, the opposition of holy and unclean represents the terms of the ideological struggle of the Gospel narrative, and the struggle is personified in the conflict of spirits. We can rule out the demon conflict as a candidate for the main plot, not only because it concludes before the plot begins but also because it sets the terms for the plot. It helps to define the plot, but it is not the plot.

The two conflicts that shape the plot itself are that of Jesus and the Judean authorities and that of Jesus and the disciples. Sociological studies that emphasize the historical action of Jesus in relation to the social structures of his day tend to favor the first plot, that between Jesus and the Judean authorities. As I have made clear above, I share this assessment, though my arguments are based on literary categories and Mark's work rather than on historical categories and Jesus' actions. Summarized, my reasons are the following.

1. The greater seriousness of the temple incident and the plot containing it recommends it as the main plot. It is the opposition of the temple authorities that results in Jesus' death. The dispute with the disciples contributes to that, but indirectly.

2. The struggle between Jesus and his disciples is narrower in scope, contained as it is within one side of the larger conflict of Jesus and his friends against the Judean authorities.

3. The subplot usually peaks before the main plot.[23] This would fit the two dramatic shapes if the Peter saying at 8:27–30 is the crisis of the subplot while the later temple incident at 11:15–19 is the crisis for the main plot. The subplot, in this pattern, serves the main plot.

The conspicuous turning point at 8:27–33 has attracted critics' attention and is commonly identified as the main crisis in the Gospel account. Not only Schweizer's outline, as we have seen, but in fact most interpretations of the Gospel arrangement make their main turn on this "hinge," as Wilfred Harrington calls it.[24] This juncture in the narrative manifestly marks a change in the disciples' relationship to Jesus. It represents the central crisis in the conflict between Jesus and the disciples. Thus, this conflict is not only a serious candidate for the main plot in Mark: for many critics who deal with the literary dimension of the work, it is perceived as the only plot.

Thematic studies that explain the Gospel in terms of suffering messiahship tend to emphasize the pattern of Jesus and his disciples, almost to the exclusion of the conflict between Jesus and the authorities. Literary studies have followed suit, impressed with the distinctive turning point at 8:27–33. But they tend to take the equally important hinge in chapter 11 for granted, as if they view the crisis in chapter 8 as Mark's literary creation but that in chapter 11 as simply part of the historical record. As a matter of fact both moments have the same literary credentials. Certainly the crisis in chapter 8 seems more pronounced in Mark than in the other Gospels and so warrants attention from the literary critics. But the temple crisis in chapter 11 is not only equally important but also equally Markan in its narrative origins. (Here it is instructive to compare John's Gospel plot, which, in chapter 11, positions the raising of Lazarus in this role.) The temple crisis, borrowed by Matthew and Luke for their Gospels, is one of Mark's major contributions to the genre. That which most clearly unites the Synoptic Gospels, which allows them to be read synoptically, is their adherence to Mark's plot. On the whole, then, the literary evidence argues for the conflict with the authorities to be counted as the main plot and the discipleship conflict as the subplot.

## Imitation: The Heart of the Subplot's Conflict

In the opening chapter of this book, with the help of J. G. Davies, I raised a question: What are we to imitate in the *imitatio Christi* to avoid being overly literal in our imitation? That is, How are we to know what in the Gospel we are invited to imitate and what is merely incidental? Now we can begin to discern the lines of an answer to this question.

The teaching of Jesus is placed in the context of a narrative in which Jesus does not speak directly to the reader, as would be the case in a collection of his sayings, but rather speaks to disciples as characters in a story. The rhetorical indirection achieved by this stratagem permits a number of effects. One is the opportunity to exploit narrative conflict as the disciples distance themselves from Jesus. Another is the introduction of a separation between the disciple-reader and the disciples-characters. As readers we can compare and contrast between ourselves and the apostles. As readers we also find our relationship to the text mirrored by the relation between Jesus and the disciples inside the text, and this is crucial for what the author has planned for us.

Disciples by definition are followers. They derive their identity to some extent from the one they follow. And so I earlier noted that

Christology informs and serves discipleship. But I have also said that the Christology of Mark is oriented to the plot, which is to say, the action of the portrayed Jesus. In the narrative this relation is acted out: "Come, follow me." The disciples adopt the identity of Jesus by doing as he does. Discipleship means doing as Jesus did — "following him" — and this means following through with the action of the main plot. It is no surprise then that the bulk of teaching is to be found in chapters 9–10 of Mark, as Jesus leads the disciples toward the climax of the narrative, in the nonviolent confrontation in the temple. His teaching very specifically orients to the plot — and his expectations of the disciples in the coming crisis. In the narrative, "to follow" is a pattern of behavior dramatized on the way to the city. They follow in his footsteps, along the road that leads to the temple. A rich man takes a different path (10:22). A blind man follows Jesus down the same road leading to Jerusalem (10:52; 11:1).

At issue in the conflict of the subplot is the disciples' *inability* to join Jesus in the main plot. They are slow to enter the role of confronting power, and once they accept this "messianic" role, they are entirely unwilling to adopt Jesus' "servant" expression of this role. The series of misunderstandings that punctuate the text describing their progress down the road to the city shows us their divergence from the pattern given by Jesus. The twelve argue over their relative status (9:34). John associates discipleship with special privileges (9:38). James and John make a bold bid for the best places in the organization, outraging the other ten, perhaps out of resentment (10:35, 41). These elaborate the fundamental difference between Jesus and his disciples that is implied in his servant model, a difference represented in the dispute between Jesus and Peter as they first set out for the city (8:32–33).

So we see here one of the advantages for Mark in situating Jesus' teaching within a narrative. The narrative context allows him to specify the meaning of the teaching. It serves as a control. When a disciple is invited to "follow" Jesus along his way, this is not simply a matter of identifying with him in a spiritual or psychological unity. It means to join with him in action, to follow in his steps, to do as he is doing. And in Mark that action is defined by the narrative plot. In this way the text resolves J. G. Davies's dilemma. By giving his Christology a narrative conformation and situating his notions of discipleship in relation to that narrative, Mark in effect links the imitation of Christ to the activity of Jesus as given in the narrative plot. In a way, this fits the exegetical view that in Mark the *imitatio Christi* follows upon the *theologia crucis* — but with the crucial proviso that the "cross" is to be interpreted more properly as a symbol of narrative events than as a pointer to a theological construct external to the narrative.

The narrative context, specifically its relation to the main plot, gives concrete meaning to imitation: follow Jesus in his confrontation and nonviolent response. Become, as he is, a nonviolent resister. Thus we can resolve the difficulty mentioned above concerning genre by understanding that the rhetorical or pedagogical program of the Gospel is embedded in the narrative plot — as an aspect of the poetics of the text.

## The Conflict Resolved?

The subplot does not reach a satisfactory resolution, however. The disciples fail to carry through their task of following Jesus. Their imitation comes up short. While they have been mandated to follow and, in the dialogue with Peter at 8:34, invited to take up their cross and follow, they drop out of the picture prematurely. Fear rather than faith prevails in their response to the call.

It is common though not essential for subplots to contribute to the main plot of the narrative of which they are a part. Evidence that this is also true in Mark's Gospel is circumstantial but strong. The failure of his foremost disciples to follow him leaves Jesus stranded and vulnerable to the designs of his enemies. In the passion account, in chapters 14–15, this is seen most clearly in the relations among the crowds, the disciples, and Peter.

The evidence is indirect, but it strongly suggests that the followers' failure made Jesus vulnerable unto death. Their mandate, as we have been reading it, was to join him in nonviolent confrontation. Certainly he is not shown asking them to defend him with weapons. And yet he *is* asking them to stay with him. To what end? What is implied in the story not taken? What do the requests Jesus makes of his followers — to follow and stay with him, but not in any violent way — bode for the coming confrontation? What do they imply for the story he proposes, a story the followers fail to carry through? One can surmise a possible prophetic campaign, but that story comes to us only as a conjecture. It is not presented in the narrative. It is a story that may have been once, but is no longer, possible. What actually happens in the narrative is their departure and his death. The resolution of the subplot in the disciples' failure makes way for the crucifixion, the working out of the main plot.

In the first part of this chapter we saw that the themes of Jesus' teaching, Messiah and servant, are integrated into the narrative. They dictate the narrative program and reveal the narrative itself as the Gospel's primary christological datum. In this second part we have seen that the teaching of Jesus not only thematizes the main plot of the narrative but also — because it is poorly received by the disciples — becomes a center of contention in itself. It is this conflict between Jesus and the disciples that specifies the subplot of Mark's narrative. What is at issue in this dispute is the invitation to imitate Jesus by joining him in the action of the main plot.

## The Reader: Discipleship and the Structure of Irony

While the christological titles and teaching are integral to the Gospel narrative, this is not the whole story. In addition to the teaching dramatized in the relation between Jesus and his disciples we also notice the titles are used outside this framework. In particular, at Mk 1:1 they are confided to the reader by the narrator. The opening verse sets up expectations for the reader outside the awareness of Jesus or his disciples, who have not at this point in the account as yet received any mandates. Jesus does not speak directly to the reader, but the narrator does.

The structuring frame we saw earlier in this chapter was based on the titles of Jesus. By carefully distinguishing that structure as mandating action *inside* the story, as part of the awareness of its characters, we can distinguish it from another very similar structure that is *outside* the story, though a part of the narrator's report to the reader/ listener. This structure also operates by christological titles. The first verse of the Gospel, Mk 1:1, stands apart from what follows as a heading for the entire work. Some have called it the "title" of the work.[25] Its double attribution to Jesus sets up a program for the narrator and reader:

The beginning of the gospel of Jesus (who is)
    (*a*) the Christ (Messiah),
    (*b*) the Son of God.

In Mk 1:1 these christological titles are divulged to the reader outside the events of the story, before the story begins. As readers we expect the themes thus singled out will be pivotal in the narrative to follow. Since we soon learn that (except for the protagonist) the characters are in the dark, our expectations shift to their attempts to discover the meaning of the titles. Situations in which the reader knows something that the characters do not represent the basic structure of situational irony. We can expect that this structure of irony relates more to the ideological relation between narrator and reader outlooks than it does to the conflictual relationship among the characters themselves.

When Peter names Jesus as Messiah at 8:29, he partially completes the narrative contract of Mk 1:1, which promises to show Jesus as "Messiah" and "Son of God." But this contract was originally issued to the reader, not to Peter, and so he does not know his (correct) answer is still incomplete. Nor was he present at the baptism of Jesus to hear the voice from heaven naming Jesus as Messiah and servant, citing Ps 2:7 and Isa 42:1, although the reader was privy to this event too. And so Peter is surprised and distraught to learn that Jesus has more to add to the title of Messiah. It is the nature of this addition that disturbs Peter, for it includes suffering and dying, features not part of the messianic agenda in the usual interpretation (8:31). Aware of the baptism message, the reader may see here Jesus' mandate to be servant, but Peter knows nothing of this, thinking that the Messiah must be aggressive and even ruthless if the movement is to overturn Roman control and restore Israel to its rightful prominence in the land.

And so, one imagines, Peter finds in this talk of suffering and dying an unwelcome note of defeatism that seriously mars the charismatic élan that made Jesus so attractive in the first place. So Peter enters into an argument with Jesus about his negative outlook. The dispute is about what direction the narrative will take from here. Jesus, in possession of information denied to Peter, can tell him that his ways are human and not divine (8:33). But since Peter did not hear the voice at the baptism, human ways are the best he can manage.

Peter, like the reader, detects a new direction appearing at this point in the narrative. Is the new direction intended for Jesus alone, or is it also for those who follow? Peter suspects the worse. It is troublesome enough that Jesus is losing his luster. Worse is that he may expect his followers to take this same next step themselves. As if to settle such doubts, Jesus immediately renegotiates the original call of 1:16–20: "If you would come after me, deny yourself, take up your cross and follow me" (8:34). I can imagine Peter, as the narrative's spokesperson for the reader-as-disciple, protesting: "You said nothing about a 'cross' back at the lake!" Clearly Jesus has raised the stakes.

But the hardest word for Peter is "deny." As the narrative unfolds we find this word belongs to him in a most excruciating way. At the end of chapter 14, in a double scene that the narrator presents as occurring simultaneously, Peter defends himself in the high priest's outer courtyard as Jesus is on trial inside, in effect, taking up his cross. This is Peter's chance to deny himself and take up the cross with Jesus, or on behalf of Jesus. Instead, he denies three times that he knows the man (14:66–72). In the narrative context, Peter's denial expresses the natural aversion to the nonviolent conflict that Jesus espouses. At the center of the story, before they have departed for Jerusalem, this future is still unclear to Peter, though he has his fears. And he has his differences with Jesus. Presumably Jesus has the proper information about how the messianic role is to be interpreted. Thus the heavenly arbiter settles the dispute between Jesus and Peter. And the disciples, including the reader of the text, are invited to observe the action of Jesus in the unfolding narrative in order to understand the meaning of Messiah as God has given it and Jesus has learned it.

The second title, "Son of God," also has a second accented moment in the narrative, and it is parallel in its dramatic emphasis to that of Peter at midpoint in the Gospel. In Mk 15:39, the centurion, observing the death of Jesus, says, "Truly this was a son of God." As with Peter's saying, this constitutes a recognition scene, and it concludes its part of the narrative.[26] The centurion gets the last line, but the line properly belongs to the disciples because this message is for them. The fact that they are no longer present to the events of the narrative, so that they are unable to receive the message, is a potent symbol of their failure.

In fulfillment of the program set out in Mk 1:1, the titles pose a set of anticipations that are resolved in two recognition scenes, featuring respectively Peter and the centurion. These are diagrammed in figure 17.

How do we get from "Messiah" to "Son of God"? "Messiah" alone is not enough — it must be supplemented by further teaching. And that teaching is provided by Jesus' lessons regarding the "servant" in chapters 9 and 10. An equation of sorts among titles is the result:

$$\text{Messiah} + \text{servant} = \text{Son of God}$$

| | | |
|---|---|---|
| Title: Mk 1:1<br>The beginning of<br>the good news of Jesus: | Mk 8:29<br>Peter | Mk 15:39<br>Centurion |
| Messiah ⟶<br>Son of God ⟶ | You are the<br>Messiah | Truly this is a<br>Son of God ⟶ |

Figure 17

The reader is expected to draw up the total.

The centurion, we must note, is on the wrong side of the conflict. More specifically, he is the narrative's main spokesperson for violence. He is the character in charge of the soldiers, who possess the official capacity for violence necessarily engaged by the council to complete its plans for Jesus. His verdict here is impressive, coming as it does from a hostile witness. While his speech suggests a conversion, it may be a further ingredient in the heavy cloud of irony that overlays the closing chapters. Its main function may be to highlight the disciples' failure to arrive at a similar enlightenment.

In general, the centurion, standing in proxy for the disciples, completes the lessons on discipleship. The series ends as it began, outside the purview of the story characters to whom it pertains. In the title, 1:1, it was in the narrative, but outside the frame of the story. In 15:39 it is concluded with a substitute character, for the disciples, the intended receivers, have in effect taken leave of the story. The only continuity in the series is that of the relation between narrator and reader.

We might recognize here the rough equivalent of Kingsbury's so-called story of Jesus mentioned at the beginning of this chapter. But now we understand it not as a plot in the narrative but rather as a structure of irony taking the form of a discourse directed by the narrator to the reader concerning the disciples' progress. It is not a story so much as it is a bridge between the action in the story and the reader's own situation.

In this major framework, which we might call the *christological structure of the text*, the narrator expands the two-part instruction to the disciples so as to include the reader. But the reader is present to the text as already knowing the "answer" — the titles to which the characters struggle are already in the reader's possession at 1:1. What the reader presumably does not know is how these titles will be fleshed out with narrative content. While the characters are moving from the action to the titles, the reader is back-filling, giving to the titles some active content. This is another way of saying that the plot specifies the Christology, this time as directed to the disciple-readers. Briefly put, the christological structure, pivoting on the titles of Messiah and servant and relating to discipleship, belongs properly to the world of the narrator and the reader, and only in a secondary way to that of Jesus and his disciples. It is because the reader is a disciple, or a possible disciple, that the christological structure is so much in the foreground.

But while the two lines of discourse — that of the narrator to the reader and that of Jesus to the disciples — can be distinguished, and should be, they also converge, with a layering effect. For the call to discipleship within the text is heard outside of it as well, in the act of reading. And the convergence of reader and character around the theme of discipleship is especially prominent in the interaction between the reader and Peter, an interaction that is real though not direct.

The preceding might be summed up by saying that Jesus' relation to the disciples inside the story replicates the narrator's relation to the reader. Jesus extends his own mandate to the plot, to the disciples, in his invitation to follow him. The invitation Jesus extends to the disciples the narrator likewise extends to the reader. The discourse that the narrator directs to the reader parallels Jesus' teaching of the disciples by way of themes that give meaning to action in the main plot. The christological structure inside the story, based on the themes of Messiah and servant and on part of the characters' awareness, is matched by the structure outside the story, based on the titles shared by the narrator and the reader but not disclosed to the characters.

In other words, the Gospel story of nonviolent confrontation and conflict resolution is not simply shown for our admiration. It does indeed have a "rhetorical" aspect that takes it beyond the interests of literary poetics to the arena of practice. It does invite us, calling us as well as showing us. It not only scripts a way of nonviolent resistance but engages us to go and do likewise.

*Chapter Six* _____

# THE AGON AND NONVIOLENT PLOT RESOLUTION

> It was like a chess game, he supposed — although he had never played chess — with the difference that he had several opponents, and while moving against one he must never forget the others who might choose that moment to move against him. And of course, he thought grimly, the stakes were higher in this game. A wrong movement could mean death.[1]

This reflective interlude catches Matt Coburn in the moments before the shoot-out that concludes *The Empty Land,* the novel I have been using to represent the story world of Louis L'Amour. The action is moving into its closing moments, the resolution of the plot. Of the three steps in the pattern of the agon — challenge, evaluation of the challenge, and response to it — this is the second. The first step dared him to clean up the town, which means in this particular moment to clean out the gunfighters lining the main street in readiness. Coburn's response will be to accept the challenge, join the shoot-out, and win it. At the end, four of the enemy are dead, though some escape. There is room for another story at another time. Typical of the resolution of conflict in such stories, the antagonists are paid back and are consequently unable or unwilling to continue the opposition. The story stops.

The agon as I defined it refers to the conflictual dimension in human interaction that corresponds to the patterns of narrative. Since in narrative this pattern includes a point of view, it can be seen from another side. In discussing the agon I noted a built-in ratcheting effect, which promotes escalation of conflict. In terms of narrative, the story does not necessarily end, although we may be ready to hear "happily ever after." The other side might just be launching a new conflict based on their perception of our unfair gains in the exchange just finished.

## Richard Horsley's Spiral of Violence

Richard Horsley has taken this pattern of escalation as his theme in *Jesus and the Spiral of Violence.*[2] The spiral pattern is borrowed from Dom Helder Camara, who uses it to picture the social dynamics found among peasant societies in today's Third World. Horsley applies it convincingly to the peasant society of Jesus' Palestinian world. The spiral is imagined in four ascending stages: (*a*) an initial state of *injustice* or structural violence, (*b*) a subsequent stage of reaction by way of *protest* and *resistance,* (*c*) a third stage of *repression* in response, and (*d*) a final stage, which consists of open *revolt.*[3] The last stage may or may not be accompanied by violence.

Horsley documents the spiral of violence in Jewish Palestine of the first century.[4] He shows evidence for each of the four stages in the pattern, from the institutional oppression of Herod the Great in 40–4 B.C.E. to the great revolt in 66–70 C.E. Examples of injustice are easily located in the rule of Herod and Rome's imperial control of Judea.

The pattern of injustice gave rise to a series of resistance movements. Passover, commemorating the liberation from Egyptian slavery, was always a tense time for the Roman governors. "Passover was a time when the underlying tensions of the imperial situation came to the surface,"[5] and it warranted close monitoring by the Roman officials. No stinting of repressive countermeasures is reported in the record. Subject peoples were kept alert to the consequences of opposing Roman rule in many ways. The presence of the Roman occupying army served to intimidate with the specter of inevitable reprisals should the locals become too independent in their activities. And crucifixion itself, as we have seen, was a primary tool in the Romans' arsenal of repressive weapons. Although "the usual historical experience is that the spiral of violence ends with repression,"[6] in Judea, the Roman repression prompted the realization of the fourth move in Horsley's spiral, that is, revolt. The main revolts in Roman times were in 4 B.C.E., 66–70 C.E., and 132–35 C.E. Two of these bracket, with thirty-five years on each side, the years of Jesus' ministry, though none coincides. These and Horsley's more extensive list of examples illustrate the various steps in the spiral, certainly a factor in first-century Judea.

## Gene Sharp's Three Moments

The Gospel tells a different story. It is one that we might perceive to be a variant, a contrasting alternative to which we can properly give the name nonviolent action. The suggestion can be placed on more secure footing by a comparison with the model of nonviolent resistance presented by Gene Sharp in his comprehensive study *The Politics of Nonviolent Action.*[7] "Nonviolent action" is understood here as a specific form of nonviolent resistance, which is for Sharp a broader concept.

Sharp's third volume addresses the "dynamics" of nonviolent action. In this volume he analyzes the drama of a nonviolent resistance, the behavioral sequence of a nonviolent action. Sharp identifies three successive moments in a dialectic of action and reaction. These moments correspond to the first three chapters of the third volume and can be labeled confrontation, repression, and nonretaliation.

Nonviolent *confrontation,* also called "challenge" by Sharp, names the moment of active resistance. Features of this moment are its nonviolent character, the initiating role that the nonviolent agent assumes, and the action's focus on the opponent's source of power. Insofar as the nonviolent action engineers a confrontation it can properly be called an initiative. Commonly it brings to the surface a history of unexpressed grievance. The initiative confronts the opponent's power in two ways — indirectly, in that it applies nonviolence to an opponent more familiar with violence, and more directly, in that it removes the very basis of the opponent's authority, namely, the consent of the governed.[8]

*Repression* names the second moment and describes the opponent's response to the nonviolent initiative. Repression is the opponent's acknowledgment of the seriousness of the challenge. It is violent or threatens violence. Essentially, in a repressive response the dominating party invokes the sanctions that buttress control. This move has a demystifying value for the nonviolent group, in that it reveals the opponent's reliance on violence in order to reinforce an eroded authority. It also has a certain disarming effect, in that it forces the opponent to play his trump, something usually more effective as a threat left in reserve. Forms of repression include information control, psychological pressures, arrests and imprisonments, and direct physical violence.[9] While the repressive forms vary, in general they trace back to a capability of employing direct physical violence.

*Nonretaliation* constitutes the third moment, in response to the repressive move. This counterresponse is essentially a refusal to counter violence with further violence. Insofar as violence invites retaliatory violence, nonretaliation is a surprise, a second initiative. The nonviolent practitioner opens a new direction for action by interrupting the pattern, becoming the agent once again. Sharp writes of "nonretaliatory suffering" in this moment and of the need for solidarity and discipline.[10]

The nonviolence of nonretaliation differs from that of the original confrontation in its ostensibly passive character, although that passivity must be understood in the context of the initiatives taken by the nonviolent agent in the first moment of resistance and in the third moment of nonretaliation. Each moment can be conceived as deliberately breaking a pattern. The confrontation nonviolently interrupts the silence of oppression; the nonretaliation nonviolently interrupts the incipient cycle of violence. Because it is active, the nonviolence of nonretaliation might better be described as nonaggressive, rather than passive.

The three moments of nonviolent action describe a pattern abstracted from the vagaries of historical praxis. In case histories of nonviolent action variations of the pattern usually occur. For instance, it is common for the first and second steps to cycle through more than one round before the third step is taken. Nonviolent confrontation leads to repression, but a more concerted display of nonviolent confrontation may be selected as the best response to the repressive move. The escalation implied in this kind of cycle would conclude, however, with the third moment of nonretaliation. The three moments can be considered as idealized versions of the main movements in a dialogic exchange of confrontative gestures.

As a gestural dialogue it compares to the agonistic pattern discussed in chapter 2, above. It is, in fact, an alternative form. As in the agon, the moves consist of social challenge and calculated response. The nonviolent action pattern goes beyond the description of the agon in typifying three particular kinds of challenge and/or response. These are designed specifically to break out of the constrictions placed by the quasi-narrative features of agonistic encounters. Whereas the agon permits two outcomes, winning or losing, the nonviolent dynamism seeks to transcend its behavioral straitjacket. Whereas in the agon refusing to fight is considered equivalent to losing, in nonviolent action the refusal to fight is presented as another kind of challenge. It challenges not only the opponent but also the rules of the game.

In this way, it interrupts Horsley's spiral of violence. Horsley is interested in affirming the resistance character of Jesus' activity, which for him means downplaying the nonviolent dimension. Thus his spiral is invoked for the purpose of demonstrating the dynamics of violence, not the workings of nonviolence. Nevertheless, the relationship is clear. The first of the four stages of the spiral is presumed in Sharp's analysis, as the situation of injustice that prompts the nonviolent action. The difference lies in the deliberate refusal to take the steps of the conventional pattern. The steps taken by the protecting group deliberately frustrate the spiral of violence by refusing the expected pattern (see fig. 18).

| Steps in the Cycles of Violence and Nonviolence | | |
| --- | --- | --- |
| Stages | Violence *Horsley* | Nonviolence *Sharp* |
| 1 | injustice | (injustice) |
| 2 | protest, resistance | nonviolent confrontation |
| 3 | repression | repression |
| 4 | revolt | nonretaliation |

Figure 18

While the four stages of the spiral of violence are thought to be characteristic of social dynamics in conflict, they are not considered inevitable. They can be understood to provide the armature upon which deliberate nonviolent action rings its changes. In fact, Horsley offers his own confirmation of the alternative pattern. Although he is not arguing in favor of nonviolence, he reports the presence of nonviolent campaigns around the time of Jesus' ministry:

> Most remarkable of all Jewish nonviolent resistance to Roman rule were the massive popular demonstrations that occurred just before or shortly after the ministry of Jesus. Among the issues evident in these protests, the most obvious is the consistently nonviolent character of Jewish resistance.[11]

In another place, he cites a passage from Josephus that illustrates the pattern hypothesized by the nonviolent theory. The setting is Pontius Pilate's ruthless rule (26–36 C.E.) and in particular the first head-on conflict between the governor and the people:

As procurator of Judea, Tiberius sent Pilate, by night and under cover, to bring into Jerusalem the images of Caesar known as standards. At daybreak, this caused an enormous disturbance among the Jews. Those nearby were alarmed at the sight since it meant that their laws had been trampled on — for those laws do not permit any image to be set up in the city. The angry city mob was joined by a huge influx of people from the countryside. The Jews rushed off to Pilate in Caesarea and begged him to remove the standards from Jerusalem and to respect their ancestral laws. When Pilate refused, they threw themselves down on the ground around his house and stayed put for five days and nights.

The next day, Pilate took his seat on the tribunal in the great stadium and summoned the crowd, pretending to be ready to give them an answer. Instead he gave a pre-arranged signal to his armed soldiers to surround the Jews. Finding themselves in a ring of troops three deep, the Jews were dumbfounded. Then Pilate declared that he would cut them down unless they accepted the images of Caesar, and nodded to the soldiers to draw their swords. As if by arrangement, the Jews all fell to the ground, extended their necks, and proclaimed that they were ready to be killed rather than transgress the law. Astonished by the intensity of their religious fervor, Pilate ordered the immediate removal of the standards from Jerusalem.[12]

The pattern is classic. The sit-down strike declares the moment of nonviolent confrontation. It evokes the repressive response of Pilate's armed soldiers. This in turn produces the nonretaliatory response of the defiantly extended necks.

## Sharp on the Gospel

As we have seen, the Gospel plot, as agon, presents in the rising action an image of popular resistance, though without the military trappings commonly associated with popular messianic movements. Now we see that nonviolent confrontation patterns, as elucidated by Sharp, allow us to make sense of the narrative resolution of Mark's account.

In the Jerusalem chapters (chs. 11–16), Mark's narrative reaches its climax and continues through the falling action to the catastrophe. Chapter 11, beginning the dramatic climax, shows Jesus taking the initiative, moving into the city and forthrightly making his case in the cleansing of the temple.[13] In response, the authorities propose to "destroy" him (11:18). The Synoptic pattern, following Mark, offers the temple cleansing as the action that precipitates the passion account. Jesus elaborates this confrontation with the controversies in the temple area of chapter 12 and the word of judgment on city and temple in chapter 13.

Momentum shifts to the other side in chapter 14, as the passion account begins and the dynamic of repression takes its turn. The outcome of repression is foreseen by Jesus, who knows how he plans to respond and prepares his followers for the worst, at the supper. This is actually the last word in a long period of preparation, given through the course of the Gospel story. After the supper, the arrest in the garden, followed by the two trials, acts out the repressive countermeasures. Jesus responds to his arrest nonviolently and nonaggressively.

The presence of other alternatives indicates that Jesus' nonviolence represents a choice, not helpless impotence. The choice is earlier explored in depth in his garden prayer. The unusual detail of the severed ear is probably to be linked to the earlier prophetic motif of "eyes and ears" symbolizing the blocked avenues to conversion, developed earlier in the Gospel (Mk 4:12; 7:6–7; 8:18).[14] Violence inhibits conversion in a radical, direct manner. The power of Jesus' decision for nonviolence is confirmed by the man in white at the empty tomb. It is even more surprisingly confirmed by the opponent, in the person of the centurion (15:39), who is none other than the strong arm of the violent opposition, its practical agent.

## Three Narrative Moves

This narrative movement can be concentrated into three moments that correspond to those of Sharp: the temple, the garden, and the cross. Each is a part of a longer action, but each is focused in a climactic scene as well (see fig. 19).

A verbal signal that accents these three crucial scenes is the word "robber" or "bandit" (*lestes*). Its only instances in Mark occur at these three moments. At the temple action, Jesus says, quoting Isa 56:7 and Jer 7:11: "My house is a house of prayer for all nations, but you have made it a *robbers'* den" (Mk 11:17). At his arrest in the garden, he responds to the armed crowd with the words: "Have you come out as against a *robber,* with swords and clubs to capture me?"

- the **temple** (chs. 11–13),   *scene:* **cleansing** (11:15–19),
- the **garden** (ch. 14),   *scene:* **arrest** (14:43–52),
- the **cross** (ch. 15),   *scene:* **mocking** (15:27–32).

Figure 19

(Mk 14:48). And the narrator informs us that on Golgotha they crucified him: "And with him they crucified two *robbers* one on his right and one on his left" (15:27).

The word *lestes* implies ruthless use of force, seizure of person or property by violent means.[15] And yet the term is used judiciously. Jesus calls the opponent party "robbers," and suggests as well that they are unable to think of him in any other way — which assessment they confirm by having him executed in the company of robbers. Their own self-understanding has constricted their view of him. Underlying this language is a radical difference between the two approaches to conflict, a difference the opponents are unable to appreciate — until the centurion's enlightenment.[16]

The meaning of violent incursion contained in the word *lestes* gives weight to our sense of aggressive encounter in the narrative movement of the Gospel. The initiative of Jesus and the counterinitiative of his opponents resemble "raids" upon enemy territory. Thus Jesus' temple cleansing can be seen as a raid upon his opponents' power base. He comes from the edge to the center of their world to place it under siege. Upon his arrival he symbolically "cleanses" that which is thought to define what is clean and what is holy. His attack strikes at the root of the temple's power to define reality.

Conversely, the appearance of the armed crowd in the garden of Gethsemane is a counterraid on Jesus' own power center. The garden is the site of his communication with his Father. Here on the Mount of Olives, standing to the east and opposite the Temple Mount, he makes his effective prayer, a prayer not possible in the temple. The arrival of the high priest's party with their armed guards is a violent incursion. It is a clandestine entry masquerading as a legal arrest, moving under cover of darkness. The circumstances do not suggest the legal warrants of justice.

A third raid does not happen, because Jesus refuses it. The third moment, that of nonretaliation, is nonaggressive. Here the element of initiative in refusing the response is apparent. And so what might have been a third raid turns into another kind of response, breaking the pattern of reciprocal raiding.

These three movements can in turn be taken to represent the main

vectors of conflict in the story. Each moment concludes a direction
of ongoing action to generate a reversed or new direction. The temple cleansing concludes the long rising action of Jesus' initiative that
began in the synagogues of Galilee. The garden arrest brings to fulfillment the decision made by the priests at the temple action (11:18).
It brings to an end their repeatedly frustrated attempts to lay hands
upon him. Finally, his refusal to respond in kind begins the movement
of dénouement that brings the action of the plot to a halt, in the acceptance of the cross. Each moment articulates a phase of the plot of
the narrative. We can see this more clearly by situating these moments
in a description of the unfolding action.

## The Move on Jerusalem

All along the road to Jerusalem, signposted by the passion predictions,
Jesus preaches a Messiah of nondestructive power, drawing upon the
servant theme of Second Isaiah. In this section the note of nonviolence
in his resistance movement comes clearer. The preparation of the inner
cadre continues. However, the suffering character of Jesus' program
of resistance is not without earlier precedent in the narrative. It has
appeared at every juncture. As noted earlier, the cure of the withered
hand identified suffering as the cost of a commitment to life-giving.
And the mission of the twelve takes place during a flashback report of
the Baptist's death (6:17–29), which casts its shadow forward to the
passion. Peter's recognition of the Messiah is immediately followed by
the first passion prediction.

   And yet life-furthering is the dominant theme of the first half of the
Gospel — all but two of the cure miracles occur there — just as life-
offering dominates the second half. The life-furthering emphasis seen
in the cures, exorcisms, and liberations from the law is an expression
of Jesus' compassion. These acts represent his challenge to authority
and serve to keep the challenge alive through the time of rising action.
The pattern of initiative leading to repression enters into a spiral of
new initiatives, leading to increased repression, until the movement is
ripe to enter Jerusalem.

   In Jerusalem the movement toward confrontation reaches its climax. We have seen that the dramatic symbolism of the temple
cleansing is interpreted by a parable in action. On the way to the temple Jesus curses a fig tree for being fruitless, and on the next morning it
is found to be withered. In the narrative sequence the fig tree account

brackets the story of the temple action, framing it with a glossing image implying that Israel is under judgment. The fig tree incident raises the questions of faith. This theme of faith has already been encountered in the series of miracle stories in chapters 4 and 5. Faith is opposed to fear. But here in Mk 11:23 faith is opposed to the Temple Mount: "Amen, I say to you, whoever says to this mountain, 'Be lifted up and thrown into the sea,' and does not doubt in his heart but believes that what he says will happen, it shall be done for him." The casting of the mountain is an expression of Jesus' action in the cleansing protest and figured in the cursing of the fig. Faith continues to mean adherence to Jesus' project and is positioned against the temple and its system.

In the dispute about authority (11:27–33), with its belated reference to John the Baptist, the narrative gives one of many ways in which the climactic confrontation recapitulates motifs of the original confrontation in the opening chapters (1:22, 27; 2:10). The confrontation itself (1:21–28; 11:15–19), the contrast between vineyard fruit and withered growth (2:21, 22; 11:20; 12:1–9), the turn toward debates covering what is "lawful" (2:26; 3:4; 12:14, 19, 28), all of these declare that a movement in the narrative is rounding off.

## Moving from Temple to Garden

If the narrative movement of chapters 1–11 presents a persistent attack on the temple-centered purity system, it culminates in a "raid" on the geographical and ritual center of that system. The attack and the raid have the character of nonviolent confrontation, in accord with Gene Sharp's first move in the dialectic of nonviolent action. In the determined response of Jesus' opponents, the second and opposing move is made, as announced at 11:18, in the middle of the temple-cleansing account:

> And the chief priests and the scribes heard it and sought a way to destroy him; for they feared him, because all the multitude was astonished at his teaching. (Mk 11:18; see 1:22)

Thus begins a movement of repression that reaches its first objective at the arrest scene in the garden. But it does not move toward that objective smoothly, for the authorities are stymied at first. Their move against Jesus falls into two stages, a public phase and a private, clandestine phase, after Judas enters the picture. In the public phase they are frustrated; later they regain their momentum.

The public stage is characterized by debates in the temple. During these Jesus is protected by the crowds who are watching him closely, positioned to notice anything untoward. The crowds serve the roles of both referee and scorekeeper in the debates. Because his opponents cannot better him in the debates, the moment of confrontation in the temple is prolonged, making what seems to them an intolerable situation even worse. Thus their first efforts at intimidation fail and even assist Jesus. Meanwhile the dramatic tension grows palpably more intense.

In the three main debate episodes of Caesar's coin (12:13–17), the resurrection question (12:18–27), and the Great Commandment (12:28–34), the issue on the table is authority, and the discussion turns on matters of law. These features repeat concerns of the initial series of debates in Mark 1–2.

In a neat convergence of two opposition groups, the Pharisees are sent by the priests to ask the question about Caesar's coin: Is it *lawful* to pay the tax? The question is a trap. Horsley points out that (*a*) the issue was already a well-defined debating point in Judea; (*b*) a negative answer would have provided grounds for arrest; and (*c*) they expected Jesus to say no, for otherwise the story does not make sense.[17] The trap pits the hated Roman authority against the Judean religious traditions ("Is it lawful...?"). Instead of addressing the question, Jesus addresses the trap, by transferring attention to the coin. Caesar's visage on the coinage is a claim to authority, which the "hypocrites" accept by carrying the coins and making use of the system. When Jesus shifts attention back to the tax question, it is on new terms, for now the Pharisees are implicated. In terms of the ongoing narrative, and apart from the precise import of the story, the trap fails. They are no closer to apprehending Jesus than before.

The Sadducees' question about resurrection also addresses the issue of authority and the Mosaic law. However, the presumption against Rome shifts, since the Sadducees were Judean allies of the imperial presence. Again the authority issue is transferred to a particular case — this time, notions of immortality. The Sadducees pit traditional notions of immortality through the family name against new-fangled ideas of resurrection. Jesus bluntly refutes them, and the narrative is no closer to resolution.

The friendly scribe, with his question about the Great Commandment, succeeds in drawing out a response that halts all further questions (12:34). Although the scribe is friendly, the law remains the issue. It seems that love of God in love of neighbor is the import of Jesus' answer and that it is the new center that replaces the temple. The scribe, realizing this, affirms that the Great Commandment "is much more than all whole burnt offerings and sacrifices" (12:33). In this narrative, the love command is the positive corollary to the temple cleansing and the warning of Mk 13:2.

The public phase of the story concludes in chapter 13 with Jesus' farewell to his disciples and his public ministry. His final critique of the temple is launched from the Mount of Olives, which serves in this narrative as Mount Anti-Zion, confronting the temple. In a moment of clairvoyance the protagonist projects his vision — a vision of the revolt of 66–70 C.E. — outside the story into the future of the listening disciples and the world of the implied reader. The destruction of the temple, contemporary with the writing of the account, is the ultimate moment in the critique of the holiness system, centered on the Holy of Holies. In Jesus' speech of chapter 13, itself a powerful word, the temple destruction is layered upon the other messages of threat, to construct an overwhelming message of conclusion to the former age.

Jesus' farewell to the public arena coincides with a shift to less public opposition by the priestly party. From chapter 14 onward they begin to operate in secret, with Judas's help. The ambiance of the feast of unleavened bread and Passover provides the ritual backdrop for the events. The liberation content of the exodus events, commemorated in Passover, colors the narrative from this point on. Judas's violation of the meal companionship underscores his complicity with the repressive countermovement that would quash the drive toward liberation in this new Passover. The first "cup prayer" is at the table; the second is in the garden. Jesus' close communion with the "Abba" God identifies the garden of Gethsemane, on the Mount of Olives, as the center of Jesus' sacred universe. With Judas as guide, the temple authorities accomplish their counterraid.

## Garden to Cross: Nonretaliation

The time of nonretaliation begins at the arrest. Because Jesus refuses to reply with a third "raid," the falling action continues, but with a difference. Though the repressive response of his opponents continues, they are not as much in control of events as they might appear to be. Jesus submits to arrest without submitting to their claims. He surrenders his body but not his struggle. He continues to withhold his consent. Although events are not under his direct control, his deliberate nonretaliation is a positive move, lending purpose to the subsequent events. The narrative manages this by showing us a Jesus in apparent control insofar as he accepts the destiny scripted for him.

Submitting to the arrest is presented as a conscious, purposeful action (Mk 14:38). Whereas the opponents' reaction to Jesus' initiative was to "destroy him," Jesus' reaction to the opponents' response is clearly one of nonretaliation. In Mark, Jesus' acceptance of this pattern is seen in his behavior at the arrest. His elected response (14:49) is juxtaposed to that of the disciple who attempts a violent defense, severing the ear of one of the guards (14:47). In the heat of confrontation, the impulse to violent self-defense, not to mention the defense of a loved one, is deliberately thwarted.

The Gospels of Matthew and Luke, each in its own way, reinforce this reading by their additions to Mark's text. Each has inserted into the pattern, precisely at the moment of immediate response to the garden arrest, an interpretive detail that supports the nonretaliatory meaning. Matthew records Jesus' saying to the disciple who acted to defend Jesus by cutting off the ear of the guard: "Put your sword back into its place; for all who take the sword will perish by the sword" (Mt 26:52). This saying of Jesus' is often cited as a recommendation of nonviolence as a policy. Now, we see that its context, as the proper moment of retaliation in the main narrative pattern of the Gospel, lends it additional significance.

Luke expands the same scene in another way. After the guard's ear is severed, Luke writes: "But Jesus said, 'No more of this!' And he touched his ear and healed him" (22:51). Apart from the tendency by some to see here an example of Luke's interest as a physician, the narrative touch supplies a contrast between false and true power — the sword versus healing. Nonviolence can be understood negatively, as the refusal of violent force or power, but the Gospel has prominently displayed the alternative and contrasting image of power as healing. Such power cannot be controlled for the purposes of domination, as can the application of coercive violence. Against the dynamic of severing, it presents the alternative dynamic of knitting the wound.

In the movement from garden to cross events move at two levels. Donald Juel tells us that "the use of double-level narrative makes possible the use of the most prominent literary feature of the passion story: irony."[18] Pilate's phrase "king of the Jews," which he decides to post on the cross itself, has a double meaning for the Christian reader. The royal charade of the Roman soldiers, decking Jesus in purple and crown, both spitting and kneeling, acts out the irony. The reader winces, knowing the truth divulged by the narrator — this is indeed the Messiah.

The irony reaches its strongest statement in the mockery directed at Jesus as he hangs upon the cross. As with the soldiers, the taunting scene at the cross combines the verbal irony of sarcasm with the situational irony of deceptive appearances. The sarcasm of the passers-by and the chief priests proposes to deflate the protagonist's royal pretensions. However, the situation as revealed to the reader by the narrator shows that Jesus is no pretender, and so the irony is turned back upon the mockers, victims of their own sarcasm.

As we have seen earlier, the messianic issue, which Jesus debated with Peter, concerns the nature of authentic power. The hidden king, unknown to those inside the story but disclosed by the narrator to the reader, operates with a hidden power. The messianic designation is intimately associated with Mark's narrative project. Situating Jesus in a sustained narrative conflict is equivalent to presenting a thesis about power relations. The narrative irony that says appearances are not what they claim to be is of a piece with the dramatic claim in this narrative that power is not what it seems. We see here, at the level of the narrative, the cultural skepticism that denies the possibility of power without violence, such as we saw at the beginning of this book. It is the confidence in violence that becomes an article of faith: the gods are on the side of the biggest battalions. It is precisely the false belief that the prophet Second Isaiah strove to overcome among the Israelite exiles in Babylon, in the 550s B.C.E., as he developed the theme of the suffering servant, so prominent in the passion account of the Gospel.

## An Empty Tomb: An Unclosed Story

Today most scholars believe that the original version of Mark's Gospel ended with 16:8. The longer endings found in different manuscripts have been appended, they believe, by various early editors who found the original ending to be too abrupt. The original would have seemed unsatisfactory on at least three accounts. First, it ends weakly, on the enclitic *gar* (for). Its lack of emphasis is disconcerting, as if the narrator's voice were to trail off into uncertainty, as if a symphony were to end on a passing note. It suggests a more complete statement has been broken off. Such an ending is very unusual but not entirely without precedent.[19]

A second problem is that the original ending omits any mention of Jesus' resurrection appearances — a situation redressed by the more familiar of the appended longer endings. The appearance accounts serve the narrative as a form of closure. In the appearances the reader is assured along with the disciples that Jesus is alive and well. The word of the "man in white" at the tomb, that "he is risen," is all very well. But one wishes to ascertain for oneself.

Third, the resurrection appearances satisfy needs of closure by bringing vanished members of the cast back on stage for a final bow, and not only Jesus, but the disciples as well. The followers of Jesus have long departed from the story. Most left the scene at the time of Jesus' arrest. Peter, to his dismay, persisted in his following to the high priest's courtyard. We would like to know that these lost followers have been reclaimed. This is one of the things that resurrection stories show us. And though Mark's man in white instructs the women to "tell his disciples," the women's fear prevents them from telling anyone. So for this, as for the other reasons, the reader is denied the satisfaction of a restful conclusion to the story.

However, the bracketing structure of anointing scenes, at 14:3–9 and 16:1, would suggest that this more unsettling ending is present here by design.[20] The anointing attempt in 16:1 returns the narrative to the situation with which the passion account began, in 14:3–9, explicitly labeled by Jesus (14:8) as a "burial anointing." As an anointing for burial, the event is incomplete in each case. In 14:3–9, the action is premature, since Jesus is still alive. In 16:1, it is too late; his body is no longer present to them. Thus the anointing is twice declared but never fully accomplished.

Like the anointing that signals it, the closure of the narrative is declared by returning to the opening event, but it does not manage to be quite complete. Its unfinished quality is intended. It is both closed and unclosed. It moves into its sequel, as was seen in chapter 13, where Jesus looked ahead to the future of the disciples and the present of the reader. That is to say, the Gospel story explicitly makes reference to the yet-to-come story of the disciples. It addresses the reader and says, "This is to be your story."

When the women come to the tomb, they find the man in white who tells them, "He has been raised; he is not here." The tomb is the wrong place to look for him. Where instead ought they look? "Go and say to his disciples and to Peter: 'He is going ahead of you into Galilee:

there you will see him as he told you.'" In terms of the narrative, as we have been reading it, this advises a return to the starting point of the narrative. The disciples are invited to begin their own enactment of the story. If the portrait of Jesus in this narrative is located in the plot, the reenactment of the narrative action of the lives of the disciples is testimony to Jesus' continued presence and the continuation of that presence. The story will not die.

In the more traditional terms of resurrection, terms that we find more satisfying because they are more familiar and not because they are less astonishing, Jesus lives. Despite the claims of cultural reality, his path through these events has been toward life. The assurance given is not unlike that offered by the story in 2 Maccabees 7, where a mother loses her seven sons to the persecuting zeal of an emperor. The brothers are able to persist in their nonviolent resistance to the very end by drawing on a tangible faith in resurrected life. *They* will be vindicated, not the emperor. Similarly, in Mark's Gospel, Jesus lives. God vindicates him, not the emperor.

And so, in the final chapter of the Gospel, the narrator reaffirms the order of "reality" conspicuous in the irony of the passion account but implied from the very first verse. Appearances are deceiving. In the power struggle portrayed by the narrative plot, the apparent victors have lost. Violence, as seen concentrated in its most representative moment, that of killing, does not prevail. In its irony the narrative finds a way out of the mythic contradiction that would hold that violence redresses, or cures, or civilizes — the cultural trap that would claim that violence can be relieved by adding more of the same.

*Chapter Seven* _____

# BREAKING THE MYTH OF VIOLENCE

In the last chapter I argued that the Gospel account interrupts the narrative impulse of the agonic plot. But the refusals of the narrative cut deeper than that. I have viewed the agon as the conflictual aspect of human interaction that corresponds to the patterns of narrative. It is this link between literature and life that is problematic in our use of violence. It is this relation that underlies the functioning of myth as expressing and reinforcing the terms of shared human experience. If Stephen Crites and others who study the mutual influence of narrative and experience are correct, narrative is a quality of human experience. In that case, the influence of verbal narrative on our behavior cannot be forsworn in itself, but it can be understood to some extent and redirected. To the extent we are aware of our primary stories, we might be able to edit them.

Narrative imposes a form on experience. The narrative constraints of the agon, with its rules of narrowed options, two sides only, point of view, and so on, illustrate vividly how narrative form can script our experience. And a powerful impulse in narrative, influencing form, is the drive toward *symmetry*. Symmetry governs the course of the story. Stories begin in the bliss of innocence ("Once upon a time..."), prior to the chastening wisdom brought on by the narrative plot, and they end in a symmetrical blissfulness ("...happily ever after"). This complacent serenity, which is interrupted by harm (as when the safe is robbed; the ranch is burned down; or the cattle, camels, sheep, and children are lost in a string of cataclysms), must be returned as closely as possible to its original condition. The repair thus takes the form of a restoration, governed by a sense of symmetry.

## Ways That Stories Tend

The impulse toward symmetry organizes the violent plot. Its formal satisfactions generate much of our emotional satisfaction in attending to these stories. The tendency for narratives to fulfill formal patterns has been much studied, and such studies help us to see how the Gospel narration dares to reject these tendencies in order to assert its values. Elli Köngäs Maranda and Pierre Maranda have published a study of folk narratives, *Structural Models in Folklore and Transformational Essays,* that provides a narrative model for conflict resolution, offering the possibility of a negative demonstration.[1] It is negative insofar as it suggests how the Gospel deviates from conventional story norms. That is, it shows us what the Gospel narrative does not do. More importantly, it suggests how the Gospel plot, in making these deviations, asserts its nonviolent character. Nonviolence — the absence of violence — is a negative concept expressing our cultural bias. As an exploration of conventional stories, the Maranda folktale study hints why the concept should take this form for us.

## Popular Stories

The Marandas studied North American myths, not ancient Semitic stories. But their study has considerable explanatory power in revealing our own experience with stories. In addition, it has been applied with some profit to biblical texts.[2] It seems to describe something that transcends the narrower genres within the province of storytelling, to reach a level of interpretation that cuts across time and cultures. Folk narratives, by their very simplicity of structure, give access to insights to the ways of story that more complex narratives may not. In this way they make valuable models for thinking about the story.

We have our own versions of folk stories. In addition to genre literature such as L'Amour's western tales, we have the simplified tales on TV screens and summertime cinema. Consider a popular although clearly violent example: George Lucas's original *Star Wars* film, which lent its name to the media designation of the Strategic Defense Initiative program. This cinematic fable has a simplified structure, good for enabling insights. It also had an enthusiastic audience response suggesting that it struck a cultural chord. In the first week of its release movie reviewers noted that audiences were spontaneously applauding at the end of the film, as the death star was destroyed. Intrigued by this report, I could not wait to see the film. Sure enough, we all cheered at the end, myself included. And yet the death star was nothing less than an artificial planet. Millions of lives were presumably extinguished. How could we in the audience have so cheerfully given our assent to this? Some of the answers to this question can be found in the formal satisfactions of symmetry.

From the beginning, during the initial skirmish between the rebels and the imperial powers, the elaborate costuming made clear to us which side we were to favor. The "enemy," outfitted in ungainly, robotlike costumes, had the impersonality of machines, in ironic contrast to the characters on our side where even the robots or "droids," though machines, had very human personalities. As regards the band of heroes, an innovative touch reinforced our identification with them: their equipment was weathered and patched. We recognized the familiar hot-rod culture of the 1950s, projected into a remote time and place. And, of course, underlying the whole is the science fiction premise: the human world struggles against outer-space aliens, doubtfully human.

But the crucial preparation for the final scene was the meaning given to the death star by its previous history. It was designed to be an instrument of global destruction. It had already obliterated a living planet — Princess Leia's home planet. This destruction was the moment in the story that actually surprised theatergoers, who were not ready for so massive an evil in what was, after all, little more than a cinematic melodrama. And yet, there it was, establishing for us the nature of the death star, and thereby ensuring, by a perverse symmetry, the final scene. There is much that is mysterious transpiring here, not the least of which is the manner in which the story elicits our strong approval for a degree of violence that would otherwise appall us deeply.

### A Story Formula

It is this set of obscure transactions between the story, the storyteller and the listeners that the Marandas' study illuminates. They borrowed a quasi-algebraic formula that Claude Lévi-Strauss made famous and adapted it to fit their own purposes.[3] The formula is basically a ratio or proportionality equation, with a twist built in. (See Appendix D for a more elaborate explanation of this pattern.) For Lévi-Strauss the formula served as a shorthand description of the tenuous balance that held among values in a myth system. But the Marandas wanted to describe a narrative, not a system of beliefs. They wanted to study how folk narratives undergo a series of changes through time. In a narrative the relations among the characters, even between characters and their constituent character traits, change as the story progresses. The

Marandas found that Lévi-Strauss's formula worked well to describe the changes they discerned.

They discovered four key moments in a narrative, corresponding to the four terms of the ratio formula. The first pair were the initial moments of identification, when we find out about the antagonist and protagonist, respectively. The second pair of moments incorporated the twist in the formula, and we can think of them as moments in which the protagonist and antagonist undergo a set of transformations.

**Two Character Identifications.** The first two terms of the formula are moments of identification. In one, the listeners or readers identify the hero; in the other, they identify the villain. It is probable that the hero enters the story first, though this is not at all necessary. Theoretically these moments are simultaneous, since there is a symmetry of opposition between them. In our *Star Wars* example, the movie opens with an escape attempt from an imperial warship, introducing us to the two sides and to some of the subsidiary heroes. In the next scene we encounter Luke Skywalker, as yet innocent of the task ahead of him, as the escapees descend into his world.

In all of this business of identification, we as readers or viewers need to figure out who is on the good side and who is in the wrong. No one provides labels though there are other strong indicators, as the western movies' cliché of white hats and black hats would remind us. But the main work of identification is by way of perceived behavior. In the Maranda formula these identifications occur in the manner of oral narrative traditions, solely through the words and behavior of the leading characters. Not until the trait is applied to the character do we know which is which. The hero acts out a value that fits into the listeners' social world. The villain's behavior violates that cultural value.

In simple stories, and maybe in more complex stories as well, the traits that mark the main characters usually express two sides of the same value. The protagonist exemplifies it; the villain violates it. If the hero is honest, the villain is a notorious liar. The listener's perception of the conflict is assisted by this heightening of the contrast. In the Gospel, Jesus' integrity is poised against the hypocrisy of his opponents. In stories that are pitched at the level of violence, this too enters the picture in terms of contrast between the two sides. The hero is against it; the villain is on easy terms with it.

Like walking or talking, listening to stories is complicated work made deceptively simple. The identifications, for instance, have us, as readers, not only identifying who is who, in the manner of labeling, but also identifying *with* the protagonist and *against* the villain. Here we take sides. We are eager to do so. Our experience of moviegoing instructs us in how we are impatient to learn whom to cheer and whom to jeer. We want these preliminaries cleared up by the time the credits have finished running.

But the two kinds of identification — the identifying *of* whom and the identifying *with/against* whom — stand in some degree of tension with each other. The loyalty accompanying the identification "with" seems to ignore the rather arbitrary character of the identification "of" — often made on the flimsiest indication of shared values. In attending to stories, we wear our hearts on our sleeves.

***Two Character Transformations.*** As the story moves to the confrontation between the two leading characters, the transformations occur in a second set of moments. Both hero and villain are transformed. The *hero* drops the ways of virtue and adopts the practices previously monopolized by the villain. At this point it is instructive to remember that it was precisely this character's commitment to the positive set of traits that identified him[4] as the hero. Even though the listeners initially identified the hero on the basis of his practice of virtue and avoidance of vice, now they approve his new way of life, as he adopts the characteristic practice of the villain. This represents the transformed identity of the hero.

It is a peculiar thing that the readers, who identified this character as the hero on the basis of his commitment to positive values, and consequently identified with the character, remain loyal although the justifications for such allegiance are now gone. There is a condition for this. The reader approves of the new mode of existence as long as the negative behavior the hero manifests is directed against the villain, who has been doing these reprehensible things to others. The symmetry of hoisting the villain with his own petard is the principle commonly called "poetic justice." The Marandas explain the acceptability of this feature in the grammatical terms of a double negative: the "negative function of the mediator [the hero] is his negative action against the negative force and is thus to be considered positive."[5]

The *villain,* in fact, is felt to deserve such treatment. The feeling against the villain runs deep, for this character has come to be equated with the evil introduced into the world of the story. The Marandas have used Lévi-Strauss's formula to great advantage in showing how deeply the villain's transformation reaches. In effect, the character and the character trait exchange positions and status. The negative value of the character trait takes on weight and substance as if it were itself a character, while the character, the villain, is diminished in personality to little more than an image or mask of the evil. The villain is submerged beneath the evil he represents to such a great extent that objectified "evil" itself becomes the functional antagonist, the "enemy." The villain is perceived as the personification of that evil. In this way the villain's transformation lays the foundation of the happy ending. In order to remove all evil from the world of the story, it becomes imperative to remove the villain. An inverse proportion seems to be at work here: the more complete the removal of the villain, the happier the ending.

This kind of exchange between a person or entity, on the one hand, and its attributes or qualities, on the other, has traditionally been called a subject/predicate reversal. The qualities predicated of a subject suddenly take on the primacy formerly enjoyed by the subject they qualified, relegating the original subject to the secondary status of predicate. Something similar was seen in the third draft of the U.S. bishops' peace letter, when the subject Jesus was demoted from the focus of allegiance to be replaced in this role by the virtues he espoused. In the revision, the virtues became the center of focus, and Jesus was now cast as their illustration. Subject and predicate exchanged places.

## Poetic Justice

Reflection lingers where it meets resistance, at certain obscurities in the pattern. The identifications are an initial example. As listeners, we do not merely identify the hero, we identify *with* the hero. Conversely, we both identify the villain and identify *against* the villain. This two-edged identification suggests our readiness to take a place in the world of the story. When we buy our ticket at the box office, we make a tacit pact to cherish someone in an anticipated, unknown drama and despise someone else. Once we have found our place among the characters, we do not easily budge. Our allegiance is firm, unto the story's end. Commitment to the characters is strong enough to sustain itself throughout the subsequent transformations of those characters. In fact, it establishes the secure footing needed to make the transformations possible. In this interplay the pattern described by the Marandas fits the structural notion of a system of interdependent relations.

The transformations when they occur offer a second kind of obscurity. Eventually our devotion to the hero is tested by his dramatic conversion to a set of behaviors that contradict those that elicited our original empathy. The principle of the "double negative" expresses our taste for punishment in the form of the satisfying symmetry of "poetic justice." The punishment must fit the crime. Certainly not all stories involve overt violence. The bully is humiliated, the liar deceived, the manipulator manipulated. But in those stories in which the villain is marked by a practical relationship to violence, the means of his downfall will certainly be violent. In such stories, the hero is "peace-loving," the proper alternative to promoting violence. Typically, he manages to overcome his principled reluctance, frequently after a struggle of conscience, and then proceeds to "do what needs to be done." As listeners, however, we do not ordinarily experience many qualms of conscience, perhaps because the hero's manifest sense of responsibility reassures us that at least someone of consequence is weighing the moral questions. After all, we have placed our destiny in his hands. And, of course, we rest content in knowing that the ugly deed will target no one but the villain, the origin of ugliness in the story. After all, the villain is not innocent, and his victims were.

## Innocence and Purgation

This too is a useful discovery. We learn that we truly believe that harming others can in fact be justified if the target of the harm is not innocent. At the beginning of the narrative all the characters are neutral; that is, they are provisionally innocent. But the villain acted against innocent parties and thus established his own lack of innocence. It seems that when the characters are neutral and cannot bias the scale, the harming action is disclosed as an evil in itself. But once our attitudes become fixed, it is no longer counted as evil — or at most is a necessary though rather satisfying evil. In short, the same act that declares and establishes evil in the story can do double duty as virtue, so long as it is justified. And what justifies it for us? It justifies itself, inasmuch as its very emergence into the world of the story constitutes the crime that legitimates its use against the character who is the instrument of that emergence.

The villain's transformation is the depersonalization that is required to make him a target of harm. No longer simply identified with the evil, he becomes its incarnation. The functional opponent is no longer the villain but evil itself, with the villain as its ready manifestation. To rid the story of evil, we need to remove the villain — and the more completely, the better.

The pattern is one of punishment as purgation, and it raises implications for our notions of conflict resolution. We might recognize in this narrative pattern a tactic of pandering to our fears and our impatience with long or difficult processes of reconciliation. These would require a degree of "faith" that we are not at this time in the story ready to tolerate. Such stories do not tend to favor negotiated results. Efforts toward reform and reconciliation that might have an equal claim to be the goal of punishment are not rewarded here. The impulse toward reconciliation presumes that the evil to be repaired is the harm done to the relationships among persons. It does not reside in the persons themselves. It originates from defects in the persons, to be sure, but the object of conflict resolution is to restore the relationships between the "terms," not simply to obliterate one of the terms. Certainly the preferred methods of addressing evil will differ, depending on whether the evil is conceived as a substance to be blotted out or a relationship to be mended.

## The Gospel Refusals

The narrative strategy delineated by the folktale study of the Marandas is rejected by the nonviolent Gospel precisely at the two points of transformation. In so doing it generates a tension within the conventional system of narrative attitudes, since it accepts in no uncertain manner the pattern of the initial identifications. We identify firmly with the hero, Jesus, and we identify firmly against his opponents. The Gospel's exaggerated antipathy toward the Pharisees has been frequently noted.[6] So we enter into the world of the story, taking our place alongside the hero. But Jesus, as hero, chooses not to carry out the subsequent required transformations and thus subverts the form.

This deliberate refusal is double; it affects both transformative moments. In the first place, Jesus deliberately rejects the transformation of the hero. He refuses to use the methods of his opponents against them. In Mark, the opponents' modus operandi is clearly labeled. As I have noted time and again, they intend to "destroy" him (3:6; 11:18). The other two Synoptics retain this language (Mt 12:14; Lk 19:47), and in fact the destructive intent of the opposition is integral to all versions of the Gospel, motivating the passion and death. The narrative portrays the garden of Gethsemane as the particular setting for

Jesus' decision in this regard. In the successive moments of his "Abba" prayer (Mk 14:36) and his arrest (Mk 14:49), Jesus resolves upon a nonviolent response to his opponents' aggression and acts upon that resolution. His crisis corresponds to that of the disciples, who sleep at the prayer and flee during the arrest. His failure to continue the ways of satisfying stories is too much for them. In the subsequent trial scenes with the Sanhedrin and with Pilate, Jesus' refusal to defend himself reinforces for the listener the deliberate character of his action.

The refusal to use force in the face of force is symmetrical with a primary theme of nonviolence theory, namely, the need to preserve a correspondence between means and ends. Thomas Merton has written: "Christian non-violence, therefore, is convinced that the manner in which the conflict for truth is waged will itself manifest or obscure the truth." Or, in A. J. Muste's succinct expression: "There is no way to peace, peace is the way."[7]

The second moment, allied with the first, in which Jesus and the Gospel effect a refusal concerns the equation of the opponents with the evil behavior they are acting out. The transformation of the villain into the image of depersonalized evil, like that of the hero into the image of the villain, is rejected. This time the hill of Golgotha is the setting. One function of the taunting of the suffering Jesus, which occurs during the trials and at the crucifixion, is to dramatize this second refusal. The two kinds of behavior are starkly juxtaposed. Here the saying reported by Luke stands as an emblem for the deliberateness of this second refusal: "Father, forgive them; they do not know what they are doing" (Lk 23:34).[8] Forgiveness is an invitation to reconciliation. The act of forgiveness decisively retains the humanness of the opponents. Here, at the moment of Jesus' execution, his saying separates the persons of his enemies from their roles as destroyers. It rather precisely rejects the narrative strategy of equating the antagonists with the evil they do and amounts to a conscious decision not to configure them as depersonalized, disposable "droids."

Jesus' forgiveness, as the second crucial deviation from standard narrative, agrees with another theme in nonviolence theory, that which asserts the primacy of love in conflict situations. Again, Thomas Merton has an appropriate comment: "He [the Christian] will not let himself be persuaded that the adversary is totally wicked and can therefore never be reasonable or well-intentioned, and hence need never be listened to."[9]

The Gospel narrative refuses to accept the usual script for action.

It does this by overruling the need for a symmetrical payback. It interrupts the cycle of challenge and response. The protagonist, Jesus, is able to overcome the pressures that would dictate a response in kind, a response that would follow the powerful constraints of narrative scripting. While the narrative does not avoid confrontation against injustices, it does abandon the prescribed modes of confrontation. In refusing to adopt the methods of the opposition, the protagonist successfully maintains his opposition to their methods. In refusing to depersonalize the enemy, the protagonist keeps the conflict within a horizon of human relationships. By refusing the expedient of obliterating the opposition, the protagonist refuses the simplistic outlook implied by violent solutions — that if we just erased those who trouble us, the world would be a happier place.

## The Quality of Innocence

The Gospel story disturbs us by challenging our usual response to the suffering of innocents. Most conspicuously this is seen in the innocent suffering of the protagonist, which arouses our pity and outrage. Our pity responds to the inevitable suffering; our outrage to the rank injustice of it. But the story also troubles us in a more insidious way insofar as Jesus refuses to defend himself in the ways we usually consider appropriate. And by refusing them, he has taught us something about the stories that organize our lives.

The story model has shown us that our willingness to inflict harm in the cause of innocent suffering operates under at least two master images. One is that of *erasure,* as if evil could be finally erased. And the other is *balance,* as if perfect symmetry could be achieved.

The first of these pursues a program of purgation and is animated by a feeling for evil as pollution and good as purity. It longs for an innocence akin to bliss, before stories begin and after they have ended. The ideal objective is innocence as ignorance of conflict, unblemished by differences. Authentic life stands outside the struggle of the story in which we find ourselves.

The model of purity, which attempts to erase the blemish of evil, interacts with the primitive idea that pain works as a purifying agent. It is a principle articulated by Rebecca West in her classic report, *Black Lamb and Grey Falcon.* West's search for the roots of violence in our time took her in 1937, under the looming shadow of Hitler's ascendancy, on a journey through Yugoslavia, site of Archduke Ferdinand's assassination and flashpoint of World War I. In recent years her book has returned to the bookstands, as we grope to understand the century's legacy of "ethnic cleansing."

West's insight relates to the two major illuminations she received on her travels, which provided her with the title for her book. The first was that of a *black lamb* sacrificed on a huge rock in Macedonia, a site of animal sacrifices from antiquity. The lamb was slaughtered by some Gypsies in an attempt to ensure the pregnancy of one of their number. Everything that was ugly and irrational in the ritual of sacrifice rose up to confront West as she witnessed this rite and faced this ancient rock covered with blood, littered with rooster heads and broken pottery:

> The man with the knife and his friends gathered round us and told us of the virtue of the place.... But the rite of the Sheep's Field was purely shameful. It was a huge and dirty lie. There is a possibility that barrenness due to the mind could be aided by a rite that evoked love and broke down peevish desires to be separate and alone, or that animated a fatigued nature by refreshment from its inner sources. But this could do nothing it promised. Women do not get children by adding to the normal act of copulation the slaughter of a lamb, the breaking of a jar, the decapitation of a cock, the stretching of wool through blood and grease. If there was a woman whose womb could be unsealed by witnessing a petty and pointless act of violence, by seeing a jet of blood fall from a lamb's throat on a rock wet with stale and stinking blood, her fertility would be the reverse of motherhood, she would have children for the purpose of hating them.[10]

It is here that West found her principle: "I knew this rock well. I had lived under the shadow of it all my life. All our Western thought is founded on this repulsive pretense that *pain is the proper price of any good thing*."[11] It is true enough that change for the good often requires a struggle. We have seen that the Gospel plot gives evidence of that life pattern. But trouble begins when we think we can turn this around, believing we can begin with the pain, as a kind of investment toward the result we want. Instead of entering a struggle for the good, a struggle that may involve a pain-filled cost, we believe that if we undergo or inflict a quota of pain we will make a down payment on the good results we desire.

The moment of the lamb at the rock is made more compelling by

another, that of the falcon. In the *grey falcon* West found the secret
that her pilgrimage aimed to discover. Here she located what she was
seeking concerning Yugoslavia as Europe's door to violence. It was
on the plain of Kossovo in Serbia, historical site of the 1389 defeat
of the Slavs by the Turks, that West heard the poem that moved her
to insight. While the historians attribute the loss to incessant quarrels
among the Slavic princes, the famous nationalist poem about the grey
falcon has it differently:

> There flies a grey bird, a falcon,
> From Jerusalem the holy,
> And in his beak he bears a swallow.
>
> That is no falcon, no grey bird,
> But it is the Saint Elijah.
> He carries no swallow,
> But a book from the Mother of God.
> He comes to the Tsar at Kossovo,
> He lays the book on the Tsar's knees.[12]

The book offers a choice to Tsar Lazar, head of the Slavic forces. He
can choose the heavenly kingdom or the earthly kingdom. If he would
choose the earthly kingdom, he will win. If he would choose the heavenly kingdom, "all your soldiers shall be destroyed, / And you, prince,
you shall be destroyed with them." The tsar chooses the heavenly
kingdom because it will last for eternity, not just for a time.

The poem troubled West like a desperate parable. Lazar was
wrong, she told herself: "He saved his soul and there followed five
hundred years when no man on these plains, nor anywhere else in Europe for hundreds of miles in any direction, was allowed to keep his
soul."[13] What West recognized with a shock, even in herself and her
pacifist friends, was the enticement of a martyrdom that combined
virtue and defeat, as if defeat were the seal of truth on one's virtue.
What West discovered was that the lamb and the falcon were two
symbols of one story or of two sides of one story. The lamb had taught
her that there was something deeply wrong with a rite that would
buy with pain "an unrelated good," its arbitrary relation confirming
that only pain, some kind of pain, must be the price of happiness. She
concluded that we have learned this lesson in our hearts, though our
minds reject it. And so we turn from the lamb to the falcon: "Our response was not to dismiss the idea as a nightmare, but to say, 'Since it
is wrong to be the priest and sacrifice the lamb, I will be the lamb and

be sacrificed by the priest.'" And doom was welcomed as the emblem of true honor and virtue.

The two stories were revealed as the two sides of one coin. They were one in their compact with death and violence as the price of virtue. To whom is the price owed? The theories are conflicted on this point, but ultimately thinking comes back to a God who is the final author of reality. The arrangement is taken to be the pattern of the real world. West's charge that we have taken the works of love and submitted them to a hostagedom of cruelty carries the theological implication that we have preferred a God of cruelty to a God of love.

A common view of the Gospel story puts it uncomfortably close to West's description. In this line of thought the Gospel becomes a story of Jesus' predetermined destiny. Rather than allowing characters to work out their destinies as the story progresses, the story has an outcome that is preordained, as characters walk through the steps laid out for them. Unlike the challenge and response of the agon, the destiny story lacks causality. Closer to pageant than drama, the plot is missing the suspense and surprise that are at the center of dramatic action. And since the plot is resolved from the very beginning, it leaves no room for conflict resolution. Those who perceive a plot of destiny in the Gospel see the narrative stepping through a set of required actions. Jesus must go to Jerusalem to die for our sins as willed by God. His death is the moment of real meaning in the account, and everything leads up to it. Framed thus, the movement of the narrative takes on a deliberate, ritual-like character, and insofar as the cross is interpreted as atonement the narrative turns into a ritual of sacrifice.

But in Mark's narrative, God is not the one who requires Jesus' death. Instead, the enemies of Jesus, and of God, exact that demand. In Mark's narrative, God mandates Jesus' struggle against these enemies. The confrontation in the temple, which stands as the culmination and climax of Jesus' campaign of challenge, is difficult to reconcile with a reading of the Gospel narrative that emphasizes ritual, since the episode would appear to critique such a perspective. The episode is explicitly placed within the tradition of such criticism by the prophetic allusions it makes to Jeremiah, Isaiah, and Zechariah.

The reading of the story that emphasizes destiny fails our proposal on both counts: it is neither a story of nonviolence nor a story of resistance. First, in this reading of the story Jesus offers *no resistance*. He does nothing aggressive that would evoke the deadly response against him, because he is incapable of objectionable behavior. His enemies plot against him and kill him without motivation beyond that of their fundamental perversity. They are incapable of anything that is not objectionable. In terms of the account, they are simply and unwittingly carrying out God's will, as is the betrayer, Judas.

Second, this version of the story also *lacks nonviolence.* On the one hand, the protagonist need make no resolve to avoid violence in his resistance, since no resistance is practiced. On the other hand, he is in complicity with a reading that emphasizes violence because he is seen as adopting and even approving his own murder. In this reading the violence receives the endorsement of God, who wills that Jesus suffer it. In this story the threat of arriving at an endorsement of nonviolence in Jesus' story is overcome by finding a positive value for violence. Thus, the reading that emphasizes ritual reinforces an understanding of violence as authentic reality, implying a violent God as the ground of its reality.

## The World of Gift and Debt

The other master image of innocence is balance, which promotes a drive toward symmetry and poetic justice. Innocence is interpreted in the language of debt, rather than stain. Those who hold this view envision a ledger that needs to be balanced. Fairness is the main consideration here; injustice needs to be balanced out. The imbalance of the unredressed fault is perceived to be the crime to be repaired. The dream that narrative has given to this image of conflict is the notion that it is possible to achieve a final balance by payback. Whereas the pollution model tries to escape the horizon of the narrative conflict into the stasis beyond story, the balance model tries to adopt a point of view outside the conflict. It pretends the balance it achieves is a neutral evening-up of scores and not just a sense of satisfaction felt on my side of the conflict, after we win. It overlooks the inescapably conditional outlook of the "point of view." I want to believe that my version of the resolution is absolute and universal. But the agonic dynamic continues, as the story is picked up on the defeated side, to live on by dreams of future payback on another day.

The justice dream of absolute symmetry intersects with the narrative of Mark more clearly at the level of the subplot, in the dispute between Jesus and his disciples over the nature of messiahship. It takes us to the biblical themes of justice. Fernando Belo, in his seminal sociohistorical study of the Gospel, *A Materialist Reading of the Gospel of Mark,* traces a second strand of social order through the biblical texts, which he places alongside the purity/pollution system elaborated by Mary Douglas. In some ways this second system is more familiar to us than the rather exotic purity system, since it understands holiness in terms of justice and moral virtue rather than purity, and turpitude as moral guilt rather than contagion.

Belo identifies the second system as one of "gift and debt":

> There is another kind of violence that must be forestalled by prohibiting it in accordance with a second system. The violence takes the form of human *aggression;* the system of prohibition I shall call the *debt system* (the word "debt" usually being translated as "sin"). Like the first system, this one involves two principles, *gift* and *debt,* which are mutually exclusive, as are pure and polluted.[14]

As a blessing, the social order of justice is a divine gift. The gift is apparent especially in the biblical theme of the land, with the rather miraculous deliverance of that land into the hands of Israel in the face of opposition by professional armies and superior military technology. But the gift needs to be maintained. This means, for instance, not only that the land must be husbanded but that its character as a gift must be remembered. Not only the gift but the very sense of giftedness must be nurtured. The land is, of course, a major symbol for the basic gift of Israel's very existence. Israel exists as a divine gift, through the exodus and the covenant, and this must be remembered. The gift must be cared for, the giftedness kept vivid.

Belo sees the sense of gift maintained in a lively spirit of generosity: "It says that what Yahweh has given to human beings, they must in turn give to their fellow humans who lack it; as they have been filled, they must in turn fill their brothers and sisters."[15] It is this spirit of generosity that governs the relations with God, as seen in the returning gifts of tithes, of sacrificial victims, of Sabbath and festival times. And it is the spirit that is to govern the people's relations with one another, as institutionalized in customs and regulations of care for the vulnerable, the widow, and the orphan, of care for the family name in the levirate laws, and of care for the quality of social life under the covenant.

The spirit of gift is no less than crucial because it addresses the covetousness that generates violent aggression. The root of antisocial evil in the gift/debt system is located in the desires thought to be of the heart.[16] The covenant commandments against stealing, adultery, and killing are prohibitions against injustice as forms of aggression and violence. To disobey is to fall into debt, or sin. The commandments against coveting address "the desire that is the origin of aggressive violence."[17]

Yet commands of the law turn out to be imperfectly equipped for the task of maintaining a generous spirit. Made specific by the common need to know just when and where it applies, the law rewards the desire to earn the "blessings" without the risk of depending upon the gift. A close reading allows one to fulfill the conditions and "earn" the good result. But, of course, this good result is no longer a "blessing" — it is "just compensation." And the spirit of gift gives way to the spirit of calculation. Covetousness has used the law to make its claims and banish the insecurity of a gift-based system.

This tension pervades the biblical history of God's people and dogs the many attempts to revive the sense of giftedness in the relation to God and to one another. Not only are gifts seized in aggressive acts of debt, or sin, but the sense of the land, the society, the family, and the self, as benefits with the character of a gift, is overwhelmed by the desires of the heart that would unravel the debt/gift system itself, to turn it into a debt/debt system.

If "debt" is usually thought of as "sin," what is a word for "gift"? Walter Brueggemann suggests we think in terms of shalom. In the biblical notion of peace we find a vision of social blessing that contains the elements of freedom and unity, justice and order. As a blessing, it is a divine gift; but it also requires work. It is a task entrusted to us as well.

Brueggemann evokes the vision of shalom by quoting certain pivotal scripture passages. One of these is Lev 26:4–6:

> Then I will give you your rains in their season, and the land shall yield its increase, and the trees of the field shall yield their fruit. And your threshing shall last to the time of vintage, and the vintage shall last to the time for sowing; and you shall eat your bread to the full, and dwell in your land securely. And I will give peace in the land, and you shall lie down, and none shall make you afraid; and I will remove evil beasts from the land, and the sword shall not go through your land.[18]

Shalom, as peace, is opposed to war and violence. As gift, it is opposed to aggressive appropriation and violence. Against the spirit of gift is the spirit of "grasp." Shalom as a vision requires the vision of gift and the suppression of grasping violence. As freedom, it means deliverance from the human perpetuation of slavery in its various forms. As prosperity, it means a level of social order in the land.

Not all social orders, of course, are expressions of justice, but as we have seen in the Exodus text about the stranger, the widow and the orphan, and the poor person, Yahweh is on the side of justice.[19] Brueggemann writes: "God is concerned for the well-being of those who lack power to secure it."[20] He then states:

> Order and justice are not the same. It is a common mistake to assume that order, simply because it is established, is an adequate representation of justice. But it is clear that the king is the agent of order. The prophets (after the manner of Moses) are the agents of justice. At times prophet and king may agree, but many times they perceive things differently and, therefore, urge very different responses.[21]

In the image of shalom we encounter a vision of the "peaceable kingdom." It is an image of what the Gospel calls the "kingdom of God." In Mark's narrative we see Jesus challenging the "order" of the social system based on purity and pollution. Historically, we understand this system to be in complicity with the grinding imperialist presence of Rome. In the terms of the narrative we witness the system to be an intolerable burden, weighing especially on the vulnerable — the poor, the stranger, the widow and orphan. As a system of preventions, it bars many within Israel, and all those outside, from the qualities of fully human life and from the sources of that life in Yahweh. As an ideological system, it teaches that these barriers and hardships for members of certain classes are the will and plan of God.

## Violence and Moral Outrage

In Mark, Jesus' proclamation of the peaceable kingdom is also a critique of the social order as it stands. The critique is found in the various violations Jesus commits against the purity restrictions. It is found in the festival spirit of the banqueting group of the Jesus movement — the community of feasters who refuse to be fasters. And it is found in his ministrations to the vulnerable, bringing to them a compassion that the standing system would not actively offer and had passively forbidden.

The depiction in Mark's narrative of a protagonist moved by compassion is one that endorses the rejection of suffering. It is a compassion that does not calculate the deservedness of pain. And when it shows Jesus moving from compassion to wrath, from addressing the pain to confronting the causes of suffering, it shows him in nonviolent conflict resolution. He refuses to use the pain that is the evil he opposes. And here is the last temptation: that compassion vitiate itself by moving to violence. The outrage evoked by blatant inhuman injustice can move to violence as forcefully as any experience.

Exculpation of self-hatred through solidarity with victims, when it joins them in violent resistance, becomes often enough a complex psychological action. It is often my past and my native community that I am battling against. Compassion begins in solidarity and the feeling of common humanity. It can turn to a rage that expresses hatred in the name of an outraged justice, or it can turn to a firm nonviolent confrontation in the Gospel pattern. Georges Casalis illustrates this paradoxical impulse, writing of his threshold experience in Algeria in 1957:

> I was at the Ouchaia Wadi, a horrible shanty-town in Algeria where men, women, and children were subsisting in an indescribable subhuman state. Suddenly, in a particularly filthy hut where I was helping distribute flour, I was overcome by an irresistible wave of class hatred. It was an experience all the more disturbing because, until that time, nothing had prepared me for it. The liberation of the area and the colonial fight for independence appealed to other motives. Here the evidence was overpowering— nothing at all could justify such misery, which was the direct result, the legitimate offspring of our conquest and occupation of that country. I can still hear one of my companions muttering, "After a hundred and thirty years of French presence..." And I know that at that moment I would have been capable of any kind of "terrorist" act, no matter what, against a system that had not only tolerated but engendered the slow and violent death of "underdeveloped" multitudes. Yet at the same time I knew that my class hatred was self-hatred, hatred of myself as a beneficiary and an accomplice of the colonial system as well as a product and an exported expression of the capitalist order. Middle-class persons who undergo such an experience, if they do not make their escape through the distractions at their disposal, cannot help hating themselves.[22]

I am not suggesting that innocence leads to violence. But there is a false innocence that can release me from awareness of complicity in evil, an awareness that stays my hand from blows. If I too am guilty, I cannot strike without qualms, recognizing myself in my victim. But if I have been delivered from the sin that needs punishment, I can be the agent of punishment, cleansing, or justice, and I can feel intense and clarified. False innocence is the kind that does not require the self-knowledge of my own cruelty. Gandhi's hedge against this was "self-suffering."[23] This is not to say that suffering is a valuable experience or that my willingness to suffer cannot convince me all the more of my special virtue, but self-suffering can provide an occasion to check to what extent I am acting out of self-interest. It is to be accompanied by a commitment to truth and love, in Gandhi's view.

Authentic compassion would maintain a priority of persons over categories. What begins in compassion can dissolve into a program of retribution in which the syndrome of poetic justice prevails. The seduction of symmetry, like the fear of pollution, leads to desperate measures. And such desperate measures can be found in those wars of virtue we call just and holy, situated on either side of nonviolent resistance. On the one hand, just wars would restore a balance shaped in the shadow of a narrative of poetic justice; on the other hand, holy wars would blot out the stain of evil where it is perceived to invade the pure world. Both would seem to be ruled by the scripts of narrative other than the narrative of Mark's scripture.

*Epilogue* _____

# Taking Stock

Perhaps we are a naturally violent species. Perhaps when caught under certain circumstances we strike out destructively as an inevitable matter of course. At least such an assumption seems a commonplace.

When Peter Berger and Thomas Luckmann attempt to lay out the social foundation of all human reality, they mysteriously exempt violent behavior. Our proclivity toward violence would seem to be prior to social constructions of the real world, as is suggested by the saying, "He who has the bigger stick has the better chance of imposing his definition of reality."[1] Our tendency toward violence is not seen as a result of social formation but rather as part of our given nature that helps to shape those social formations. Likewise, when René Girard views sacrifice as a social process that has arisen to deflect violent behavior from the members of one's own society onto victims who are deemed unacceptable persons,[2] he would seem to have grouped us with the predatory animals and conceded the question. Violence is presumed to be a constant force, like a psychological drive that can at best be diverted, but never blocked, if we wish to avoid explosive outbreaks.

And yet we are allowed to wonder why violent activity, if it is inevitable and natural, is so fervently argued as necessary. We can wonder why the belief in a violent human nature needs continual reinforcement if it is an inevitable pattern. Why do we need to be convinced of something about which we have no choices? It is this question that allowed us to spot the myth of constructive violence, for myth achieves its effects by masquerading as natural. It comes to us as a given, a part of the real world. And it is constantly reinforced by stories. My surmise and my thesis are that the Gospel, this violent story with its nonviolent hero, breaks the myth of violence. After exploring this idea in its many dimensions, it is time to take stock.

The story of constructive violence confers a sense of confidence in its workings that has created theological dissonance in dealing with the Gospel narrative. Almost without their noticing, theologians who address these issues run up against an obstacle, like a boulder beneath the surface of a river that diverts its flow. The unseen obstacle is the myth, and the displacement in the stream is the loss of narrative. In the opening chapter we saw three examples of this: the "Christian realism" of Reinhold Niebuhr, the theology of revolution developed by J. G. Davies, and the pastoral letter *The Challenge of Peace,* published by the U.S. Catholic bishops. In each case we witness a neglect of narrative. And in each case the narrative of Mark offers a reply.

Niebuhr avoided narrative by framing his position in the exclusive context of the teaching of Jesus. This made it possible to deny any traces of nonviolent resistance in the New Testament. The teaching of Jesus was identified as one of absolute nonresistance. But Mark's narrative shows us otherwise. In its rising and falling action it depicts the development of a resistance movement and its nonviolent resolution. Furthermore, the resistance, while mainly imaged in the rising action, is also present in the falling action, as Jesus refuses to respond to his opponents with the destructive methods they espouse. Similarly, nonviolence informs the rising action as well as the falling. In his healing manner, Jesus confronts the social system at every level from the beginning.

Davies questioned the nonviolent imitation of Christ, arguing that Christ's life need not be reproduced in every detail. What indeed is to be imitated? Is nonviolent resistance a detail? What is central and what is peripheral in the Gospel? Mark's narrative addresses the question in the way it shapes the story plot. The conflict identifies the central issue of the narrative, the bone of its contention. In the main plot we have the image of nonviolent conflict resolution. In the subplot of the Gospel, Jesus also struggles with the disciples, who are loath to follow him to Jerusalem. The call they receive to imitate him as disciples works out as an invitation to join him in the main plot. And so the "rhetorical" dimension of the Gospel, which at first we rejected as foreign to the narrative, now is found to have a place in it. Far from being extraneous to the narrative, it is in fact embedded in the "poetics" of the plot.

The pastoral letter *The Challenge of Peace* avoided narrative in its third edition by shifting its center of gravity from the person of Jesus (showing the way) to a set of virtues with Jesus in the role of their primary exemplar. Propositional forms of truth are favored as a more secure guide for the transition of Gospel values across the ages from Mark's time to our own. They offer points of guidance for discovering our own way to peace. As a matter of fact, Mark's narrative does indeed present Jesus as teaching concepts, which appear in the form of messianic titles. But these are under the control of the narrator, and serve the purposes of the narrative insofar as they explain the action in its resisting and nonviolent aspects. The narrative is not an illustration of the propositional truth of Jesus' teaching; instead, the teaching explains the action of the plot.

In short, the portrait of Jesus is not to be found in the characterization of the Gospel narrative, but rather in its plot. The action of the plot is the image of Christ in the Gospel. It is one that responds to the question about how we are to love under conditions of conflict, which are the only conditions we know.

Underlying the narrative conflict is a theory of power. At one level the struggle between Jesus and the Judean authorities has to do with his refusal to accept their authority. But this struggle is animated by a conflict between two spirits, holy and unclean. And this spiritual conflict presupposes two claims of power. In Mark's narrative, destructive power is demonic, the province of the "unclean." Nondestructive, healing power is "holy." The parties of the social conflict are assimilated to these values, as Jesus becomes the "Holy One" and the Judean authorities demonstrate their allegiance to the unclean spirit world.

The struggle between theories of power is a battle of outlooks. It is an ideological struggle that Jesus wages against the temple as the hub of the Judean worldview. It also is also a battle he engages with the disciples, who eventually abandon him in consequence. Like the authorities, the disciples fail to understand; their hearts, like those of their opponents, are hardened. This struggle over the hearts and minds of the disciples occupies Jesus throughout the central section of the narrative, right up to the climactic events in Jerusalem.

But in teaching the disciples, Jesus teaches the reader. His guidance of the disciples in the story replicates the role of the narrator as regards the reader. As readers we too hear the call to follow, and each of us is invited to adopt the pattern of the plot as the image of Christ. Just as Jesus is engaged in a war of outlooks, so clearly is Mark. The Gospel text is Mark's campaign in the movement Jesus started; it is Mark's offensive in the war of outlooks, which is a war about the need for wars. At stake are the hearts and minds of those who would read this work, who are among the second and subsequent generations of the followers of Jesus.

# Appendix A

# EXEGETICAL OUTLINES

One place to begin looking for the major form of Mark's discourse is the formal outlines of exegetes. While these scholars are seldom concerned about the narrative as story, they do give the Gospel a very close reading in search of theological development. Their discernment of fissures, seams, and turning points in the unfolding account is worth positing for a starting point.

Two of the better accepted of such outlines are those of Eduard Schweizer and Norman Perrin.[1] Both studies recognize three major turning points in the action before Jesus arrives at Jerusalem. These involve significant decisions taken toward Jesus by various groups in the Gospel, and each marks the conclusion of a main segment of the story.

- In Mk 3:6, the Pharisees join with the Herodians against Jesus.

- In 6:6a, Jesus' hometown of Nazareth rejects him.

- In 8:27–30, Peter, in the name of the twelve, declares him the Messiah.

In particular, the outline of Eduard Schweizer promises a certain serendipity. It has been widely accepted, being subsequently reproduced with only minor points of difference in current commentaries.[2] Thus it is not only accepted; it is also familiar. Schweizer names certain features not mentioned by Perrin. One of these is the division of the Gospel into two major parts, at 8:30/31. This has been identified by Gilbert G. Bilezikian as the crisis of the dramatic form of Mark's narrative.[3] After Peter's profession of Jesus' messiahship, the story turns its attention toward Jerusalem. It shifts, as it were, from a major to a minor key. Exegetes conventionally view the part that follows this central pivot as being organized in this way: the journey to Jerusalem concludes with the end of chapter 10; Jesus works in the city in a climate of rising tension in chapters 11–13; and the passion account fills out the Gospel.

In its main lines, Schweizer's outline takes the form sketched in figure 20. The titles I have given the various sections are my own, not his. They represent the approach I take to the material in chapter 3, above. However, the dimensions of the parts are essentially the same.

|              |            |                                |
|--------------|------------|--------------------------------|
|              | 1:1–13     | Title and Prologue (the Baptist) |
| I. Through Galilee | 1:14–3:12 | The First Week             |
|              | 3:13–6:6a  | The New Family                 |
|              | 6:6b–8:30  | Loaves and Other Stories       |
| II. To Jerusalem | 8:31–10:52 | Road to Jerusalem           |
|              | 11:1–13:37 | Confrontation in the Temple    |
|              | 14:1–16:8  | Passion and Empty Tomb         |

Figure 20

The outline is suggestive for narrative thinking, and the three decisions taken toward Jesus that characterize the episodes that conclude the three segments of part 1 especially offer clues in this direction. They can be taken to represent the climactic moments of three "acts" of the drama. But the narrative structure is complex. One feature of this complexity is the fact that the three acts of the first half of the Gospel, in accordance with the doublet-based thrust of our study, are contained in dual patterns, or brackets, with the concluding "decision taken toward Jesus" situated as the second member in each case. The first member immediately follows the introductory summary and discipleship unit in all three cases. Opening Schweizer's outline further, to include the brackets, we arrive at the general outline sketched in figure 21.

The bracketing items have an integrating function for the respective sections of the account, each "act." In each case, the first bracketing item establishes the terms of conflict that come to fruition in the second bracketing item of that section. As commentators have noted, Mark's duality is not simply repetition — it is often progressive. Some development occurs. In these instances the second moment of a repeated motif or unity does not simply repeat, but it advances beyond the first. When such dual structures are used as a framing device, they invite the reader to suppose that the intervening recitation accounts for the advance in narrative status. Such duality is of narrative use if it describes the departure point and terminus of a stretch of text.

The two synagogue miracles are unique (the only other synagogue episode in the Gospel is the rejection at Nazareth) in that in only these two cases does Jesus happen upon the sufferer to be cured ("In the

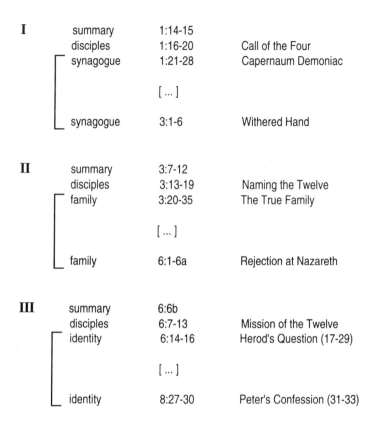

| I | summary | 1:14-15 | |
|---|---|---|---|
| | disciples | 1:16-20 | Call of the Four |
| | synagogue | 1:21-28 | Capernaum Demoniac |
| | [ ... ] | | |
| | synagogue | 3:1-6 | Withered Hand |
| II | summary | 3:7-12 | |
| | disciples | 3:13-19 | Naming the Twelve |
| | family | 3:20-35 | The True Family |
| | [ ... ] | | |
| | family | 6:1-6a | Rejection at Nazareth |
| III | summary | 6:6b | |
| | disciples | 6:7-13 | Mission of the Twelve |
| | identity | 6:14-16 | Herod's Question (17-29) |
| | [ ... ] | | |
| | identity | 8:27-30 | Peter's Confession (31-33) |

Figure 21

synagogue there was a man who had ... "). Together, the two accounts define a redactionally constructed week, comparable to the final week of the Gospel, also a redactional construct. The dynamic element is the verb "destroy," given in two assertions (1:24; 3:6), first posited as Jesus' intention, then as that of his opponents. This sequence, or act, moves from one to the other.

The two "family" episodes are the only instances in which Jesus' relatives come into the Gospel story. Again the problem is set up in 3:20–35, which establishes their doubt about him, and comes to a resolution in 6:4, when his hometown rejects him. The conflict is posed in terms of the old family and the new (3:31–35) and is developed in terms of insiders and outsiders. It represents a period when his disciples are "with him" (3:14) in a sort of apprenticeship.

In the third act, the two "identity" sayings are verbally parallel and frame a sequence in which the question of Jesus' identity is raised. The problem is resolved with Peter's recognition of Jesus as Messiah. This section moves beyond the previous one insofar as the disciples move beyond apprenticeship to delegated ministry. The question of identity is a matter of conflict since the disciples' delegated action depends upon the answer to that question.

Insofar as these brackets involve the terms of conflict as it unfolds in the account, they can be said to have a narrative function. Bracketing items usually perform the rhetorical task of identifying a didactic or conceptual theme. In this case, instead, their work of integration is carried out on the plane of conflict among characters. Given these circumstances, we would seem to have warrant for seeking our clues to the narrative movement of the whole in these elements of the work.

*Appendix B* _____

# NARRATIVE TRANSFORMATIONS

Tzvetan Todorov's experiments in narrative grammar[1] involve a theory that can be adapted to my notion of narrative movement within the individual "acts" of Mark's narrative. Todorov wondered whether units of language larger than the sentence might similarly exhibit verbal structures. Was there a grammar of stories? One product of his fruitful inquiry was the proposal that transformations could be charted in the progressive situations of a story. How does the ending differ from the beginning? Todorov thought that these could be identified, clearly stated, and classified. His grammar would search out and identify those episodes in a narrative that described the passage from one state of the story world to another.[2] He summarizes the matter:

> A sequence implies the existence of two distinct situations each of which can be described with the help of a small number of propositions; between at least one proposition of each situation, there must exist a relation of transformation.[3]

In other words, narrative movement can be demonstrated to exist if we can identify two states, one early and one late, that represent the before and after moments of a narrative. We should be able to locate or formulate statements that adequately express each of these two situations, so that when they are compared they show a relation of "transformation." This relation of transformation would be similar to that of verbs in ordinary grammar. Thus the difference between two grammatical versions of a sentence can imply a narrative event. To say, "Hank will commit a crime," and then to say, "Hank has committed a crime," is to put the same sentence into two grammatical formulations. But when placed next to each other in this manner, they imply a story. In fact, for Todorov they define a story.[4]

His grammar of narrative transformations has proven difficult to apply. But it points us in a helpful direction. What I have done with Todorov's theory is to borrow the notion that a statement of the state of affairs in two different parts of the story can be investigated to determine if a change occurs that would be recognized as a narrative shift, a forward movement. When a stretch of text is framed by similar stories in Mark's characteristic dual pattern, we can ask if the second is a transformation of the first and then how the intervening episodes contribute to the change. For a redactor working with pre-existing narrative materials, setting up such dualities would seem to be an obvious and natural way to create narrative. It would seem to be equally natural for a reader to recognize the narrator's intent as signaling narrative development.

In each of the Markan dual structures framing the three acts of the drama, we can discern a narrative transformation in the manner of Todorov. For example, the synagogue of 1:21–28 precedes the synagogue of the man with the withered hand (3:1–6). These two events, framing a "redactional week," provide the two instances in which Jesus simply encounters a supplicant ("There was a man who…"). But what sets the two moments off as the beginning and end of a narrative moment is the play on the word *destroy:*

1:24: "What have you to do with us, Jesus of Nazareth? Have you come *to destroy* us?"

3:6: The Pharisees went out and immediately took counsel with the Herodians against him, how *to destroy* him.

Figure 22

This gives us the transformation we have used in the text (see fig. 22). As we have noted, the movement proceeds from Jesus' initiative in the Capernaum synagogue (1:21–28) to the clear decision to destroy him, in the second synagogue episode.

*Appendix C* _____

# JESUS AS PROPHET —
# NOTES ON THE TEMPLE ACTION

I began this book by considering what seems to be our cultural predilection to deny nonviolent resistance on the grounds that any form of active resistance, if effective, must be violent. We encounter that attitude again as we observe Jesus moving from compassion to wrath. Anger, we feel, must be a form of violence. Conflict itself, in fact, strikes us as somehow violent. In the temple events the confrontational work of Jesus reaches a climax, and its appearance of violence presents a problem. A partial answer to this frequently felt doubt is found by placing the temple action among the prophetic traditions. The prophetic interpretation of Jesus' temple action by the narrator places that action in a context that draws upon a history of telling the truth to power without embracing its methods.

The prophetic interpretation of this event is primarily managed by the scriptural references, particularly in the writings of the prophets, which reach a peak of intensity here. The text is structured by an account of days, representing a week, from 11:1 to 16:2 — a week that offers another parallel to the redactional week that opens the conflict at the beginning of the Gospel.[1] The first three days of the final week show us the entry, the temple cleansing, and the temple debates (11:20–12:47).

But the events in chapter 11 and on up to 12:12 display their own unity. Commentators[2] have noticed the balanced form of the fig tree story (set out by the difference from Matthew) bracketing the temple cleansing and have viewed this as a parable in action. Further, on each side of this we see units featuring Psalm 118. The first of these is the triumphal entry with its quoted text (11:9):

Hosanna! Blessed is he who comes in the name of the Lord. (Ps 118:26)

The second text is the parable of the vineyard renters, with its lesson (12:10–11):

> The very stone which the builders rejected
> has become the head of the corner;
> this was the Lord's doing,
> and it is marvelous in our eyes. (Ps 118:22–23)

Psalm 118 puts the whole in an ambiance of the feast of Tabernacles, with its eschatological overtones. This feast of the vineyard harvest is associated with the building of the temple and gave its liturgy to the ceremony of its rededication. In Zechariah 14 we see how the ingathering of the grape harvest had become an image of the final eschatological ingathering of peoples. A cluster of related texts is indirectly referenced here, having to do with the eschatological ingathering. One of these is Isa 56:1–8, cited in the cleansing episode.

The same psalm was recited at Passover, which fits Mark's chronology better. In this regard it commemorated the liberationist origins of Israel. It was an opportunity to celebrate nationalist hopes in the midst of Roman oppression. The double theme seems operative here — the nationalist hope and the eschatological realization of God's kingdom. Many felt they were one and the same. In the course of the narration they are clearly separated. By the time we arrive at the second citation of the psalm, at 12:12, the advent of God's kingdom coincides with the rejection of Israelite nationalism, as represented by its current leaders.

The move that opens the wedge between nationalist hope and God's kingdom occurs during the parade that enters the city. In joining the procession, Jesus evokes Zec 9:9–10, as a reinterpretation of the procession. The passage from Zechariah celebrates the "Prince of Peace" under the aegis of disarmament. The text evokes a triumphal military entry after conquest, but without the military. In adding Jesus' contribution to the parade, the narrator changes its meaning. The interplay of Old Testament citations sets up the tensions of the climactic scene in Mark, between the militant and the prophetic, between the expectation and the action.

After entering the city and temple, Jesus returns to Bethany for the night. The fig tree episode on the following day has a symbolic meaning signaled by the discourse — "and it wasn't time yet." The discovery of the withered state of the fig, following the temple incident, gives us a textbook example of Mark's brackets. That is, the two moments of curse and withering provide a commentary on the temple cleansing within the bracketing. The cleansing is a judgment upon the temple itself, as the language of paradox tries to express — a curse on the source of blessing, a "cleansing" of the holy. In terms of the language of the social topography, the purity system itself is undone, as it is turned inside out.

The symbolism of this event is rooted in the prophetic tradition. Israel is repeatedly pictured under the image of fig, vine, or olive tree (see Mk 12:1–12, following Isaiah 5). In Hos 9:15–16 and Hos 2:11–12, we see the prophetic motif of Israel under judgment. More pertinently, in Jer 8:13 we find this motif in close proximity to the passage cited at Mk 11:17 (Jer 7:11). In Jeremiah's text it follows upon his famous temple sermon, with its blistering judgment. The Revised Standard Version's translation of a difficult Hebrew text reads:

> When I would gather them, says the Lord, there are no grapes on the vine, nor figs on the fig tree; even the leaves are withered, and what I gave them has passed away from them. (Jer 8:13)

At the center of this elaborate narrative construction is the event of the cleansing itself. The action, an "exorcism" of the merchants, refers to Zec 14:21 — a chapter that has already been cited twice. In this sense, then, the action of the episode has its origins in prophecy. Insofar as this is the action that is perceived by readers as violent, it is partially accounted for by seeing it as an expression of prophetic judgment on the temple.

This is the lesson of the cursed and withered fig (11:12–14, 20–25). This also is the lesson of the parable of the vineyard tenants (12:1–12). It is the lesson of the faith that would "say to this mountain, 'Be taken up and thrown into the sea'" (11:23). And especially it is the lesson of the two prophetic citations uttered by Jesus at the pitch of this action — Isa 56:7 ("My house shall be a house of prayer for all nations...") and Jer 7:11 ("...but you have made it a robber's den").

The citation of Jeremiah is especially damning, as it refers to the occasion in which Jeremiah condemned the temple cult, not long before the temple of Solomon was destroyed. The text is a reference to Jeremiah's temple sermon of 609 B.C.E. In this stunning speech Jeremiah uses the covenant conditions of Sinai to launch a direct assault on the temple cult. He calls the temple a "hideout" (robber's den) where the complacent Israelite betrayers of the covenant could come to offer sacrifices, make amends, and be free of the con-

|  | | Nationalist Hopes | Eschatological Ingathering | Prophetic Judgment |
|---|---|---|---|---|
| Entry 11:1–11 | | | | |
| | 11:1 | | Zec 14:4 | |
| | 11:2 | | Zec 9:9–10 | |
| | 11:9 | Ps 118:25 | Zec 14:16 | |
| Fig cursed 11:12–14 | | | | Hos 2:11–12 |
| | 11:13 | | | Hos 9:16 |
| Cleansing 11:15–19 | | | | |
| | 11:15 | | | Hos 9:15 |
| | 11:16 | | Zec 14:21 | |
| | 11:17 | | **Isa 56:7** | **Jer 7:11** |
| Fig withered 11:20–26 | | | | |
| | 11:20 | | | Jer 8:13 |
| Parable 12:1–12 | | | | Isa 5:1–7 |
| | 12:1 | | | Jer 2:21 |
| | | | | Ezk 19:10 |
| | 12:10 | Ps 118:22–23 | | |

Figure 23

sequences of their crimes. In Jeremiah 26, one of his disciples has written about the consequences for him of these actions. He was arrested and charged with serious crimes, but he refused to speak up in his own defense. The story of Jesus unfolds in pronounced homage to these precedents.

The fuller passage from Isaiah is 56:1–8. It speaks in eschatological terms of when, in the fullness of time, eunuchs and gentiles will be welcomed into the Holy Place. Usually seen as an expression of post-exilic universalism (in tension with the strong particularism of this age), it delivers its message in the language of purity rules — revoking them, in fact. In Mark's version (alone) the gentile dimension of the allusion is indexed by extending the allusion to include the words "for all nations [gentiles]."

The Isaian text pertains especially to the function of the temple "cleansing." The symmetry between the healings of the unclean, especially the gentiles, at the beginning of the journey to Jerusalem and the cleansing of the temple at the journey's end is encapsulated in the Isaian quote. The fuller passage, Isa 56:1–8, looks upon the future arrival of the eschatological moment, when the temple will be opened up to eunuchs and gentiles. The ritually unclean will even become temple priests (Isa 66:21)!

As the temple cleansing is the climax of the action in Mark, the text's use of allusion to prophetic texts reaches its climax as well. The prophetic allusions interpret the action of Jesus as one of truth telling. It is a nonviolent prophetic confrontation. Its gestures dramatize rather than destroy. In fact, they dramatize destruction in order to protest it. The rich clustering of allusion in these events is collected in figure 23.

*Appendix D* _____

# THE STORY FORMULA

Pierre Maranda and Elli Köngäs Maranda borrowed from Claude Lévi-Strauss a quasi-algebraic formula that he devised to illustrate the system of social values implied in a body of myths.[1] To illustrate the relations among contradictory cultural values, as mediated by the workings of myth, Lévi-Strauss had drawn upon mathematical function theory, the theory of dependent variables. To nonmathematicians this looks more complex than it is. It simply formalizes the pervasive algebraic reality that some elements in an equation or system depend for their value on other elements. For instance, in the equation $y=2x$, the value of $y$ depends on that of $x$. Since the artifacts of human culture, including myth and narrative, typically exhibit such patterns of dependence, this kind of notation understandably attracted the attention of Lévi-Strauss.

Lévi-Strauss's myth formula, as presented by the Marandas,[2] reads:

$$fx(a) : fy(b) :: fx(b) : fa\text{-}l(y)$$

They comment:

> Levi-Strauss' formula borrows its symbolism from the alphabet of function theory but the connection with this mathematical field should not be carried further. He himself has never seen it as anything more than "a drawing" to illustrate the "double twist which is translated with respect to the passage from metaphors to metonymies and vice-versa."[3]

The notation $f$ indicates function. Here the elements $a$ and $b$ are specified by the functions $fx$ and $fy$. For mathematicians this is elementary; for nonmathematicians (like myself) it can be confusing. Furthermore, Lévi-Strauss readily conceded that he was not proposing a mathematical law for myth but merely borrowing the convenient symbolism of math in order to demonstrate certain characteristic peculiarities he found in the mythic process. Since this is not convenient for all, substituting a simpler notation seems in order.

The Marandas used Lévi-Strauss's ideas to illustrate the plots of narratives. In the language of structuralism, they converted a synchronic structure to diachronic purposes. This means they had to convert a theory concerning relations among abstract values into a theory that plots shifting relations among the main characters in a story as it unfolds. The Marandas converted Levi-Strauss's nonlinear concept into a linear model of narrative line, or plot. They note:

> In other words, if a given actor (a) is specified by a negative function fx (and thus becomes a villain), and another one (b) by a positive function fy (and thus becomes a hero), (b) is capable of assuming in turn also the negative function, which process leads to a "victory" so much more complete that [it] proceeds from the "ruin" of the term (a) and thus definitely establishes the positive value (y) of the final outcome. This time as a term, (y) is specified by a function which is the inverse of the first term.... Finally, it might be useful to point out that the two first members of the formula refer to the setting up of the conflict, the third to the turning point of the plot, while the last member refers to the final situation.[4]

Their use of the theory is flexible. They too are not trying to suggest a law for narrative plot, so much as they want to illustrate conventions of storytelling. My use of their ideas is in a similar vein, though it takes a further departure. I am not so much concerned to say that this is what stories always do, as to call upon our memory of experiencing stories to indicate certain tendencies of plot direction. These can be imagined as directions plots tend to take, as if they were structural properties of the narrative genre itself, or they can be imagined as a set of expectations common to listeners and readers. The main thing is that the theory identifies conventions that can be fulfilled or frustrated. Popular forms of narrative tend to fulfill these expectations; more artistically self-conscious efforts tend to frustrate them.

## The Terms

In formalizing the changing relations among characters in a story, some terms need to be defined. The simplest formulation, involving the two main characters and their characteristic traits, would be something like this:

$a$ = a character
$b$ = another character
$x$ = negative traits
$y$ = positive traits

Here $a$ and $b$ are substantives while $x$ and $y$ are values that potentially qualify them. In grammatical language, $a$ and $b$ are nouns, and $x$ and $y$ are adjectives; or $a$ and $b$ are subjects, and $x$ and $y$ are predicates. In narrative language, they represent characters and their traits. The Marandas use the language of actors and roles, which are taken to correspond to terms and functions. The characters are empty of value until they combine with traits. This combination — a "term" — can be represented by attaching the trait, in parenthesis, to the character. Thus $a$ is an unidentified character, but $a(x)$ is the villain, the character identified by negative traits. Similarly, $b(y)$ is the hero, the character identified by the positive traits. Thus:

$a(x)$ = villain
$b(y)$ = hero

The advantage of this abstract consideration is that it allows us to think about the hero and the villain apart from their identifying features. We realize that their roles as hero and villain derive from the application of these values, pro and con.

We are also given to suspect that the positive or negative values are culturally determined. Which is to say that stories so arrange matters that the protagonist shares certain values with the readers of the story. There is a consensus of sorts on what constitutes good. Since human beings strive after goods, though they may disagree about what may constitute those goods, we can also assume that another story is possible in any given plot. This is the story seen from the antagonist's viewpoint. What motivates the villain's participation in the struggle is not a simpleminded devotion to evil (despite the wiles of stories and storytellers) but a "heretical" reading of what is good. And so we can imagine that $x$ and $y$ might be otherwise invested in their assignments of positive or negative value.

## The Formula

The formula devised from these terms was used by Lévi-Strauss to illustrate what he saw as an unusual double reversal occurring in myth. The Marandas used it to demonstrate a similar double reversal in the plots of narratives. In their version, the formula showed how the plots of longer folk narratives unfold in four major moments. In our version their formula would look like this:

$$a(x) : b(y) :: b(x) : y(-a)$$

This can be recognized as a version of the formula for continuous analogy: "*a* is to *b* as *b* is to *c*." However, the four terms of the analogy are complex terms, each combining a character and a trait, in the manner we have just examined. The fourth term depicts the double reversal that Lévi-Strauss and the Marandas were at pains to exploit. In *y(-a)* the function and term are reversed, and the new function is negated. This will interest us as well, but not to the exclusion of the other three terms. All are very interesting.

Each of the four terms represents a moment in the logic of the unfolding narrative. Each moment represents a particular relation between one of the two main characters and one of the character traits. These moments contain shifts in the relations between the protagonist and the antagonist and between these two and the readers. For convenience, these moments can be grouped in two pairs: the moments of identification and the moments of transformation. The formula as a whole charts the course of a narrative from beginning to conclusion in terms of the changing relations of the protagonist and antagonist.

In the moments of transformation, the hero trades in his or her defining character traits for those of the villain, to become *b(x)*. On the other hand, the villain shows a double twist. The fourth place in the formula does not give us *a(y)*, as expected, but a version of *y(a)*. The symbol *y*, which up until now represented positive traits — the good values attached to the hero — now becomes a substantive in its own right, as if it were a character in the story. Not only do the term and function exchange roles in the Maranda formula, but the new function is negated: *a* becomes -*a*.[5] Since *a* is the villain, the negation of *a* represents the removal of this character as a force in the story. And since *(-a)* is now a function, it is upon this function that the happy state of *y* depends.

# NOTES

## Chapter One: Louis L'Amour and the Myth of Constructive Violence

1. For guidance in the world of Louis L'Amour, see Robert Weinberg, *The Louis L'Amour Companion* (New York: Bantam, 1994).

2. Louis L'Amour, *The Sackett Companion: A Personal Guide to the Sackett Novels* (New York: Bantam, 1988).

3. Louis L'Amour, *Jubal Sackett* (New York: Bantam, 1985), appendix, 340.

4. Bruce Malina, *The New Testament World: Insights from Cultural Anthropology* (Atlanta: John Knox, 1981), 25–50.

5. John Howard Yoder, *When War Is Unjust: Being Honest in Just-War Thinking* (Minneapolis: Augsburg, 1984), 79.

6. Stephen Crites, "The Narrative Quality of Experience," in *Why Narrative? Readings in Narrative Theology*, ed. Stanley Hauerwas and L. Gregory Jones (Grand Rapids: Eerdmans, 1989), 65–88; originally appearing in the *Journal of the American Academy of Religion* 39, no. 3 (September 1971): 291–311. See also Terrence Tilley, *Theology of Story* (Collegeville, Minn.: Liturgical, 1985), 23–26.

7. In the L'Amour story collection *Riding for the Brand* (New York: Bantam, 1986), we find a representative concentration of stories concerned with the enforcement of narrative constraints ensuring a violent resolution. See "His Brother's Debt," in which the heroine accuses the hero of being "yellow," and "Fork Your Own Broncs," which has a Quaker for a protagonist. In the end each redeems his reputation with mayhem. See also in the collection "A Strong Land Growing."

8. This list is scarcely exhaustive. Other features shared by the narrative and anthropological patterns can be easily added to it. Thus, clarity of form characterizes the patterns, for purposes of communication (since one of the chief aspects of the patterns is its function as dialogue). Both incorporate a drive toward symmetry in action and reaction, which in turn leads toward a final stasis in which these are imagined to be in some future balance. Within this symmetry, and subverting it, is the need, relating to the basic partisanship of conflict, to establish an edge over one's opponent, leading to the escalation of conflict. A stylistic elegance is favored in the most desirable playing-out of the pattern.

9. Louis L'Amour, *The Empty Land* (New York: Bantam, 1969), 125.

10. This aspect of narrative emerges from the narrative point of view and is appropriately called ideological. A narrative's ideological point of view is generally understood in narrative analysis to represent the worldview adopted by the author, by the narrative voice used by the author, or by characters in the story. For the narrative use of the term "ideology," see Boris Uspensky, *A Poetics of*

*Composition: The Structure of the Artistic Text and Typology of a Composi-
tional Form,* trans. Valentina Zavarin and Susan Wittig (Berkeley: University of
California Press, 1973), 8. Also appropriate in the present context is the classic
notion of Karl Mannheim of ideology as the undergirding of the sociology of
knowledge. Insofar as society is seen as determining the content as well as the
appearance of human thinking, with the exception of certain mathematical sci-
ences, "point of view" is socially important in determining what is thought to be
"real." See Karl Mannheim, *Ideology and Utopia: An Introduction to the Sociology of Knowledge,* trans. Louis Wirth and Edward Shils (New York: Harcourt,
Brace and World, 1936), 75ff. See also Peter Berger and Thomas Luckmann,
*The Social Construction of Reality: A Treatise in the Sociology of Knowledge*
(Garden City, N.Y.: Doubleday, 1966), 9–10.

    11. John Dominic Crossan, *The Dark Interval* (Sonoma, Calif.: Polebridge,
1988). The apt phrasing is borrowed from Tilley, *Theology,* 40, 46.

    12. See, for instance, Claude Lévi-Strauss, "The Structural Study of Myth,"
*Structural Anthropology* (New York: Basic Books, 1963), 1: esp. 229.

    13. The contradiction mediation of Lévi-Strauss's theory is actually included
in Crossan's theory as well (see Crossan, *Dark Interval,* 32–34). It is apparent
that the L'Amour westerns mediate a deeper cultural rift that allows us to think
of the American continent as a blank slate awaiting the European arrival —
L'Amour's title is "The Empty Land." When we say that it was "discovered" by
Columbus, and subsequently "colonized" and "settled," we speak as if it were
previously unoccupied. The actual historical experience of forcibly wresting it
away from the occupants contradicts this irenic vision, and our stories mediate
the contradiction. Certainly the role of Native Americans in the "cowboy and
Indian" movies is closer to the bone of the dynamic. But our focus here is on
those stories that have abstracted, or mediated, the problem to concentrate on
violence itself and its necessity for *any* civilizing function.

    14. Crites, "Narrative Quality," 65–88.

    15. Robert Jewett, *The Captain America Complex: The Dilemma of Zeal-
ous Nationalism* (Philadelphia: Westminster, 1973), 29–30. See also Ernest Lee
Tuveson, *Redeemer Nation: The Idea of America's Millennial Role* (Chicago:
University of Chicago Press, 1968). Jewett writes elsewhere (27): "Early Puritans
in New England derived from the book of Revelation the dualistic world view
and the belief that violence would inaugurate God's kingdom."

    16. Quoted in *Gandhi on Non-violence: Selected Texts from Mohandas K.
Gandhi's "Non-violence in Peace and War,"* ed. Thomas Merton (New York:
New Directions, 1964), 40.

    17. Reinhold Niebuhr, "Why the Christian Church is not Pacifist," in *Chris-
tianity and Power Politics* (New York: Scribner's, 1940), and *An Interpretation
of Christian Ethics* (New York: Seabury, 1979).

    18. Niebuhr, *Christianity and Power Politics,* 9–10.

    19. J. G. Davies, *Christians, Politics, and Violent Revolution* (Maryknoll,
N.Y.: Orbis, 1976), 25.

    20. National Conference of Catholic Bishops, *The Challenge of Peace: God's
Promise and Our Response. A Pastoral Letter on War and Peace* (Washington,
D.C.: United States Catholic Conference, 1983).

    21. Jim Castelli, *The Bishops and the Bomb: Waging Peace in a Nuclear Age*
(Garden City, N.Y.: Doubleday, 1983), 133.

22. One of these was restored in the final draft. The stronger of the two was left on the cutting room floor. It read: "Jesus commanded his followers to love each other as he had loved them (Jn 15:12). A love which gives life, which forgives always, which even sacrifices one's own life that others might live in the knowledge of God is the love commanded of all who follow Jesus. Further, this love, if it is to be like his, is marked by mercy, gentleness, and non-violence" (*Origins* 12, no. 20 [October 28, 1982]: 310).

23. See *Origins* 12, no. 20 (October 28, 1982): 310 (2d draft, par. 32), and *Challenge of Peace,* par. 55; emphasis added.

## Chapter Two: On Reading Ancient Texts

1. See Elisabeth Struthers Malbon, "Narrative Criticism: How Does the Story Mean?" in *Mark and Method: New Approaches in Biblical Studies,* ed. Janice Capel Anderson and Stephen D. Moore (Minneapolis: Fortress, 1992), 27.

2. Messages lost through distorted signals are the concern of information theory and the central theme of the definitive studies by Claude Shannon (with Warren Weaver, *The Mathematical Theory of Communication* [Urbana: University of Illinois Press, 1949]). Shannon illustrates his theory of communication with a visual diagram that serves as a model for many of the theories in narrative criticism (see fig. 24).

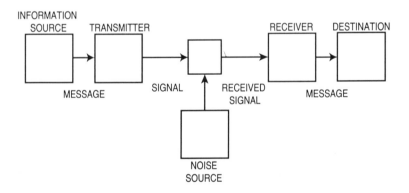

Schematic diagram of general communication system

Figure 24

3. Anne Mangel, "Maxwell, Demon, Entropy, Information," in *Mindful Pleasures: Essays on Thomas Pynchon,* ed. George Levine and David Leverenz (Boston: Little, Brown and Co., 1976), 95–96

4. D. E. Nineham, *Saint Mark* (London: Penguin, 1963), 351–53; Wilfred Harrington, *Mark* (Wilmington, Del.: Glazier, 1979), 202–4. Identifying "the desolating sacrilege" as a historical event of Mark's day, Nineham questions what it could be and provides a few candidates: it may refer to the fall of Jerusalem, as it seems to do in Luke's Gospel. Or, given the personal grammar of the

passage, it may refer to the Roman presence in the temple area. Or it may mean, very specifically, Caligula's attempt to have his statue set up in the temple, which would provide a closer fit with the precedent of Antioches Epiphanes. Harrington's commentary covers the same ground, adding the destruction of the temple as itself a candidate. He calls it the "parousia of Satan" and the climax of the antitemple theme in Mark.

5. See Wayne Booth, *The Rhetoric of Fiction* (Chicago: University of Chicago Press), 79–81, 138–39.

6. Robert Scholes, *Structuralism in Literature: An Introduction* (New Haven: Yale University Press, 1974), 26.

7. Ibid., 27.

8. Here I would differ from those theorists, such as Robert Fowler (*Let the Reader Understand: Reader-Response Criticism and the Gospel of Mark* [Minneapolis: Fortress, 1991], 45) and Augustine Stock (*Call to Discipleship* [Wilmington, Del.: Glazier, 1982], 9–10), who assimilate Mark's text to oral speech categories. The absence of the sender in the case of ancient writings, with the consequent reliance upon the text as the sole means of contact, separates such texts definitively from spoken messages with their characteristic immediacy. Spoken communication implies feedback.

We begin to see more clearly that the image of oral narration given by a written text is an illusion. When Huck Finn seems to be chatting away, the oral conversation is a calculated effect. We have nothing oral in the text; it is written — which is to say that the temporal experience of oral storytelling, including the listening experience of having the story unfold in the teller's good time, is present in a written text only by sleight of hand. What we have is a *spatial* representation of a *temporal* experience. The written text is linear (and unidirectional), not temporal. Nor is the reading experience temporal except in the banal sense in which all human experience unfolds in time. Just as it takes time to study, let us say, a nonlinear road map, so it takes time to examine a linear text from one end to the other. See Shlomith Rimmon-Kenan, "Text-time," in *Narrative Fiction: Contemporary Poetics* (London: Methuen, 1983), 44–45.

It is this one-directional linearity, especially on first reading, that effects the illusion of storyteller's time. But the situations of reading and listening are radically different, with different kinds of constraints, as even the most unselfconscious of readers demonstrates when he or she checks the ending of a mystery novel. And the absolute difference this make for writing, as distinct from telling, is confronted by the reader along with the problems and opportunities of the spatial, configured text. To treat the written Gospel as oral is a case of category confusion; oral strategies of storytelling do not apply *prima facie* to written texts.

9. The difference between genre and literary form is generally one of size and complexity. See James L. Bailey and Lyle D. Vander Broek, *Literary Forms in the New Testament: A Handbook* (Louisville: Westminster John Knox, 1992), 13–14: "Whereas literary forms can be short and structurally simple, [genres] are longer pieces that may themselves contain a number of shorter literary forms."

10. Bruce J. Malina, *The New Testament World: Insights from Cultural Anthropology* (Atlanta: John Knox, 1981), 2.

11. See Bailey and Vander Broek, *Literary Forms,* 14–16.

12. Ibid., 15.

13. See, for instance, Raymond E. Brown, *The Critical Meaning of the Bible* (New York: Paulist, 1981), 23–29.

14. Frank Kermode, *The Genesis of Secrecy* (Cambridge, Mass.: Harvard University Press, 1979), 163.

15. T. R. Wright, *Theology and Literature* (London: Basil Blackwell, 1988), 72: "It [Mark's Gospel] is not, fortunately, entirely original, otherwise it would indeed prove to be unreadable." And Kermode, *Genesis*, 162: "Yet the statement that Mark founded a new genre does not entail that it is unrelated to all others. If it had been so it would have been practically unreadable."

16. Kermode, *Genesis*, 162.

17. Jonathan Culler, *Structuralist Poetics: Structuralism, Linguistics, and the Study of Literature* (Ithaca, N.Y.: Cornell University Press, 1975), 136. Perhaps such naturalization is noticeable to us when a Shakespearean character thinks aloud, for we are observing across cultural divides. Yet the soliloquy is one of the few ways in which characters can share feelings or thoughts with an audience. It is done today on TV or film by a voice-over. The character's voice is heard, perhaps in musing tones, while the character is shown with lips unmoving. We automatically conclude: thoughts are being shared. These conventions do not bother us. Once we see how they operate, we take them to represent reality, and they seem natural enough. They have been "naturalized," that is. The conventions of genre, in this sense, are agreed upon procedures that allow us to take in a story and not be too bothered by the medium. In a sense, the conventions carry much of the message, and the conventions are in turn carried by the culture.

18. John Lyons, *Chomsky* (London: Fontana, 1974), 37ff., is one text that discusses competence, performance, and the role of native speakers in Chomsky's work.

19. Kermode, *Genesis*, 163.

20. This seems to have happened with Mary Ann Tolbert's "authorial audience" (*Sowing the Gospel: Mark's World in Literary-Historical Perspective* [Minneapolis: Fortress, 1989], 52–55).

21. An apparent difficulty seems to loom here. Presumably this study of the Gospel considers its message significant and even normative for Christians, or it would not be worth pursuing. However, when we abandon "author's intent" in favor of twentieth-century reading options, we seem to be jettisoning any possibility of appealing to the Christ of the Gospel for precedent. Are we not simply looking in a mirror? But to pose the question in this manner is to assume we have a choice in the matter, and I have been trying to insist we do not. The most competent reading of ancient texts implies the wisest use of modern genres as working contexts. The bind in which we find ourselves is another version of the classic hermeneutical circle. But we can pose the matter differently. The allegiance to Jesus is prior to any appeal to the written text and is the reason for such an appeal. The engagement with the text is performed within the framework of an interpretive community, and the existence of such a community implies a consensus on genre. The fundamentalist has learned to ask certain questions of the text. The genre is assumed to be a form of oracle, with each syllable full of portent. The redaction critic sees a theological treatise obscured by narrative. As is apparent, I object to their respective projects as pivoting on genre error. In turn I can anticipate their objections to my efforts as misunder-

standing the Gospel genre, as neglecting either the plain, historical truth or the theological core.

22. David E. Aune, *The New Testament in Its Literary Environment* (Philadelphia: Westminster, 1987), 47.

23. Tolbert, *Sowing the Gospel,* 60:

> Attempting to account for that difference may provide a new starting point for developing a plausible hypothesis concerning the genre of the Gospels: perhaps they belong to the realm of *popular culture and popular literature.* If so, then Xenophon's *Memorabilia* stands in the same relationship to the Gospel of Mark that Dostoyevsky's *Crime and Punishment* stands to Agatha Christie's *The Murder of Roger Ackroyd:* one is written for the literate elite of culture, the other is accessible to middle- and lower-class masses; one is individualized, subtle, ambiguous, and profound, the other is conventionalized, pellucid, stereotypical, and repetitious; one is an example of self-conscious literate culture, the other of popular culture. The study of popular culture has been a major component of literary scholarship for many years, but only relatively recently have scholars begun to realize that popular cultures existed alongside "elite" cultures well back in history, back behind the pulp novels of the nineteenth century, back behind the Middle English verse romances of the medieval period, back, in fact, at least to the classical world.

24. Ibid., 63–64, 67.

25. An influential reading of Mark's Gospel as tragicomedy has been offered by Dan O. Via, Jr. In this regard, see his books *Kerygma and Comedy in the New Testament: A Structuralist Approach to Hermeneutic* (Philadelphia: Fortress, 1975), ch. 4, and *The Ethics of Mark's Gospel — In the Middle of Time* (Philadelphia: Fortress, 1985).

26. Sam Smiley, *Playwriting: The Structure of Action* (Englewood Cliffs, N.J.: Prentice-Hall, 1971), 47.

27. Ibid., 48.

28. Ibid., 48, 96–97.

29. Some which need to be mentioned are: David Rhoads and Donald Michie, *Mark as Story: An Introduction to the Narrative of a Gospel* (Philadelphia: Fortress, 1982); Stephen D. Moore, *Literary Criticism and the Gospels: The Theoretical Challenge* (New Haven: Yale University Press, 1989); and Tolbert, *Sowing the Gospel.*

30. William A. Beardslee, *Literary Criticism of the New Testament* (Philadelphia: Fortress, 1970), 3–4:

> With some oversimplification one can say that there are two main lines of tradition in literary criticism, using the term in its narrower sense of studies of literary form. One of these lines, descending from Aristotle's *Rhetoric,* treats the form as the vehicle for a content which can stand in its own right, apart from the form. Form, from this point of view, becomes simply a means for effectively (persuasively) communicating the content, which in turn is thought of as an idea.... Within studies of literature, however, a second line of tradition, descending from a very much

more important work of Aristotle, the *Poetics,* has been more influential than the rhetorical tradition. This type of criticism regards literary form as an essential part of the function of the work, and not as a separable, instrumental addition to the intellectual content.

31. Because some books about narrative use literary works to explore the theoretical dimensions of narrative while others use narrative theory to explore the meaning of individual narrative works, we can speak of *narratology* as theoretical and *narrative criticism* as focused on particular works, in the manner of Moore, *Literary Criticism,* 51: "Narratology is about theory, narrative criticism is about exegesis." In this chapter I will make use of the various possibilities of narrative theory as they pertain to my task.

32. Jonathan Culler, *The Pursuit of Signs: Semiotics, Literature, Deconstruction* (Ithaca, N.Y.: Cornell University Press, 1981), 170. Culler writes: "There is considerable variety among these traditions, and of course each theorist has concepts or categories of his own, but if these theorists agree on anything it is this: that the theory of narrative requires a distinction between what I shall call 'story' — a sequence of actions or events, conceived as independent of their manifestation in discourse — and what I shall call 'discourse,' the discursive presentation or narration of events" (169–70).

33. For this aspect of the Gospel narrative, see the seminal article by Norman R. Petersen, "'Point of View' in Mark's Narrative," *Semeia* 12 (1978): 97–121.

34. Rhoads and Michie, *Mark as Story,* 43.

35. Malbon, "Narrative Criticism," 27. Seymour Chatman has given us the definitive elaboration of the model in *Story and Discourse: Narrative Structure in Fiction and Film* (Ithaca, N.Y.: Cornell University Press, 1978), 151 (see fig. 25).

Narrative Text

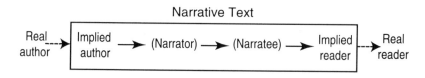

Figure 25

Moore, *Literary Criticism,* 46, offers one of the most concise descriptions of this diagram:

The communication from the real (actual, historical) author to the real reader is conducted instrumentally through the personae within the box. Distinguished from the flesh-and-blood author is the *implied author.* This term denotes the complex image of the real author that the reader infers as s/he reads — a selecting, structuring, and presiding intelligence, discerned indirectly in the text, like God in his/her creation. The author's generation of this textual second self is a profoundly rhetorical act (e.g., Luke 1:1–4). The *narrator* is also said to be immanent in the text as the voice that tells the story, a voice which may or may not be that of one of the characters. The principal New Testament examples of narrators who do participate in the story as characters are John of Revelation, and the "we"-narrator of Luke-Acts (see Acts 16:11ff.). The narrative voice is the instrument by means of which the story-world, and the image of its author-creator, is transmitted (a bearer of divine messages, if you will). The *narratee is* defined as the narrator's immediate addressee (e.g., Theophilus in Luke-Acts), and the *implied reader* as the (generally more oblique) image of "the reader in the text": the reader presupposed or produced by the text as (in some theories) its ideal interpreter.

36. Fowler, *Let the Reader Understand*, 35–38.

37. Booth, *Rhetoric of Fiction*. "Implied author" is typically invoked in cases of the "unreliable narrator." Huck Finn, as both narrator and protagonist of Mark Twain's novel, is the textbook example of the unreliable narrator insofar as he habitually "stretches" the truth. To account for the reader's awareness of this inaccuracy in the only account on the page, critics posit a second point of view in the text, that of the implied author. As if winking to the reader over the narrator's shoulder, the implied author communicates an awareness of the narrator's lack of reliability to the reader. But the notion of implied author might be extended to include other traces of authorial process as implied in the text. *Redaction* — piecing together a text from prior texts and editorially smoothing it — is such a process, and it is inferred from implications in the text. Furthermore, it is quite distinct from narration and, in fact, may even threaten to subvert narrative. Here we seem to have good reason for positing the distinction between implied author and narrator and using it to our benefit in literary studies of the Gospel texts. Such an understanding underlies the interpretation of "blocking the action" in the narrative plotting of Mark's account, in the next chapter.

38. As C. Hugh Holman and William Harmon (*A Handbook to Literature*, 6th ed. [New York: Macmillan, 1992], 361) put it: "Because the plot consists of characters performing actions in incidents that comprise a 'single, whole, and complete' action, this relation involves conflict between opposing forces.... Without conflict, plot hardly exists. We must have a Claudius flouting a Hamlet, an Iago making an Othello jealous, if we are to have plot."

39. Rhoads and Michie, *Mark as Story*, 103. The book's chapter on character is found on pp. 101–42. The authors helpfully enumerate and describe the main traits of the character Jesus, as well as those of the religious authorities and the group of disciples. Although this line of thought is not developed in their treatment, it is revealing to notice how the character traits they have isolated in fact shape the contrasts between Jesus and these two groups that the authors have named as producing the major conflicts in the Gospel narrative. The complexity of the apparently "rounded" character of Jesus is largely a direct reflection of the complexity of the plotted action. A concise chart presents the traits of Jesus alongside the contrasting traits of his opponents (see fig. 26; page nos. are from Rhoads and Michie).

40. For a more elaborate study of the oppositional groups in Mark, see Elizabeth Struthers Malbon, "The Jewish Leaders in the Gospel of Mark: A Literary Study of Marcan Characterization," *Journal of Biblical Literature* 108, no. 2 (summer 1989): 259–81.

| Jesus | Religious Authorities |
|---|---|
| • authority from God (105) | • spiritual blindness (118) |
| • integrity (104, 108) | • hypocrisy |
| • serving others, not lording over others (109) | • lording over others (119) |
| • losing his life (111) | • saving their lives (121) |

| Jesus | Disciples |
|---|---|
| • faith (108) | • fear, lack of faith (124) |
| • renouncing self, losing life (111) | • resistance to death, lack of self-renunciation (125) |
| • being least (111) | • arguing about who is greatest (125) |

Figure 26


41. See, for instance, Sean Freyne, *The World of the New Testament* (Wilmington, Del.: Glazier, 1983), 100–105, 110–18.


## Chapter Three: The Gospel as Agon

1. See Paul Ricoeur, *Time and Narrative,* trans. Kathleen McLaughlin and David Pellauer (Chicago: University of Chicago, 1984), 1:38–45.

2. Ibid., 41. On p. 42 he adds: "Aristotle says nothing against episodes as episodes. What he proscribes are not episodes but the episodic texture, the plot where the episodes follow one another by chance. The episodes, controlled by the plot, are what give amplitude to the work and thus a 'magnitude.' "

3. Norman Petersen, "The Composition of Mark 4:1–8:26," *Harvard Theological Review* 73 (1980): 186–87.

4. For descriptions of episodic structure and parataxis, see C. Hugh Holman and William Harmon, *A Handbook to Literature*, 6th ed. (New York: Macmillan, 1992), 175, 343.

5. Robert M. Fowler, *Let the Reader Understand: Reader-Response Criticism and the Gospel of Mark* (Minneapolis: Fortress, 1991), 149–50.

6. Frans Neirynck, *Duality in Mark: Contributions to the Study of the Markan Redaction* (Leuven: Leuven University Press, 1972).

7. Walter J. Ong, *Orality and Literacy* (London and New York: Methuen, 1982), 148.

8. See, for example, Holman and Harmon, *Handbook,* 207.

9. Ibid., 132, 153.

10. These are not to be confused with the complication and climax, also called respectively the *epitasis* and the *catastasis.* Writing about "dramatic structure," Holman and Harmon tell us (*Handbook,* 153):

The rising action (or complication) is set in motion by the exciting force (in *Hamlet* the ghost's revelation to Hamlet of the murder) and continues through successive stages of conflict between the hero and the counter-players up to the climax or turning point (in *Hamlet* the hesitating failure of the hero to kill Claudius at prayer). The ancients called this part the epitasis.

The falling action stresses the activity of the forces opposing the hero and, although some suspense must be maintained, the trend must lead logically to the disaster with which the tragedy is to close. The falling action, called by the ancients the catastasis, is often set in movement by a single event called the tragic force, closely related to the climax and bearing the same relation to the falling action as the exciting force does to the rising action.... In *Hamlet* it is the blind stabbing of Polonius, which sends Hamlet away from the court just as he appears about to succeed in his plans.

11. See ibid., 153.

12. As *paired* events, they are unique to Mark. The exorcism in the Capernaum synagogue is the public opening move of Jesus in this Gospel. In expelling the "unclean" spirit from the Holy Place, Jesus performs a "cleansing," as he will again in the temple. In Matthew, this dramatic flourish is missing, replaced by the Sermon on the Mount (Matthew 5–7), even though Matthew retains Mark's notice of Jesus' success, appended now to the Sermon (Mk 1:22; Mt 7:28–29). Luke, for his part, keeps the Capernaum event but bumps it from its privileged position by preceding it with his version of the Nazareth rejection. The Nazareth event serves Luke well as an inaugural episode for the double work of Luke-Acts, but the Capernaum synagogue story becomes, in his use of it, simply another incident demonstrating the style and content of Jesus' ministry.

13. Whereas Luke omits the Bethany anointing, having opted for another similar account placed earlier in the Gospel (Lk 7:36–50), Matthew omits the final anointing, apparently coping with some of the awkwardness in Mark's account of the women attempting a burial anointing that they already understand they cannot accomplish.

14. D. E. Nineham, *Saint Mark* (London: Penguin, 1963), 372–73.

15. Eduard Schweizer, "Mark's Contribution to the Quest of the Historical Jesus," *New Testament Studies* 10 (1964): 421–32.

16. To name three who have seen fit to borrow a version of it: Wilfred Harrington, *Mark* (Collegeville, Minn.: Liturgical Press, 1991), 1; Edward J. Mally, "The Gospel according to Mark," in *Jerome Biblical Commentary*, 1st ed. (Englewood Cliffs, N.J.: Prentice-Hall, 1968), 23–24; Daniel Harrington, "The Gospel according to Mark," in *Jerome Biblical Commentary*, 2d ed. (Englewood Cliffs, N.J.: Prentice-Hall, 1990), 598.

17. Tzvetan Todorov, *The Poetics of Prose*, trans. Richard Howard (Ithaca, N.Y.: Cornell University Press, 1977), 108ff.

18. See Robert Fowler, *Let the Reader Understand*, 136–37, for his account of Matthew's "filling the gaps" in Mark. Other Gospels seem to assume causal relations equivalent to those I have claimed for Mark. For instance, in John's Gospel, which is independent of Mark, the loaves miracle is seen to lead rather directly to thoughts of kingship (Jn 6:15), similar to the way Mark's movement from loaves through identity questions leads to Peter's pronouncement of Jesus as Messiah. Also in John, we see that the Messiah belongs in Jerusalem — so

much so that he puts Jesus in Jerusalem as early as chapter 2, after the messianic recognition in Jn 1:41. In John's Gospel, the prophet's place in which he is without honor is Jerusalem (Jn 4:44), not Nazareth, as in the Synoptics. In Mark, the messianic recognition generates the movement toward the city in a similar way. And in Luke's Gospel the sense of a deliberate move toward the city is developed elaborately (see John Yoder, *The Politics of Jesus* [Grand Rapids: Eerdmans, 1972], 43ff.). Here Luke expands upon something already present in Mark.

19. Of the twenty-two instances in which Mark uses the word *artos* ("bread" or "loaves"), nineteen are found in this section: 6:8, 36, 37, 38, 41 [2x], 44, 52; 7:2, 5, 27; 8:4, 5, 6, 14 [2x], 16, 17, 19.

20. Just as the Messiah Jesus contrasts to King Herod, so the Baptist, as the one who comes before (9:11), contrasts with Peter and the disciples, who "come after" (1:17).

21. See 1:24 as the text parallel to 3:6; also see 3:22–30.

22. Calendar notices can be found at Mk 11:12, 20: 14:1; 15:1, 42; 16:1.

23. Ched Myers, *Binding the Strong Man: A Political Reading of Mark's Story of Jesus* (Maryknoll, N.Y.: Orbis, 1988), 300.

24. The scriptural link between wrath and compassion is found in the prophetic tradition, as it is grounded in the covenant law of Moses. This is seen clearly in the prophetic theme of the widow and the orphan, which derives from the Exodus law code, at Ex 22:20–26:

> You shall not wrong a stranger or oppress him, for you were strangers in the land of Egypt. You shall not afflict any widow or orphan. If you do afflict them, and they cry out to me, I will surely hear their cry; and my wrath will burn, and I will kill you with the sword, and your wives shall become widows and your children fatherless.
>
> If you lend money to any of my people with you who is poor, you shall not be to him as a creditor, and you shall not exact interest from him. If ever you take your neighbor's garment in pledge, you shall restore it to him before the sun goes down; for that is his only covering, it is his mantle for his body; in what else shall he sleep? And if he cries to me, I will hear, for I am compassionate.

It is the text that generates the theme of the cry of the poor. It moves in two sweeps, vv. 21–24 and 25–27 (see fig. 27). Each part has three moments, in parallel motion.

This remarkable passage states a social program for Israel. The stranger, the widow and orphan, and the poor are all vulnerable, and the prophets take up their cause, under the rubric of "the widow and orphan" (Isa 1:17; Ezk 22:7, etc.), gauging the health of God's people by the criterion of the welfare of the widow and orphan. In this regard, the parallel placement of wrath and compassion in vv. 24 and 27 is striking. Clearly wrath is the complementary side of mercy. The text is precise, and the objects of these two divine attributes are specified — the compassion for the vulnerable, the wrath for those who would exploit them. It is in the spirit of this text, and its history of prophetic vigilance, that Jesus enters the Holy City and its temple.

| 21 | Do not exploit | 25–26 | Do not exploit |
|----|----------------|-------|----------------|
|    | the stranger   |       | the poor       |
| 22 | the widow and orphan | | |
| 23 | If they cry out<br>I will hear them | 27 | If they cry out<br>I will hear them |
| 24 | for I am a God of<br>WRATH | | for I am a God of<br>COMPASSION |

Figure 27

25. George Pixley (*God's Kingdom: A Guide for Biblical Study* [Maryknoll, N.Y.: Orbis, 1977]) sees in the choice of the temple as the ultimate target of Jesus' challenge a strategic decision in an ideological battle:

> The Jesus movement saw the principal obstacle to the realization of God's kingdom in Palestine to be the temple and the class structure that it supported.... Because the class domination of the priests rested principally on a deep-seated ideology, the strategy of the Jesus movement was one of ideological attack. Our Gospels give ample evidence that Jesus was executed by a broad coalition of groups that for different reasons were threatened by this historical project. (72)

Pixley contrasts Jesus' strategy with that of the Zealots:

> The Zealots saw the Roman presence as the principal cause of the oppression of the Palestinian population. And the only way to rid the country of a military domination was by military means. Jesus and his movement, however, did not see Rome as the principal enemy. In their priorities, it was first necessary to do away with the temple domination. For this they had to avoid provoking military conflicts. Our hypothesis does not hold Jesus to have categorically rejected military tactics. It does hold that he did not espouse them for ridding the country of priestly oppression. (82)

This view of Jesus' nonviolence is purely tactical. Pixley resists any suggestion that it might be more than this:

> According to the reading of the Gospels that makes this a way of nonviolence that Jesus taught as universally valid, Jesus did not intend to have enemies. Their enmity was due to their hostilities, and Jesus' only response was to avoid provocation.
>
> This reading of the Gospels is attractive to a sector of the modern church. However, it does not seem to apply to what the gospel narrative tells us of Jesus. (81)

## Chapter Four: The Symbolism of Power

1. Arthur Conan Doyle, "The Five Orange Pips," in *The Complete Sherlock Holmes* (Garden City, N.Y.: Doubleday, 1938), 253.

2. Robert S. Paul, *Whatever Happened to Sherlock Holmes? Detective Fiction, Popular Theology, and Society* (Carbondale: Southern Illinois University Press, 1991), 53.

3. For definitions of holiness and uncleanness, see Mary Douglas, *Purity and Danger: An Analysis of Concepts of Pollution and Taboo* (London: Routledge and Kegan Paul, 1966), esp. 2–7, 35, 98; Bruce J. Malina, *The New Testament World: Insights from Cultural Anthropology* (Atlanta: John Knox, 1981), ch. 6; Jerome H. Neyrey, "The Idea of Purity in Mark's Gospel," *Semeia* 35 (1986): 91–128; John L. McKenzie, "Holy," in *The Dictionary of the Bible* (Milwaukee: Bruce, 1965), 365–67.

4. Douglas, *Purity and Danger,* 35.

5. Ibid., 98.

6. Neyrey, "Idea of Purity," 96. See also Douglas, *Purity and Danger,* 51–53.

7. Neyrey, "Idea of Purity," 95. See also Malina, *New Testament World,* 122–54. These works develop the ideas of Mary Douglas as found in her works, especially *Purity and Danger.*

8. See D. E. Nineham, *Saint Mark* (London: Penguin, 1963), 191–93, for comment on how the evangelists seem to take a more radical stance than Jesus (in the belief of this commentator) concerning abrogating the old law, including the entire set of food laws in Leviticus. In the episode of Mk 7:1–23, what began as a clarification of the oral tradition becomes an erasure of sections of the *written* law and a general *monitum* about traditions as such.

9. Elizabeth S. Malbon (*Narrative Space and Mythic Meaning in Mark* [San Francisco: Harper and Row, 1986]) has produced a rather complete structural study of the spatial relations in Mark. Malbon shows the logical and mythological relations in the narrative world of the Gospel. The spatial relations in her study fall into the three categories of geopolitical, topographical, and architectural. Cities, towns, and regions are seen as geopolitical while buildings such as houses and synagogues are architectural. Topographical relations refer to the physical features of the land, such as mountains and seas. Malbon describes the *grammar* of the symbolic language of which Mark's narrative is an extended statement, a *discourse.* This expression or discourse, in the actual telling, favors certain terms, terms foregrounded by the dualistic and chiastic texture of the narrative.

10. Douglas, *Purity and Danger,* 94–113.

11. Ibid., 114–15. The following statements by Douglas are also relevant here:

Van Gennep shows how thresholds symbolize beginnings of new statuses. Why does the bridegroom carry his bride over the lintel? Because the step, the beam and the door posts make a frame which is the necessary everyday condition of entering a house. The homely experience of going through a door is able to express so many kinds of entrance. So also are cross roads and arches new seasons, new clothes and the rest. No experience is too lowly to be taken up in ritual and given a lofty meaning. (114)

Even more direct is the symbolism worked upon the human body. The body is a model which can stand for any bounded system. Its boundaries can represent any boundaries which are threatened or precarious.

The body is a complex structure. The functions of its different parts and their relation afford a source of symbols for other complex structures. We cannot possibly interpret rituals concerning excreta, breast milk, saliva and the rest unless we are prepared to see in the body a symbol of society, and to see the powers and dangers credited to social structure reproduced in small on the human body. (115)

All margins are dangerous. If they are pulled this way or that the shape of fundamental experience is altered. Any structure of ideas is vulnerable at its margins. We should expect the orifices of the body to symbolize its specially vulnerable points. Matter issuing from them is marginal stuff of the most obvious kind. Spittle, blood, milk, urine, faeces or tears by simply issuing forth have traversed the boundary of the body. (121)

12. This may be the first usage of this combination. Examples cited prior to Mark (see Friedrich Hauck, "Akathartos," in *The Theological Dictionary of the New Testament* [Grand Rapids: Eerdmans, 1967], 3:428–29) tend to conflate all demonic "spirit" terms in early literature, with no clear early examples of this precise formulation. Whether or not Mark originated this precise formulation, it is clear that he exploits its semantic possibilities.

13. Fernando Belo, in *A Materialist Reading of the Gospel of Mark,* trans. Matthew J. O'Connell (Maryknoll, N.Y.: Orbis, 1975), has a similar system, with his *eye, hand,* and *foot* code. The present version is more directly derived from the text, I believe.

14. Richard Horsley, *Jesus and the Spiral of Violence: Popular Jewish Resistance in Roman Palestine* (San Francisco: Harper and Row, 1987), 178–80.

15. Commentators are at a loss to account for this group literally. The simplest reading would see the phrase as narrative shorthand for effecting a transition from one group to the other.

16. Frank Kermode, *The Genesis of Secrecy: On the Interpretation of Narrative* (Cambridge, Mass.; Harvard University Press, 1979), 135.

17. For an interpretation of violence as instrumentally amplified strength, as opposed to power, see Hannah Arendt, *On Violence* (New York: Harcourt, Brace and World, 1969), 44.

18. A synoptic diagram of the instances of faith and fear in this section is given in figure 28.

19. See, Nineham, *Mark,* 187–98, and Wilfred Harrington, *Mark* (Wilmington, Del.: Glazier, 1979), 95–102.

20. As in the encounter with the leper (1:40–45), Jesus is sought out by someone excluded from Jewish society. Like the case of the paralytic (2:1–12), a supplicant manages to reach Jesus although the door of the house seems closed to entry. As with the Gerasene demoniac (5:1–20), we witness an exorcism among gentiles. Like the woman with the hemorrhage (5:25–34), this woman evinces an aggressive faith. As with Jairus (5:21–24, 35–43), a parent is desperately concerned about a daughter. In addition, the episode distinctly echoes the inaugural elements of the Capernaum demoniac (1:21–28). There Jesus broke into the old order, represented by the synagogue, with his new reality that comes to be represented by the house. In the present instance, the woman forces an entry into the house, to beg a share in the new reality.

|  | Fear | Faith |
|---|---|---|
| The Stilling of the Storm (4:35–41) | "afraid" | "faith" |
| The Exorcism of the Gerasene Demoniac (5:1-20) |  |  |
| Restoration of Jairus's Daughter (5:21–24, 35–43) | "fear" | "believe" |
| The Woman with an Issue of Blood (5:25–34) | "fear" | "faith" |
| Jesus Rejected at Nazareth 6:1-6 |  | "unbelief" |

Figure 28

21. Harrington, *Mark,* 103.

22. Nineham, *Mark,* 205–7.

23. Harrington notes that it is "Mark" (or the narrator) who has placed this story outside Galilee. The elaborate identification of the woman as Greek and Syro-Phoenician makes sense historically only if the encounter takes place in Jewish territory.

24. Harrington, *Mark,* 103.

25. Douglas, *Purity and Danger,* 49–50.

26. Ched Myers, *Binding the Strong Man: A Political Reading of Mark's Story of Jesus* (Maryknoll, N.Y.: Orbis, 1988), 141–52.

27. John Pilch, "Healing in Mark: A Social Science Analysis," *Biblical Theological Bulletin* 15, no. 4 (1985): 149.

28. Americans with Disabilities Act of 1990 (PL 101–336, 26 July 1990), 104, in *United States Statutes at Large,* 327–78. A government brochure entitled *Facts about the Americans with Disabilities Act* begins with these words: "Title I of the Americans with Disabilities Act of 1990, which takes effect July 26, 1992, prohibits private employers, state and local governments, employment agencies and labor unions from discriminating against qualified individuals with disabilities in job application procedures, hiring, firing, advancement, compensation, job training, and other terms, conditions, and privileges of employment."

29. One of the problems with the purity model of society of Mary Douglas is that it sees the inclusive impulse as only a weak version of the purity system. "Weak grid" has no ideal (equivalent to purity) in its own right. This seems inadequate.

30. Pilch, "Healing," 149.

31. Myers, *Binding the Strong Man,* 147.

32. Horsley, *Jesus,* 324.

33. Mary Douglas, *Natural Symbols: Explorations in Cosmology* (New York: Vintage, 1970), 178–79.

34. Gene Sharp, *The Politics of Nonviolent Action* (Boston: Porter Sargent, 1973), 4.

35. This is Ched Myers's evocative term for the ideological struggle that engages Jesus and the Judean authorities (*Binding the Strong Man*, 14–21). This struggle is also a part of the narrator's engagement with the reader.

## Chapter Five: Jesus and His Disciples

1. See, for example, Wilfred Harrington, *Mark* (Wilmington, Del.: Glazier, 1991), xviii–xx; Paul Achtemeier, *Mark* (Philadelphia: Fortress, 1986), 59; or Augustine Stock, *Call to Discipleship* (Wilmington, Del.: Glazier, 1982), 135.

2. Examples of this tradition in specific relation to Mark's Gospel would be Norman Perrin, *A Modern Pilgrimage in New Testament Christology* (Philadelphia: Fortress, 1974), and Jack Dean Kingsbury, *The Christology of Mark's Gospel* (Philadelphia: Fortress, 1983). Although these two authors are on opposite sides of a debate about "corrective Christology," they share a common exegetical method.

3. Jack Dean Kingsbury, *Conflict in Mark: Jesus, Authorities, Disciples* (Minneapolis: Fortress Press, 1989), 29. This would agree with my conclusions. However, instead of concluding that two conflicts indicate two plots, the main plot and the subplot, Kingsbury moves away from the conflicts themselves to focus his attention on the parties involved. This allows him to discern three stories, one each for Jesus, for the authorities, and for the disciples. A closer look, however, shows that Kingsbury is not as far from my position as this turn of thought would suggest. His second and third stories are the same as the main plot and subplot as I have determined them. His departure from my approach is to be found in his story of Jesus. Here narrative does not provide the setting for the titles so much as it dissolves itself into the series. Narrative movement is seen as progressive disclosure of truth.

4. For example, Harrington, *Mark*, 8; D. E. Nineham, *Saint Mark* (London: Penguin, 1963), 62.

5. Robert Tannehill, "The Gospel of Mark as Narrative Christology," *Semeia* 16 (1979): 60.

6. I will take particular advantage of two studies: Richard Horsley and John S. Hanson, *Bandits, Prophets, and Messiahs: Popular Movements at the Time of Jesus* (San Francisco: Harper and Row, 1985), and John E. Stambaugh and David L. Balch, *The New Testament in Its Social Environment* (Philadelphia: Westminster, 1986).

7. Horsley and Hanson, *Bandits*, 110.

8. Ibid., 117.

9. Horsley points to the signs in the Gospel texts that suggest the arrival of the messianic kingdom. In his view there are primarily two of these: the banqueting, which was equated with his group; and the relief given to the sick and demon-possessed. As regards the feasting, he notes that the wider Synoptic tradition witnesses to Jesus' reputation for eating and drinking. This apparently was distinctive enough to be an identifying characteristic. In addition, the early church would seem to have continued the practice and the reputation. The festive meals that grew into the Eucharist cannot adequately be explained except as a continuation of Jesus' practice. The evidence "makes it clear that Jesus' festive 'eating and drinking' was a present celebration of the banquet of the kingdom,

the consummation of which he referred to in the saying about many coming from east and west to sit at table with Abraham, Isaac, and Jacob (Matthew 8:11 and parallels)" (Richard Horsley, *Jesus and the Spiral of Violence: Popular Jewish Resistance in Roman Palestine* [San Francisco: Harper and Row, 1987], 179). The feeding stories also pertain. The two great events in Mk 6:30–44 and 8:1–10 are "to be understood as portrayals of how God was finally feeding the people with miraculous abundance despite appearances of paucity" (ibid.). In Mark's narrative these two events are named in the flurry of questions Jesus directs at the disciples during the last boat crossing (8:14–21), in what I have called a "quiz." It moves the first half toward its conclusion.

The other main indication of the kingdom already arrived was the personal restoration of people's lives in healings and exorcisms. More than any particular cure story, it is Jesus' general reputation as a healer and exorcist that is historically grounded. Viewing the individual stories as types, Horsley notes how they conform to the categories that would be caused by social stress — "fever, lameness or paralysis, consumption, hemorrhage, deafness and dumbness, blindness, epilepsy, deformity, and dropsy." These were the problems commonly dealt with by the prophet-healers of the day. In fact, the activities of Jesus that give evidence of the kingdom-made-present are the same activities that provided us with the bodily symbols of mouth and hand, namely, the cures and meals. In Mark 2 debates about the disciples' feasting contrasted them with the feasting Pharisees, and this had followed a series of cures in which Jesus' activity was seen in the powerful word, overcoming his opponents' silence. The word and the meals indicate the power of the kingdom at work, and the power is of the Holy Spirit. The feeding stories participate in this symbolism insofar as they are parallel to the parables in chapter 4, similarly harnessed to lake crossings. The parables are the seed of the word, while the feedings are the loaves of the messianic teaching and care.

10. See Peter Berger and Thomas Luckmann, *The Social Construction of Reality: A Treatise in the Sociology of Knowledge* (Garden City, N.Y.: Doubleday, 1966), 108: "The appearance of an alternative symbolic universe poses a threat because its very existence demonstrates empirically that one's own universe is less than inevitable.... This shocking fact must be accounted for theoretically, if nothing more. Of course it may also happen that the alternative universe has missionary appeal. Individuals or groups within one's own society might be tempted to 'emigrate' from the traditional universe or, even more serious a danger, to change the old in the image of the new."

11. Elizabeth Janeway, *Powers of the Weak* (New York: Morrow Quill, 1981), 81–82.

12. See Stambaugh and Balch, *New Testament*, 113. We do know that slaves were, in general, at the bottom of the social hierarchy and that the Greek philosophers rated slaves as less than human because they were committed to manual labor. Roman law viewed them as property. We also notice the vast range of conditions within slavery itself — from the "chattel gangs on ships, farms, road construction, or mining," who were treated as commodities, through the foreman slaves delegated with managing family businesses, to the household slaves who were entrusted with educating the children and who had legal rights to make contracts, owned their own property, and were treated as family members. It would seem that slavery was so integral to the workings of pretechnical

societies that civilization without it was inconceivable for those societies. But the "ambivalent position" of slaves suggests their social position was not simply that of the lowest legal status, but also it stood in some ways as a parallel, lateral society. Of course, that would increase any social threat they represented — as an "alien" presence they would need strict controls.

13. A parallelism governs the teachings that follow the three passion predictions in chapters 8–10 of Mark, connecting the first, featuring Peter, and the third, featuring James and John. Involved in the parallelism are key symbols for the respective teachings — for Peter, the *cross* (8:34); for James and John, the *servant/slave* (10:44–45). Thus the two symbols are linked in Mark's text.

14. Part of the public ritual of crucifixion was for the prisoner to carry his own cross — apparently the crossbar — to the site of execution. One can see this as a gesture of power on the part of Rome. The rebel is forced not only to submit but to cooperate in his own punishment as a demonstration of submission. At the same time, one can imagine it becoming on the part of rebel groups a symbol of defiant resistance against the oppressive regime, turning it into a badge of honor. For instance, S. G. F. Brandon (*Jesus and the Zealots: A Study of the Political Factor in Primitive Christianity* [New York: Scribner's, 1967], 57) has suggested that "taking up the cross" may originally have a been phrase used in recruiting Jewish insurgents on the part of groups regularly crucified for their guerrilla activities. "Join us in our cause," it would imply, "and have a cross prepared with your name on it. Be proud of that response by imperialist Rome. It means we are threatening it." This may offer a precedent for certain aspects of crucifixion language in the Gospel. In Mk 8:24, Jesus informs Peter that the follower should live by three imperatives:

> deny yourself
> take up your cross
> follow me

Mark may be exploiting rebel traditions, for the linguistic situation is parallel.

15. Myers, *Binding the Strong Man,* 279.

16. Stambaugh and Balch, *New Testament,* 115.

17. See Roland De Vaux, *Studies in Old Testament Sacrifice* (Cardiff: University of Wales Press, 1964); Frances M. Young, *Sacrifice and the Death of Christ* (Philadelphia: Westminster, 1975); and Robert J. Daly, *The Origins of the Christian Doctrine of Sacrifice* (Philadelphia: Fortress, 1978), 55–56. The issue is the problematic notion that the sacrificial victim takes the place of the worshiper. De Vaux (*Studies,* 90–98) insists there is nothing of substitution in the Old Testament sin-offering (*asham*), which is at the basis of much of this thinking, but rather the blood itself is seen to expiate sin by the life it is thought to be. Young echoes this sentiment in her study (*Sacrifice,* 28ff.). Daly (*Origins,* 25–35) goes further and attempts to account for the lapse into substitutionary thinking, which he notes is the basis of Anselm's theory of the sacrificial death of Christ. He cites the influences of the Passover, Isa 53:10–12, martyrdom theories in both the Jewish and Christian traditions, and Lev 17:11, as translated by the Septuagint.

18. Gene Sharp, *The Politics of Nonviolent Action* (Boston: Porter Sargent, 1973), 452.

19. David Rhoads and Donald Michie, *Mark as Story: An Introduction to the Narrative of a Gospel* (Philadelphia: Fortress, 1982), 73, 101.

20. C. Hugh Holman and William Harmon, *A Handbook to Literature*, 6th ed. (New York: Macmillan, 1992), 462.

21. James M. Robinson, *The Problem of History in Mark* (London: SCM, 1957). The apocalyptic aspect of this Gospel is prominent enough to prompt critics to claim it as the primary genre of the Gospel; see, for example, Howard Clark Kee, *Community of the New Age: Studies in Mark's Gospel* (Philadelphia: Westminster, 1977), 63–93; Norman Perrin and Dennis C. Duling, *The New Testament: An Introduction,* 2d ed. (New York: Harcourt, Brace, Jovanovich, 1982), 237–39.

22. Rhoads and Michie, *Mark as Story,* 77.

23. Sam Smiley, *Playwriting: The Structure of Action* (Englewood Cliffs, N.J.: Prentice-Hall, 1971), 57.

24. Harrington, *Mark,* 123. See also Stock, *Call to Discipleship,* 28, and Gilbert G. Bilezikian, *The Liberated Gospel: A Comparison of the Gospel of Mark and Greek Tragedy* (Grand Rapids: Baker, 1977), 76–78, for literary versions of this pervasive view.

25. Harrington, *Mark,* 2. The traditional title, "The Gospel according to Mark," is not part of the original text. The final phrase of the opening verse, "the Son of God," is omitted in some early manuscripts but is present in others, so its authenticity is disputed. Apart from this its narrative value is clear.

26. The final position of this verse is especially apparent if we remember that 15:42–16:8 forms the second member of the bracketing pair that frame the passion account, or falling action of the plot. In this understanding, Mk 14:1–11 stands as the opening member and first anointing sequence. Mark 15:42 begins the second anointing sequence. The centurion's words are nearly the last ones apart from this bracket.

## Chapter Six: The Agon and Nonviolent Plot Resolution

1. Louis L'Amour, *The Empty Land* (New York: Bantam, 1988), 159.

2. Richard Horsley, *Jesus and the Spiral of Violence: Popular Jewish Resistance in Roman Palestine* (San Francisco: Harper and Row, 1987).

3. Ibid., 22–28.

4. Ibid., 29–58.

5. Ibid., 34.

6. Ibid., 49.

7. Gene Sharp, *The Politics of Nonviolent Action* (Cambridge, Mass.: Harvard University Press, 1973), vol. 3, pt. 3.

8. Ibid., 451–520, esp. 452–53.

9. Ibid., 521–71, esp. 535, 537–47.

10. Ibid., 573–655, esp. 587–97.

11. Horsley, *Jesus,* 99.

12. Richard Horsley and John S. Hanson, *Bandits, Prophets, and Messiahs: Popular Movements at the Time of Jesus* (San Francisco: Harper and Row, 1985), 38–39, quoting Josephus, *Jewish Wars* 2.169–74.

13. The cleansing of the temple is commonly cited as evidence that Jesus acted with violence. If this were true, of course, it would vitiate any notion of this being the climactic moment of nonviolent confrontation. Against this popular view, certain points need to be made. First, the theories of Jesus' violence almost always invoke the "whip of cords" mentioned in Jn 2:15, a separate, non-Synoptic tradition. In John the cleansing does not occur at the climactic moment of the narrative; other redactional purposes are at work. Second, Mark's conception of the action is unmistakably prophetic, which is to say the events are intended to be seen in the tradition of the dramatic word of judgment (Jer 19:1; 20:5; 27:1–22; etc.).

In the narrative segment surrounding the temple action (Mark 11:1–12:12) (bracketed by the pericopes featuring Psalm 118, the "tabernacles" processional hymn [Mk 11:9; 12:10–11]), the following prophetic texts are cited or alluded to: Zec 14:4, 16 (Mk 11:1ff.); Zec 9:9 (Mk 11:7, 10); Zec 14:21 (Mk 11:15); Isa 56:7 and Jer 7:11 (Mk 11:17); Jer 8:13 (esp. Masoretic text) and parallels (Mk 11:20–21); and Isa 5:1–7 (Mk 12:1–10). These texts focus on two themes — the final ingathering of the nations into Jerusalem and the prophetic judgment of the city and the temple. Presumably Mark intends a fruitful combination of the two themes.

14. Although I have not developed it in these pages, the "eyes and ears" motif in the central part of Mark's text represents an extension of the body symbolism in the narration, taking it beyond "mouth" and "hand." The closed eyes and ears characterize the disciples' conflict with Jesus in the subplot and align their failure with the intransigence of the Judean authorities. A fuller treatment of this symbolism would include its relation to the last four healing stories, involving blindness (8:22–26; 10:46–52) and deafness (7:31–37; 9:14–29), and their background in the prophetic literature. Thus the deaf-mute in Mk 7:32 relates to Isa 35:5, and the strategic prophetic citations at Mk 4:11, 7:6–7, and 8:18 set the motif in the framework of prophetic traditions.

15. K. H. Rengsdorf, "Lestes," in *Theological Dictionary of the New Testament* (Grand Rapids: Eerdmans, 1967), 4:257–58.

16. The garden can be the scene of both the second moment of repression and the third moment of nonretaliation because isolating special narrative scenes to represent different moments in the dialectic of interaction is artificial, although it is an artifice of the narrative itself. In fact, the actions of confrontation, repression, and nonretaliation undergo narrative development. The developments are interrelated in the same dialectical interaction and culminate in the special "moments." As Jesus' building confrontation peaks at the temple action, the repression takes serious shape (Mk 11:18). When the repression moves into overt action in the garden arrest, the nonretaliatory response begins, to culminate at the cross.

17. Horsley, *Jesus,* 307–8.

18. Donald Juel, *Messiah and Temple: The Trial of Jesus in the Gospel of Mark,* Society of Biblical Literature Dissertation series, no. 31 (Missoula, Mont.: Scholars Press, 1977), 47.

19. For a review of the issues involved in the shorter and longer endings, D. E. Nineham, *Saint Mark* (London: Penguin, 1963), 439ff., is nicely comprehensive without being overwhelming.

20. This bracket was seen earlier as part of a sandwiched pair: 14:1–2, 3–9, 10–11; and 15:42–47; 16:1, 28.

## Chapter Seven: Breaking the Myth of Violence

1. Elli Köngäs Maranda and Pierre Maranda, *Structural Models in Folklore and Transformational Essays* (The Hague: Mouton, 1971), 24–35.
2. As an example, a discussion of the Marandas' use of the Lévi-Strauss formula and application to the biblical book of Job can be found in Robert M. Polzin, *Biblical Structuralism: Method and Subjectivity in the Study of Ancient Texts* (Philadelphia: Fortress, 1977), 74–83.
3. Claude Lévi-Strauss, "The Structural Study of Myth," in *Structural Anthropology* (New York: Basic Books, 1963), 1:228.
4. The masculine pronouns in this pattern reflect the agon as discussed in chapter 1, with its distinct slots for male and female roles.
5. Maranda and Maranda, *Structural Models,* 26–27. The Marandas include a footnote on the ability of the hero (the mediator) to assume the negative function: "The negative function of the mediator is his negative action against the negative force and is thus to be considered positive, that is, as specified by the same function as the first term, the mediator cancels out the first term's action." (26, n. 23).
6. See, for example, D. E. Nineham, *Saint Mark* (London: Penguin, 1963), 100.
7. Merton, *Faith and Violence* (Notre Dame, Ind.: University of Notre Dame Press, 1968), 23. As for Muste's aphorism, see John Howard Yoder, *Nevertheless: A Meditation on the Varieties and Shortcomings of Religious Pacifism* (Scottsdale, Pa.: Herald Press, 1971), 68.
8. This text is disputed. But as Bruce Metzger (*A Textual Commentary on the Greek New Testament* [United Bible Societies, 1971], 180) points out: "At the same time, the logion, though probably not a part of the original Gospel of Luke, bears self-evident tokens of its dominical origin." The central place of forgiveness in the meaning of Jesus' life and work is recognized by placing the text at this point of the narrative when the impulse to forgive would receive its most severe test. Without the reality it expresses, Jesus' teaching on unconditional forgiveness would seem empty indeed. Luke 23:34 makes the claim that forgiveness dominated the whole of Jesus' activity. The claim made here is parallel: forgiveness is Jesus' final word, directed toward those who were instrumental in bringing about his final moment. The resurrection appearances perform a similar function for the disciples. To those last seen fleeing the confrontation in the garden, Jesus says, "Peace be with you!" (Jn 20:19, 21, 26).
9. Merton, *Faith and Violence,* 19.
10. Rebecca West, *Black Lamb and Grey Falcon: A Journey through Yugoslavia* (New York: Viking, 1941), 824, 826.
11. Ibid., 827; emphasis added.
12. Ibid., 910.
13. Ibid., 911.
14. Fernando Belo, *A Materialist Reading of the Gospel of Mark,* trans. Matthew J. O'Connell (Maryknoll, N.Y.: Orbis, 1975), 39.

15. Ibid., 50.

16. Ibid., 48.

17. Ibid., 44.

18. Walter Brueggemann, *Living toward a Vision: Biblical Reflections on Shalom* (Philadelphia: United Church Press, 1976), 15: Brueggemann's translation.

19. For the text of the passage, see n. 24 to ch. 3, above.

20. Brueggemann, *Living toward a Vision,* 105.

21. Ibid., 106–7.

22. Georges Casalis, *Correct Ideas Don't Fall from the Skies: Elements for an Inductive Theology,* trans. Jeanne Marie Lyons and Michael John (Maryknoll, N.Y.: Orbis, 1984), 3.

23. Joan Bondurant, *The Conquest of Violence: The Gandhian Philosophy of Conflict* (Berkeley: University of California Press, 1965), 26–29.

## Epilogue

1. Peter Berger and Thomas Luckmann, *The Social Construction of Reality: A Treatise in the Sociology of Knowledge* (Garden City, N.Y.: Doubleday, 1966), 109.

2. René Girard, *Violence and the Sacred,* trans. Patrick Gregory (Baltimore: Johns Hopkins University Press, 1977), 4.

## Appendix A: Exegetical Outlines

1. Eduard Schweizer, "Mark's Contribution to the Quest of the Historical Jesus," *New Testament Studies* 10 (1964): 421–32; Norman Perrin and Dennis C. Duling, *The New Testament: An Introduction,* 2d ed. (New York: Harcourt, Brace, Jovanovich, 1982), 244–47.

2. To name three: Wilfred Harrington, *Mark* (Collegeville, Minn.: Liturgical Press, 1991), 1; Edward J. Mally, "The Gospel according to Mark," in *Jerome Biblical Commentary,* 1st ed. (Englewood Cliffs, N.J.: Prentice-Hall, 1968), 23–24; Daniel Harrington, "The Gospel according to Mark," in *New Jerome Biblical Commentary* (Englewood Cliffs, N.J.: Prentice-Hall, 1990), 598.

3. Gilbert G. Bilezikian, *The Liberated Gospel: A Comparison of the Gospel of Mark and Greek Tragedy* (Grand Rapids: Baker, 1977).

## Appendix B: Narrative Transformations

1. Tzvetan Todorov, *The Poetics of Prose,* Richard Howard, trans. (Ithaca, N.Y.: Cornell University Press, 1977), 108ff.

2. Ibid., 111.

3. Ibid., 232.

4. Todorov lists six examples of "simple" transformation and six examples of "complex" transformation. The sixth form of simple transformation, that of status, seems most pertinent to my purposes. Of this Todorov (ibid., 227–28)

says: "Taking the term 'status' in Whorf's sense, we may thus designate the re-placement of the positive form of a predicate by the negative form or by the contrary form. As we know, English expresses negation by 'not,' and opposition by a lexical substitution. This group of transformations was already pointed out, very briefly, by Propp; it is the same type of operation that Lévi-Strauss in par-ticular refers to when he speaks of transformations ('we may treat "violation" as the converse of "prohibition," and the latter as a negative transformation of "injunction"'); he is followed by Greimas, who relies on the logical models described by Brøndal and Blanché."

## *Appendix C: Jesus as Prophet — Notes on the Temple Action*

1. The initial week is discussed in some detail in ch. 4. The calendar notices in Mark's final week are found at Mk 11:12, 20; 14:1, 12; 15:1; 16:1, 2.

2. For example, Augustine Stock, *Call to Discipleship* (Wilmington, Del.: Glazier, 1982), 164.

## *Appendix D: The Story Formula*

1. Elli Köngäs Maranda and Pierre Maranda, *Structural Models in Folklore and Transformational Essays* (The Hague: Mouton, 1971), 24–35.

2. Ibid., 26.

3. Ibid., 28.

4. Ibid., 26–27.

5. In the actual formulation, the function is $(a\text{-}1)$, indicating the excess of negation that generates the further cycles of the narrative impulse. While this is extremely important in the patterns studied by Lévi-Strauss and the Marandas, it is excessively confusing for our purposes.

# Bibliography

Achtemeier, Paul J. *Mark*. Philadelphia: Fortress, 1986.

Arendt, Hannah. *Between Past and Future: Eight Exercises in Political Thought.* New York: Viking, 1961.

———. *On Violence.* New York: Harcourt, Brace and World, 1969.

Aristotle. *The Basic Works.* Edited by Richard McKeon. New York: Random House, 1941.

Aune, David E. *The New Testament in Its Literary Environment.* Philadelphia: Westminster, 1987.

———, ed. *Greco-Roman Literature and the New Testament: Selected Forms and Genres.* Atlanta: Scholars Press, 1988.

Bailey, James L., and Lyle D. Vander Broek. *Literary Forms in the New Testament: A Handbook.* Louisville: Westminster John Knox, 1992.

Barthes, Roland. *Mythologies.* New York: Hill and Wang, 1975.

Beardslee, William A. *Literary Criticism of the New Testament.* Philadelphia: Fortress, 1970.

Belo, Fernando. *A Materialist Reading of the Gospel of Mark.* Translated by Matthew J. O'Connell. Maryknoll, N.Y.: Orbis, 1975.

Berger, Peter, and Thomas Luckmann. *The Social Construction of Reality: A Treatise in the Sociology of Knowledge.* Garden City, N.Y.: Doubleday, 1966.

Best, Ernest. *Mark: The Gospel as Story.* Edinburgh: T and T Clark, 1983.

Bilezikian, Gilbert G. *The Liberated Gospel: A Comparison of the Gospel of Mark and Greek Tragedy.* Grand Rapids: Baker, 1977.

Bondurant, Joan. *The Conquest of Violence: The Gandhian Philosophy of Conflict.* Berkeley: University of California Press, 1965.

Booth, Wayne. *The Rhetoric of Fiction.* Chicago: University of Chicago Press, 1961.

Boucher, Madeleine I. *The Parables.* Wilmington, Del.: Glazier, 1983.

Brandon, S. G. F. *Jesus and the Zealots: A Study of the Political Factor in Primitive Christianity.* New York: Scribner's, 1967.

Brown, Raymond E. *The Critical Meaning of the Bible.* New York: Paulist, 1981.

Brueggemann, Walter. *Living toward a Vision: Biblical Reflections on Shalom.* Philadelphia: United Church Press, 1976.

Casalis, Georges. *Correct Ideas Don't Fall from the Skies: Elements for an Inductive Theology.* Translated by Jeanne Marie Lyons and Michael John. Maryknoll, N.Y.: Orbis, 1984.

Castelli, Jim. *The Bishops and the Bomb: Waging Peace in a Nuclear Age.* Garden City, N.Y.: Doubleday, 1983.

Chatman, Seymour. *Story and Discourse: Narrative Structure in Fiction and Film.* Ithaca, N.Y.: Cornell University Press, 1978.

Crites, Stephen. "The Narrative Quality of Experience." In *Why Narrative? Readings in Narrative Theology.* Edited by Stanley Hauerwas and L. Gregory Jones. Grand Rapids: Eerdmans, 1989.

Crossan, John Dominic. *In Parables.* San Francisco: Harper and Row, 1973.

———. *The Dark Interval.* Sonoma, Calif.: Polebridge, 1988.

Culler, Jonathan. *Structuralist Poetics: Structuralism, Linguistics, and the Study of Literature.* Ithaca, N.Y.: Cornell University Press, 1975.

———. *The Pursuit of Signs: Semiotics, Literature, Deconstruction.* Ithaca, N.Y.: Cornell University Press, 1981.

Daly, Robert J. *The Origins of the Christian Doctrine of Sacrifice.* Philadelphia: Fortress, 1978.

Davies, J. G. *Christians, Politics, and Violent Revolution.* Maryknoll, N.Y.: Orbis, 1976.

De Vaux, Roland. *Studies in Old Testament Sacrifice.* Cardiff: University of Wales Press, 1964.

Douglas, Mary. *Natural Symbols: Explorations in Cosmology.* New York: Vintage, 1970.

———. *Purity and Danger: An Analysis of Concepts of Pollution and Taboo.* London: Routledge and Kegan Paul, 1966.

Doyle, Arthur Conan. "The Five Orange Pips." In *The Complete Sherlock Holmes.* Garden City, N.Y.: Doubleday, 1938.

Dubrow, Heather. *Genre.* London and New York: Methuen, 1982.

Fowler, Robert M. *Let the Reader Understand: Reader-Response Criticism and the Gospel of Mark.* Minneapolis: Fortress, 1991.

Freyne, Sean. *The World of the New Testament.* Wilmington, Del.: Glazier, 1983.

Gandhi, Mohandas K. *Gandhi on Non-violence: Selected Texts from Mohandas K. Gandhi's "Non-violence in Peace and War."* Edited by Thomas Merton. New York: New Directions, 1964.

Genette, Gérard. *Narrative Discourse: An Essay in Method.* Translated by Jane E. Lewin. Ithaca, N.Y.: Cornell University Press, 1980.

Gregg, Richard B. *The Power of Nonviolence.* New York: Schocken, 1960.

Harrington, Daniel. "The Gospel according to Mark." In *Jerome Biblical Commentary.* 2d ed. Englewood Cliffs, N.J.: Prentice-Hall, 1990.

Harrington, Wilfred. *Mark.* Wilmington, Del.: Glazier, 1979.

Heil, John Paul. *The Gospel of Mark as a Model for Action: A Reader-Response Commentary.* New York: Paulist, 1992.

Hengel, Martin. *Was Jesus a Revolutionist?* Translated by William Klassen. Philadelphia: Fortress, 1971.

Holman, C. Hugh, and William Harmon. *A Handbook to Literature.* 6th ed. New York: Macmillan, 1992.

Horsley, Richard. *Jesus and the Spiral of Violence: Popular Jewish Resistance in Roman Palestine.* San Francisco: Harper and Row, 1987.

Horsley, Richard, and John S. Hanson. *Bandits, Prophets, and Messiahs: Popular Movements at the Time of Jesus.* San Francisco: Harper and Row, 1985.

Janeway, Elizabeth. *Powers of the Weak.* New York: Morrow Quill, 1981.

Jewett, Robert. *The Captain America Complex: The Dilemma of Zealous Nationalism.* Philadelphia: Westminster, 1973.

Juel, Donald. *Messiah and Temple: The Trial of Jesus in the Gospel of Mark.* Society of Biblical Literature Dissertation series, no. 31. Missoula, Mont.: Scholars Press, 1977.

Kähler, Martin. *The So-Called Historical Jesus and the Historic Biblical Christ.* Philadelphia: Fortress, 1964.

Kelber, Werner H. *The Oral and the Written Gospel: The Hermeneutics of Speaking and Writing in the Synoptic Tradition, Mark, Paul, and Q.* Philadelphia: Fortress, 1983.

Kermode, Frank. *The Genesis of Secrecy.* Cambridge, Mass.: Harvard University Press, 1979.

King, Martin Luther, Jr. *Letter to the Birmingham City Jail.* Philadelphia: American Friends Service Committee, 1963.

Kingsbury, Jack Dean. *Conflict in Mark: Jesus, Authorities, Disciples.* Minneapolis: Fortress, 1989.

———. *The Christology of Mark's Gospel.* Philadelphia: Fortress, 1983.

L'Amour, Louis. *The Empty Land.* New York: Bantam, 1969.

———. *Jubal Sackett.* New York: Bantam, 1985.

———. *Riding for the Brand.* New York: Bantam, 1986.

———. *The Sackett Companion: A Personal Guide to the Sackett Novels.* New York: Bantam, 1988.

Lévi-Strauss, Claude. "The Structural Study of Myth." In *Structural Anthropology.* Vol 1. New York: Basic Books, 1963.

Lodge, David. *After Bakhtin: Essays on Fiction and Criticism.* London: Routledge, 1990.

———. *Working with Structuralism: Essays and Reviews on Nineteenth- and Twentieth-Century Literature.* London: Routledge and Kegan, 1981.

Lyons, John. *Chomsky.* London: Fontana, 1974.

Malbon, Elizabeth Struthers. "The Jewish Leaders in the Gospel of Mark: A Literary Study of Marcan Characterization." *Journal of Biblical Literature* 108, no. 2 (summer 1989): 259–81.

———. "Narrative Criticism: How Does the Story Mean?" In *Mark and Method: New Approaches in Biblical Studies.* Edited by Janice Capel Anderson and Stephen D. Moore. Minneapolis: Fortress, 1992.

———. *Narrative Space and Mythic Meaning in Mark.* San Francisco: Harper and Row, 1986.

Malina, Bruce J. *The New Testament World: Insights from Cultural Anthropology.* Atlanta: John Knox, 1981.

Mally, Edward J. "The Gospel according to Mark." In *Jerome Biblical Commentary.* 1st ed. Englewood Cliffs, N.J.: Prentice-Hall, 1968.

Mangel, Anne. "Maxwell, Demon, Entropy, Information." In *Mindful Pleasures: Essays on Thomas Pynchon.* Edited by George Levine and David Leverenz. Boston: Little, Brown and Co., 1976.

Mannheim, Karl. *Ideology and Utopia: An Introduction to the Sociology of Knowledge.* Translated by Louis Wirth and Edward Shils. New York: Harcourt, Brace and World, 1936.

Maranda, Elli Köngäs, and Pierre Maranda. *Structural Models in Folklore and Transformational Essays.* The Hague: Mouton, 1971.

McKenzie, John L. *Dictionary of the Bible*. Milwaukee: Bruce, 1965.

Merton, Thomas. *Faith and Violence*. Notre Dame, Ind.: University of Notre Dame Press, 1968.

Metzger, Bruce. *A Textual Commentary on the Greek New Testament*. United Bible Societies, 1971.

Moore, Stephen D. *Literary Criticism and the Gospels: The Theoretical Challenge*. New Haven: Yale University Press, 1989.

Muecke, D. C. *Irony and the Ironic*. London: Methuen, 1982.

Myers, Ched. *Binding the Strong Man: A Political Reading of Mark's Story of Jesus*. Maryknoll, N.Y.: Orbis, 1988.

National Conference of Catholic Bishops. *The Challenge of Peace: God's Promise and Our Response: A Pastoral Letter on War and Peace*. Washington, D.C.: United States Catholic Conference, 1983.

Neirynck, Frans. *Duality in Mark: Contributions to the Study of the Markan Redaction*. Leuven: Leuven University Press, 1972.

Neyrey, Jerome H. "The Idea of Purity in Mark's Gospel." *Semeia* 35 (1986): 91–128.

Niebuhr, Reinhold. *An Interpretation of Christian Ethics*. New York: Seabury, 1979.

———. "Why the Christian Church Is Not Pacifist." In *Christianity and Power Politics*. New York: Scribner's, 1940.

Nineham, D. E. *Saint Mark*. London: Penguin, 1963.

Ong, Walter J. *Orality and Literacy*. London and New York: Methuen, 1982.

Paul, Robert S. *Whatever Happened to Sherlock Holmes? Detective Fiction, Popular Theology, and Society*. Carbondale: Southern Illinois University Press, 1991.

Perrin, Norman. *A Modern Pilgrimage in New Testament Christology*. Philadelphia: Fortress, 1974.

Petersen, Norman R. "The Composition of Mark 4:1–8:26." *Harvard Theological Review* 73 (1980): 186–87.

———. *Literary Criticism for New Testament Critics*. Philadelphia: Fortress, 1978.

———. " 'Point of View' in Mark's Narrative." *Semeia* 12 (1978): 97–121.

Pilch, John. "Healing in Mark: A Social Science Analysis." *Biblical Theology Bulletin* 15, no. 4 (1985): 142ff.

Pixley, George. *God's Kingdom: A Guide for Biblical Study*. Maryknoll, N.Y.: Orbis, 1977.

Polzin, Robert M. *Biblical Structuralism: Method and Subjectivity in the Study of Ancient Texts*. Philadelphia: Fortress, 1977.

Prince, Gerald. *Narratology: The Form and Functioning of Narrative*. Berlin: Mouton, 1982.

Rengsdorf, K. H. "Lestes." In *Theological Dictionary of the New Testament*, 4:257–58. Grand Rapids: Eerdmans, 1967.

Rhoads, David, and Donald Michie. *Mark as Story: An Introduction to the Narrative of a Gospel*. Philadelphia: Fortress, 1982.

Ricoeur, Paul. *Time and Narrative*. Translated by Kathleen McLaughlin and David Pellauer. Chicago: University of Chicago, 1984.

Rimmon-Kenan, Shlomith. *Narrative Fiction: Contemporary Poetics*. London: Methuen 1983.

Robinson, James M. *The Problem of History in Mark.* London: SCM, 1957.

Scholes, Robert. *Structuralism in Literature: An Introduction.* New Haven: Yale University Press, 1974.

Schweizer, Eduard. "Mark's Contribution to the Quest of the Historical Jesus." *New Testament Studies* 10 (1964): 421–32.

Shannon, Claude E., and Warren Weaver. *The Mathematical Theory of Communication.* Urbana: University of Illinois Press, 1949.

Sharp, Gene. *The Politics of Nonviolent Action.* Boston: Porter Sargent, 1973.

Smiley, Sam. *Playwriting: The Structure of Action.* Englewood Cliffs, N.J.: Prentice-Hall, 1971.

Stambaugh, John E., and David L. Balch. *The New Testament in Its Social Environment.* Philadelphia: Westminster, 1986.

Standaert, Benot. *L'évangile selon Marc: Commentaire.* Paris: Cerf, 1983.

Stock, Augustine. *Call to Discipleship.* Wilmington, Del.: Glazier, 1982.

———. *The Method and Message of Mark.* Wilmington, Del.: Glazier, 1989.

Tannehill, Robert. "The Gospel of Mark as Narrative Christology." *Semeia* 16 (1979): 57–95.

Tilley, Terrence. *Theology of Story.* Collegeville, Minn.: Liturgical Press, 1985.

Todorov, Tzvetan. *Genres in Discourse.* Translated by Catherine Porter. Cambridge: Cambridge University Press, 1990.

———. *The Poetics of Prose.* Translated by Richard Howard. Ithaca, N.Y.: Cornell University Press, 1977.

Tolbert, Mary Ann. *Sowing the Gospel: Mark's World in Literary-Historical Perspective.* Minneapolis: Fortress, 1989.

Tuveson, Ernest Lee. *Redeemer Nation: The Idea of America's Millennial Role.* Chicago: University of Chicago Press, 1968.

Uspensky, Boris. *A Poetics of Composition: The Structure of the Artistic Text and Typology of a Compositional Form.* Translated by Valentina Zavarin and Susan Wittig. Berkeley: University of California Press, 1973.

Via, Dan O., Jr. *The Ethics of Mark's Gospel — In the Middle of Time.* Philadelphia: Fortress, 1985.

———. *Kerygma and Comedy in the New Testament: A Structuralist Approach to Hermeneutic.* Philadelphia: Fortress, 1975.

Waetjen, Herman C. *A Reordering of Power: A Socio-political Reading of Mark's Gospel.* Minneapolis: Fortress, 1989.

Weeden, Theodore J. *Traditions in Conflict.* Philadelphia: Fortress, 1971.

Weinberg, Robert. *The Louis L'Amour Companion.* New York: Bantam, 1994.

West, Rebecca. *Black Lamb and Grey Falcon: A Journey through Yugoslavia.* New York: Viking, 1941.

Wright, T. R. *Theology and Literature.* London: Blackwell, 1988.

Yoder, John Howard. *Nevertheless: The Varieties and Shortcomings of Religious Pacifism.* Scottdale, Pa.: Herald, 1971.

———. *The Politics of Jesus.* Grand Rapids: Eerdmans, 1972.

———. *When War Is Unjust: Being Honest in Just-War Thinking.* Minneapolis: Augsburg, 1984.

Young, Frances M. *Sacrifice and the Death of Christ.* Philadelphia: Westminster, 1975.

# SCRIPTURE INDEX

## HEBREW SCRIPTURES

**Genesis**

| | |
|---|---|
| 22 | 94 |

**Exodus**

| | |
|---|---|
| 22:20-26 | 179-80 n. 24 |
| 22:31 | 81 |

**Leviticus**

| | |
|---|---|
| 13-14 | 77 |
| 15 | 77 |
| 15:31 | 77 |
| 26:4-6 | 145 |

**Psalms**

| | |
|---|---|
| 2:7 | 94, 96, 110 |
| 118 | 159-60 |
| 118:22-23 | 160, 162 |
| 118:25 | 162 |
| 118:26 | 159 |

**Isaiah**

| | |
|---|---|
| 5:1-7 | 162 |
| 15 | 161 |
| 35:5 | 188 n. 14 |
| 42:1 | 94, 110 |
| 42:1b | 96 |
| 56:1-8 | 84, 160, 162 |
| 56:7 | 82, 84, 120, 161, 162 |
| 66:21 | 163 |

**Jeremiah**

| | |
|---|---|
| 2:21 | 162 |
| 7 | 43 |
| 7:11 | 120, 161, 162 |
| 8:13 | 161, 162 |
| 26 | 43, 162 |

**Ezekiel**

| | |
|---|---|
| 19:10 | 162 |

**Hosea**

| | |
|---|---|
| 2:11-12 | 161, 162 |
| 9:15 | 162 |
| 9:15-16 | 161 |
| 9:16 | 162 |

**Zechariah**

| | |
|---|---|
| 9:9-10 | 56, 160, 162 |
| 14 | 160 |
| 14:4 | 162 |
| 14:16 | 162 |
| 14:21 | 161, 162 |

**2 Maccabees**

| | |
|---|---|
| 7 | 129 |

## NEW TESTAMENT

**Matthew**

| | |
|---|---|
| 2:1-12 | 55 |
| 12:15 | 52 |
| 20:29-34 | 55 |
| 26:52 | 126 |

**Mark**

| | |
|---|---|
| 1-2 | 124 |
| 1-13 | 44, 46, 47, 49 |
| 1:1 | 110, 111, 112, 113 |
| 1:1-13 | 154 |
| 1:2-8 | 45 |
| 1:8 | 70 |
| 1:9-11 | 45 |
| 1:11 | 94, 96, 109 |
| 1:14 | 45 |
| 1:14-15 | 155 |
| 1:14-3:6 | 51-52 |
| 1:14-3:12 | 154 |
| 1:15-17 | 74 |
| 1:16-20 | 95, 110, 155 |
| 1:21-28 | 47, 51, 58, 69, 123, 155, 158 |

**Mark (continued)**

| | |
|---|---|
| 1:22 | 73, 123 |
| 1:24 | 48, 51, 71, 155, 158 |
| 1:25 | 69 |
| 1:25–26 | 47 |
| 1:26 | 69 |
| 1:27 | 123 |
| 1:29–31 | 74, 78 |
| 1:32–33 | 72 |
| 1:41 | 74 |
| 1:45 | 72, 74, 102 |
| 2:1–3:6 | 47 |
| 2:2 | 72 |
| 2:7 | 73 |
| 2:9 | 73 |
| 2:10 | 123 |
| 2:15–17 | 79 |
| 2:16 | 74 |
| 2:21 | 123 |
| 2:22 | 123 |
| 2:26 | 123 |
| 3:1–6 | 51, 56, 73, 74, 155, 158 |
| 3:4 | 57, 123 |
| 3:6 | xv, 18, 48, 51, 57, 153, 155, 158 |
| 3:7–12 | 155 |
| 3:7–6:6 | 52–53 |
| 3:13–19 | 155 |
| 3:13–6:6a | 154 |
| 3:14 | 52, 53, 155 |
| 3:20–21 | 53 |
| 3:20–35 | 53, 155 |
| 3:27 | 69, 76 |
| 3:29 | 104 |
| 3:31–35 | 155 |
| 4:1–34 | 52, 97 |
| 4:11 | 188 n. 14 |
| 4:12 | 120 |
| 4:35–41 | 76 |
| 5:1–20 | 75, 76, 82 |
| 5:8 | 69 |
| 5:21–24 | 78 |
| 5:25–34 | 76 |
| 5:30 | 77 |
| 5:36–45 | 78 |
| 6:1–6 | 53, 75, 78 |
| 6:1–6a | 155 |
| 6:4 | 155 |
| 6:6a | 153 |
| 6:6b | 155 |
| 6:6b–8:30 | 154 |

| | |
|---|---|
| 6:7–13 | 155 |
| 6:7–8:30 | 54–55 |
| 6:14–16 | 54, 155 |
| 6:16 | 54 |
| 6:17–29 | 122, 155 |
| 6:30–44 | 185 n. 9 |
| 6:31–44 | 80 |
| 7:1–23 | 74, 79–80, 97, 181 n. 8 |
| 7:1–8:26 | 82 |
| 7:6–7 | 120, 188 n. 14 |
| 7:15–19 | 68 |
| 7:19 | 81 |
| 7:24–30 | 79, 80 |
| 7:27 | 81 |
| 7:31–37 | 70, 79, 80 |
| 7:32 | 188 n. 14 |
| 8:1–10 | 185 n. 9 |
| 8:1–11 | 80 |
| 8:12–21 | 185 n. 9 |
| 8:18 | 120, 188 n. 14 |
| 8:22–26 | 55, 70 |
| 8:24 | 186 n. 14 |
| 8:27–30 | 54, 105, 153, 155 |
| 8:27–33 | 98, 106 |
| 8:29 | 54, 95, 96, 110, 112 |
| 8:30 | 95 |
| 8:30/31 | 153 |
| 8:31 | 55, 110 |
| 8:31–33 | 95, 155 |
| 8:31–10:52 | 55–56, 154 |
| 8:32–33 | 95, 107 |
| 8:33 | 110 |
| 8:34 | 110 |
| 8:35 | 102 |
| 9:7 | 95, 96 |
| 9:12 | 54 |
| 9:30–31 | 55 |
| 9:35 | 96 |
| 10 | 153 |
| 10:33–34 | 55 |
| 10:35–40 | 45 |
| 10:43–44 | 96 |
| 10:44 | 100 |
| 10:45 | 93, 101, 102 |
| 10:46–52 | 55 |
| 11–13 | 121, 153 |
| 11:1 | 162 |
| 11:1–11 | 162 |
| 11:1–12:12 | 188 n. 13 |
| 11:1–13:37 | 57–58, 154 |
| 11:1–16:2 | 159 |

11:2 — 162
11:9 — 159, 162
11:10 — 58
11:11 — 58
11:12–14 — 84, 161, 162
11:13 — 162
11:14 — 82
11:15 — 47, 162
11:15–19 — 59, 105, 121, 123, 162
11:16 — 162
11:17 — xi, 84, 120, 161, 162
11:18 — 43, 48, 56, 57, 59, 122, 123, 188 n. 16,
11:20 — 123, 162
11:20–23 — 84
11:20–25 — 161
11:20–26 — 162
11:20–12:47 — 159
11:23 — 123, 161
11:23–26 — 84
11:27–33 — 123
12 — 43
12:1 — 162
12:1–9 — 123
12:1–12 — 161, 162
12:1–37 — 47
12:9 — 48, 59
12:10 — 162
12:10–11 — 160
12:12 — 159, 160
12:13–17 — 124
12:14 — 123
12:18–27 — 124
12:19 — 123
12:28 — 123
12:28–34 — 124
12:33 — 57, 125
12:34 — 125
13:2 — 59, 125
13:14 — 21–23, 35, 96
13:21–22 — 98
14 — 121
14–15 — 44
14–16 — 44, 46, 47, 49, 96
14:1–2 — 48
14:1–11 — 45, 48, 187 n. 26
14:1–16:8 — 60–62, 154
14:3 — 49

14:3–9 — 48, 49, 128
14:8 — 128
14:10 — 60
14:10–11 — 48
14:12–31 — 45
14:18 — 49
14:23 — 45
14:32–42 — 45
14:36 — 45
14:38 — 126
14:41–42 — 45
14:42 — 61
14:43–52 — 45, 121
14:47 — 126
14:48 — xi, 120–21
14:49 — 126
14:58 — 59
14:66–72 — 111
15 — 121
15:1 — 61
15:6–15 — 102
15:7 — 98
15:15 — 61
15:16–20 — 77
15:27 — xi, 121
15:27–32 — 121
15:29 — 59
15:38 — 84
15:39 — 111, 112, 120
15:42 — 187 n. 26
15:42–16:8 — 187 n. 26
15:42–16:18 — 48
15:43 — 60, 61
15:44 — 61
15:45 — 61
16:1 — 49, 128
16:8 — 127

**Luke**
22:51 — 126
23:34 — 138, 189 n. 8

**John**
2:15 — 188 n. 13
11 — 43
11:50 — 43
20:19 — 189 n. 8
20:21 — 189 n. 8
20:26 — 189 n. 8

# General Index

agon, the: defined, 4–6, 8; L'Amour and, xv; narrative and, 6–8, 130; narrative outlook and, 11; nonviolent action and, 117; nonviolent plot resolution and, 115–29; violent plot resolution and, 114
*Alexandria Quartet* (Durrell), 33
Americans with Disabilities Act of 1990, 86, 183 n. 28
antagonists. *See* villains
anti-Semitism, xiii
"apologues," 12
Arendt, Hannah, 182 n. 17
Aristotle, 32, 40, 177 n. 2

Bailey, James L., 25, 172 n. 9
Bailie, Gil, ix–x
Bar Kokhba rebellion, 97
Beardslee, William, 32, 174–75 n. 30
Belo, Fernando, 143–44, 182 n. 13
*Bendigo Shafter* (L'Amour), 1
Berger, Peter, 99, 149, 185 n. 10
Bilezikian, Gilbert G., 153
*Black Lamb and Grey Falcon* (West), 139–42
Booth, Wayne, 35
Brandon, S. G. F., 186 n. 14
Brueggemann, Walter, 145–46

Camara, Dom Helder, 115
Casalis, Georges, 147
*Catcher in the Rye* (Salinger), 33
Catholic Church: nonviolence and, 16–17. *See also The Challenge of Peace: God's Promise and Our Response*
Catholic Worker movement, 58
*Cat's Cradle* (Vonnegut), 64
*The Challenge of Peace: God's Promise and Our Response,* 16, 135, 150–51, 171 n. 22

Chatman, Seymour, 175 n. 35
Chomsky, Noam, 13, 28
Christian realism, 14–15, 39
christological titles, 93–94
Christology, 93, 99–103
civilizing violence, xiv, xv, 8–11
comedy, 31, 32
communication theory, 20–21, 171 n. 2
Conan Doyle, Arthur, 63–65
conflict: the agon and, 7–8; destruction and, 59; distinguishing levels of, in Mark, 103–6; imitation of Christ and, 106–8; narrative and, 17–18; the object of resolution of, 137; plot and, 36–38; terminology of, 47–48; two main instances of, in Mark, 93–94; violence contrasted with, xiv
constructive violence, 1–4, 149–50
Crites, Stephen, 6, 13–14, 130
Crossan, John Dominic, 12, 13, 38, 170 n. 13
crucifixion, 101, 115, 186 n. 14
*The Crying of Lot 49* (Pynchon), 20–21
Culler, Jonathan, 27, 28, 33, 175 n. 32
cures. *See* healings, Jesus'

Daly, Robert J., 186 n. 17
Davies, J. G., 15–16, 106, 107, 150
Day, Dorothy, 58
debt, 143–46
destruction, xiv, 47–48, 59, 78–79
De Vaux, Roland, 186 n. 17
dialogic structure, 6–7
disciples, the: Jesus' teaching and, 93–103, 109–13; the subplot of Mark and, 103–9; theories of power and, 151

202

discourse: story and, 32–36
disease: defined, 85–86
*Doctor Frankenstein* (Shelley), 64
Douglas, Mary, 66, 68, 69–70, 89,
    144, 181–82 n. 11, 183 n. 29
Durrell, Lawrence, 33

*The Empty Land* (L'Amour), 4, 8–9,
    10, 92, 114
ethnic cleansing, 140

"The Five Orange Pips" (Conan
    Doyle), 63
forgiveness, 189 n. 8
Fowler, Robert, 41, 172 n. 8
Freytag, Gustav, 42–43
fundamentalism, 173 n. 21

Gandhi, Mahatma, xiv, 14, 15, 16,
    148
genre theory, 24–32, 172 n. 9, 173
    n. 21, 174 n. 23
gentiles, the, 79–83
gift, 143–46
Girard, René, 149
*Godspell*, 45
Gulf War, the, x

*Hamlet* (Shakespeare) 46, 104, 177–
    78 n. 10
Hanson, John, 97
Harmon, William, 176 n. 38, 177–78
    n. 10
Harrington, Wilfred, 22, 80, 105, 172
    n. 4, 183 n. 23
healings, Jesus': faith/fear distinction
    and, 75–79; the gentiles and,
    79–82; holy/unclean distinction
    and, 69, 72–74; as precursors of
    the kingdom, 185 n. 9; as social
    metaphors, 85–91
heroes, 4, 10, 133–37, 166
historical criticism, 26–28
Holman, C. Hugh, 176 n. 38, 177–78
    n. 10
Holocaust, the, xiii
holy, the: Jesus' healings and the motif
    of, 79–82; power and the symbolic
    language of, 65–75; the temple

cleansing and the motif of, 83–85;
    the unclean and, 151. *See also*
    purity
Horsley, Richard, 88, 97, 98, 115,
    118–19, 124, 184–85 n. 9
*The Hound of the Baskervilles* (Conan
    Doyle), 64

ideology, x, 92, 169–70 n. 10, 180
    n. 25
illness: defined, 85–86
imitation of Christ, 14–15, 106–8,
    150
implied author, 35, 175 n. 35, 176
    n. 37
implied reader, 22, 27, 34–35, 96–97,
    175–76 n. 35
information theory. *See* communica-
    tion theory
innocence, 136–37, 139–43, 147–48
irony, 109–12, 127

James, Henry, 41
Janeway, Elizabeth, 100
Jesus: breaking the pattern of violence,
    137–39; christological titles of,
    109–12; complexity of characteri-
    zation of, 36–37; in the dramatic
    movement of Mark's plot, 50–62;
    family of, 37; healings of, 69, 75–
    82, 85–91, 185 n. 9; holy/unclean
    distinction and, 68–69, 70–75;
    misreadings of the story of, 142–
    43; nonviolence of, 15, 16–17,
    99–103, 120, 122–29, 150–51, 180
    n. 25; purity/pollution system chal-
    lenged by, 146; readers as followers
    of, 151–52; scholars' theories on
    violence of, 188 n. 13; structure of
    Mark's plot and, 43–50; teaching
    of, 93–103; teaching of, as subplot,
    103–9; teaching on forgiveness,
    189 n. 8; temple cleansing by,
    83–85, 159–63
Jewett, Robert, 170 n. 15
Jewish resistance groups, 118–19
Josephus, 118
*Jubal Sackett* (L'Amour), 3
Juel, Donald, 126

justice, 143–46. *See also* poetic justice
just-war theory, 6, 16, 148

Kermode, Frank, 26, 27, 28, 79, 173
n. 15
King, Martin Luther, Jr., xiv, 14
kingdom of God: gentiles and, 82, 83;
servant theme and, 100; shalom
and, 146; signs of the coming of
the, 184–85 n. 9
Kingsbury, Jack Dean, 93–94, 112,
184 n. 2, 184 n. 3

L'Amour, Louis: the agon in the
works of, 7; biographical notes
on, 1–4; civilizing violence and,
xv; Conan Doyle compared to, 64;
constructive violence in the works
of, 11–14; ideological component
of narratives of, 92; plot resolution
in the works of, 114; women and
civilizing violence in the works of,
8–11
*Lando* (L'Amour), 2
*lestes,* 120–21
Lévi-Strauss, Claude, 13, 132, 134,
164–67, 170 n. 13, 191 n. 5
literary criticism, 26–28, 172 n. 9,
174–75 n. 30
Luckmann, Thomas, 149, 185 n. 10
Lyons, John, 173 n. 18

Malbon, Elizabeth S., 181 n. 9
Malina, Bruce, 4–5, 24–25, 66
Mangel, Anne, 20–21
Mannheim, Karl, 170 n. 10
Maranda, Elli Köngäs, 131, 132, 133,
134, 135, 137, 164–67, 189 n. 5,
191 n. 5
Maranda, Pierre, 131, 132, 133, 134,
135, 137, 164–67, 189 n. 5, 191
n. 5
melodrama, 31
Merton, Thomas, 138
Messiah: christological lessons regarding the theme of, 96–98; Jesus as
servant and, 93–96, 103; power of,
127; as title, 110–12
Metzger, Bruce, 189 n. 8

Michie, Donald, 34, 36, 103–4, 176
n. 39
miracles. *See* healings, Jesus'
*Moby Dick* (Melville), 33
Moore, Stephen D., 175 n. 31, 175
n. 35
movies, x, 131–32, 133, 134
Muste, A. J., 138
Myers, Ched, 58, 85, 88, 89, 101, 184
n. 35
myth: constructive violence and, 1–4,
149–50; Jesus and the, of violence,
137–39; Lévi-Strauss's algebraic
formula regarding, 164–67; the
narrative quality of violence and,
11–14; violence and, 130–37

narrative: the agon and, 6–8; conflict
and, 17–18; experience and, 130;
the form of, 2–8; the Gospels and
popular, 30–32; grammar of, 157–
58; ideology and, 169–70 n. 10; as
legitimizing violence, x; Marandas's
theory of, 165–67; myth, violence,
and, 11–14; oral, 172 n. 8; types of,
33–34; violence in popular, 130–
37. *See also* narrative criticism;
narrative outlook
narrative criticism, 32–38, 175 n. 31
narrative outlook, xv, 8, 11
narratology, 175 n. 31
Native Americans, 170 n. 13
Neirynck, Frans, 41
Neyrey, Jerome, 66, 68
Niebuhr, Reinhold, 14–15, 39, 150
Nineham, D. E., 22, 49, 171–72 n. 4,
181 n. 8
nonretaliation, 117, 118, 121, 125–26
nonviolence: challenges to Christian,
14–16; the church and, 16–17;
correspondence of means and ends
in the theory of, 138; cultural bias
against, 131; definition of, xiii–xiv;
the Gospel refusals and, 137–39;
of Jesus, 15, 16–17, 99–103, 120,
122–29, 150–51, 180 n. 25; of
Jewish resistance groups, 118–19;
as a menace in L'Amour's works,
9–11; negation of, in some readings

of the Gospel, 142–43; primacy of love in the theory of, 138; theme of substitution and, 102. *See also* nonviolent action

nonviolent action: definition of, xiii–xiv; final stages of Jesus', 122–29; Jesus' healings and, 89–91; stages of, 116–19. *See also* nonviolence

omniscient narrator, 33–34
Ong, Walter, 42
oral narration, 172 n. 8
original readers, 28

parables, 12
Paul, Robert, 64
Perrin, Norman, 153, 184 n. 2
Petersen, Norman, 41
Pilate, Pontius, 118–19
Pilch, John, 85–86, 87
Pixley, George, 180 n. 25
plot: the agon and nonviolent resolution of, 114–29; blocking the action of Mark's, 43–50; conflict and, 36–38; a defense of Mark's, 40–41; defined, 35; distinguishing Mark's subplot from the main, 103–6; dramatic movement in Mark's, 50–62; the Marandas's theory of, 165–67
poetic justice, 134, 135–36, 148
*Poetics* (Aristotle), 32
point of view: the "balance model" and, 143; ideology and, 169–70 n. 10; L'Amour's, 8; narrative outlook and, 11; omniscient narrators and, 34; in popular narratives, 7
political violence, 6
pollution. *See* unclean, the
power: faith/fear distinction and Jesus', 75–79; Isaiah's image of, 99–100; Mark's language of, 65–75; theories of, 151
protagonists. *See* heroes
purity, 139, 146. *See also* holy, the
Pynchon, Thomas, 20

*Rambo*, x
reader-response theory, 35

readers: ancient texts and, 19–24; discipleship, the structure of irony, and, 109–13; genre theory, ancient texts, and, 24–32. *See also* implied reader; original readers; reader-response theory; real reader
Reagan, Ronald, 2, 3
real author, 175 n. 35
real reader, 27, 28, 35, 175 n. 35
redaction, 176 n. 37
redaction criticism, 173 n. 21
redemptive violence, xiv
resurrection stories, 128
revolution. *See* theology/ethics of revolution
*Rhetoric* (Aristotle), 32
Rhoads, David, 34, 36, 103–4, 176 n. 39
Ricoeur, Paul, 177 n. 2
ritual, 65–75, 142–43
Robinson, James, 104

*Sackett* (L'Amour), 9
*Sackett Companion* (L'Amour), 2
"Sackett" stories (L'Amour), 2–3, 9
sacrifice, x, 139–40, 186 n. 17
scapegoats, ix–x
Scholes, Robert, 23
Schott, Jan, 16
Schweizer, Eduard, 50, 105, 153–54
servant, Jesus as, 93–96, 99–103
Shakespeare, William, 35. See also *Hamlet* (Shakespeare)
shalom, 145–46
Shannon, Claude, 20, 23, 171 n. 2
Sharp, Gene, 29, 89, 102, 116–20, 123
Shelley, Mary, 64
slavery, 100–101, 185–86 n. 12
Smiley, Sam, 31
Soelle, Dorothee, xiii
soliloquy, 173 n. 17
Son of God: as title, 94, 110, 111–13
*The Sound and the Fury* (Faulkner), 33
spiral of violence, x, 115, 118
*Star Wars*, x, 131–32, 133
Stock, Augustine, 172 n. 8
story: defined, 35

subject/predicate reversal, 135
symmetry, 130–32, 143, 169 n. 8

television, 131
theology/ethics of revolution, 15–16,
    150
therapeutic violence, xiv
titles, christological, 93–94, 109–12
Todorov, Tzvetan, 28, 50–51, 157–58,
    190–91 n. 4
Tolbert, Mary Ann, 30–31, 173 n. 20,
    174 n. 23
tragedy, 31, 32
Twain, Mark, 176 n. 37

unclean, the: the holy and, 151; Jesus'
    challenge of the system based on
    purity and, 146; Jesus' healings and
    the motif of, 79–82; power and the
    symbolic language of, 65–75; the
    temple cleansing and the motif of,
    83–85
Uspensky, Boris, 34

Vander Broek, Lyle D., 25, 172 n. 9
Via, Dan O., Jr., 174 n. 25
villains, 4, 10, 133–37, 166
violence: the agonistic pattern and, 6;
    conflict contrasted with, xiv;
destruction compared with, xiv; the
    Gerasene demoniac and, 76–77;
    the gift/debt system and, 143–46;
    Gospel misreadings that emphasize,
    143; instrumental, 6; Jesus breaking
    the myth of, 137–39; moral outrage
    and, 146–48; the myth of the
    naturalness of, 149–50; narratives
    and the legitimation of, x; in
    nineteenth- and twentieth-century
    fiction, 64; political, 6; in popular
    stories, 130–37; theology and, ix;
    theories of the temple cleansing
    as revealing Jesus', 188 n. 13;
    types of, xiv. *See also* civilizing
    violence; redemptive violence;
    spiral of violence; therapeutic
    violence
Vonnegut, Kurt, 64

West, Rebecca, 139–42
Wink, Walter, ix, x
World War II, x
Wright, T. R., 173 n. 15

Yoder, John, 6
Young, Frances M., 186 n. 17

Zealots, the, 180 n. 25